Financing the
2004 Election

FINANCING THE 2004 ELECTION

DAVID B. MAGLEBY

ANTHONY CORRADO

KELLY D. PATTERSON

editors

BROOKINGS INSTITUTION PRESS
Washington, D.C.

ABOUT BROOKINGS

The Brookings Institution is a private nonprofit organization devoted to research, education, and publication on important issues of domestic and foreign policy. Its principal purpose is to bring the highest quality independent research and analysis to bear on current and emerging policy problems. Interpretations or conclusions in Brookings publications should be understood to be solely those of the authors.

Copyright © 2006
THE BROOKINGS INSTITUTION
1775 Massachusetts Avenue, N.W., Washington, D.C. 20036
www.brookings.edu

Library of Congress Cataloging-in-Publication data

Financing the 2004 election / David B. Magleby, Anthony Corrado,
    Kelly D. Patterson, editors.
      p.   cm.
    Includes bibliographical references and index.
    ISBN-13: 978-0-8157-5439-8 (pbk. : alk. paper)
    ISBN-10: 0-8157-5439-6 (pbk. : alk. paper)
    1. Campaign funds—United States. 2. Presidents—United States—Election—
    2004—Finance. 3. United States. Congress—Elections, 2004— Finance.
    4. United States—Politics and government—2001– I. Magleby, David B.
    II. Corrado, Anthony, 1957– III. Patterson, Kelly D. IV. Title.
    JK1991.F57 2006
    324.7'80973090511—dc22   2006012478

9 8 7 6 5 4 3 2 1

The paper used in this publication meets minimum requirements of the American National Standard for Information Sciences—Permanence of Paper for Printed Library Materials: ANSI Z39.48-1992.

Typeset in Sabon

Composition by Cynthia Stock
Silver Spring, Maryland

Printed by R. R. Donnelley
Harrisonburg, Virginia

For
Alma Woodruff Magleby Jr.
Anthony Corrado Sr.
and
Dale Powell Patterson

Contents

List of Tables and Figures

Tables

Figures

Acknowledgments

This book continues a publishing tradition that began some years ago. That tradition was initiated in 1960 by Herbert E. Alexander, who wrote or co-wrote a volume examining elections every four years through 1992. The discipline owes him a debt of gratitude for having the foresight to begin such an important series. John C. Green continued the tradition by compiling and editing the 1996 work, and David B. Magleby edited the volume covering the 2000 election cycle. That book, which focused on the role money played in that historic election, continued to provide scholars with the longitudinal comparisons that make the volumes so important.

For this work on the financing of the 2004 election, the editorial team was expanded to include Kelly D. Patterson and Anthony J. Corrado. Kelly's understanding of elections generally and observations of campaign finance in particular past races provided important insights. Tony is among the most knowledgeable scholars of the Bipartisan Campaign Reform Act (BCRA) and of campaign finance in particular. Adding Tony and Kelly to the editorial team strengthened this volume. As editors, we wanted to continue the tradition of this series by providing full and accurate reporting of federal campaign finance in 2004, while also offering a thorough assessment of the first general election under BCRA. The chapters here have been written by experts, many of whom have written chapters for earlier editions. We are extremely fortunate to have such capable scholars who are willing to share their insights into the election process.

The knowledge and experience of scholars cannot be disseminated without the assistance and support of others. Our research on the 2004 election was generously funded by grants from the Carnegie Corporation of New York, the JEHT Foundation, and the Joyce Foundation. We express appreciation to Carnegie Strengthening U.S. Democracy Program Chair Geraldine Mannion, JEHT Senior Program Manager Kristin Engberg, and Joyce Vice President and Money and Politics Program Officer Lawrence Hansen for their trust and confidence in our work. This volume could not have been possible without their belief in the importance of continuing this series.

We also want to recognize the many people at Brigham Young University (BYU) and the Center for the Study of Elections and Democracy (CSED) who have worked on this project. Stephanie Perry Curtis, Kristina Gale, Betsey Gimbel Hawkins, Richard Hawkins, and Nisha Riggs did whatever was necessary to help us and the other authors in this book. Stephanie, Kristina, Betsey, and Richard, all recent BYU graduates, worked on the project for more than a year. Nisha joined the team later. We appreciate their dedication to helping us find, interpret, and present the data. For a book that relies so much on different kinds of data, this is no small task. BYU undergraduates Emily McClintock, John Baxter Oliphant, Chad Pugh, and Paul Russell also supported these efforts, as did Katie Varney of Colby College. We are fortunate to work at academic institutions where the mentoring of undergraduates is valued. Brook Roper and Scott Cameron provided editorial assistance. We also want to thank individuals in the Office of Research and Creative Activities at BYU. Professor Gary R. Reynolds, Melvin Carr, Kathleen Rugg, and Nancy A. Davis helped us keep all of the accounts straight.

We are most appreciative of the faith that Mary Kwak and Chris Kelaher at Brookings showed in the project. We are grateful to Janet Walker for her hard work and professionalism in steering this project through to publication.

We believe the durability of this series is a rarity. Not many titles in the discipline have the combination of interest and usefulness to span so many decades. We trust that the series' longevity indicates the perspective and wisdom provided. During the research and production of this book, we all had the opportunity to reflect on these two intangible qualities, instilled by our own fathers. We thank them for their efforts in imparting these gifts to us and encouraging us to share them with the generations to follow.

FINANCING THE 2004 ELECTION

ONE   *Change and Continuity in the Financing of Federal Elections*

DAVID B. MAGLEBY

The federal election of 2004 centered on the contest for the presidency. Even though races for the White House traditionally overshadow congressional contests, the extent to which parties, groups, and individuals concentrated resources on this contest was unusual. According to Bob Farmer, a veteran of five presidential campaigns and John Kerry's treasurer in the primaries, it was "much larger than anything I've seen in the past. The stakes . . . very high."[1] This heightened interest drew record levels of money and resources. By most measures, it was the longest, most expensive, and most closely followed presidential election in decades.

Part of the reason 2004 was especially focused on the presidency was the intensity of feeling for and against the incumbent president, George W. Bush. These sentiments ran deep and motivated people to contribute to candidates, party committees, and interest groups. The Bush administration's response to the terrorist attacks on September 11, 2001—its "war on terror"—was the dominant theme of the campaign and an element behind sentiment on both sides. Central to the war on terror was the deployment of American forces to Afghanistan and Iraq. President Bush, in the first presidential debate, framed the issue as follows: "In Iraq, we saw a threat, and we realized that after September the 11th, we must take threats seriously, before they fully materialize. . . . Iraq is a central part in the war on terror. That's why [Abu Musab al-Zarqawi] and his people are trying to fight us. Their hope is that we grow weary and we leave."[2]

Bush's foreign policy unleashed a flow of rhetoric. Opponents, especially of the war in Iraq, voiced a variety of complaints. Some favored the war but thought the administration had not committed enough force, others challenged its justification, and still others thought there were more important security threats. Critics such as George Soros called the neoconservatives piloting Bush's foreign policy a "bunch of extremists guided by a crude form of social Darwinism."[3] Supporters like Vice President Richard Cheney warned that if John Kerry were elected, "the danger is that we'll get hit again" by terrorists.[4]

Another unusual aspect of 2004 was the lingering effect of the disputed outcome of the 2000 presidential election. Because Democrat Al Gore had won the popular vote and Bush's Electoral College victory was the result of judicial proceedings, the Democratic Party and several key constituent groups felt the election had been stolen. One group organized itself around the mantra "Redefeat Bush" and on its website sold posters, bumper stickers, yard signs, t-shirts, and even condoms urging voters to reject Bush a second time.[5] The perception that minority and urban voters had been unfairly treated in the controversy over the Florida ballot counting fueled the anger even more. In the politics of the 2004 election, lessons learned from the disputed 2000 election not only influenced voter mobilization strategy but also fundraising.

Emotions ran equally high among those voters inclined to support President Bush. Within his own party, Bush enjoyed an unchallenged bid for renomination.[6] In mid-September 2003, 63 percent of Bush supporters were "very enthusiastic" about his candidacy for president.[7] In September 2004, 59 percent still saw in Bush the personality and leadership qualities desirable in a president.[8] An additional strength in the eyes of most voters was that he shared their moral values.

For the Democrats, winning back the White House in 2004 offered the best chance at regaining control over one of the branches of the national government. The high probability that whoever was elected president in 2004 would be able to determine the future orientation of the Supreme Court was especially important to pro-choice groups.[9]

This consideration led many interest groups to shift their electioneering more toward the presidential race and away from congressional contests. The shift also owed much to the fact that most competitive U.S. Senate races in 2004 were on Republican turf, and because of partisan gerrymandering there were relatively few competitive U.S. House contests, making the prospect of a shift in party control remote. Organized labor, the League of Conservation Voters (LCV), NARAL Pro-Choice America, the Sierra Club, and the Association of Trial Lawyers of America were among those that devoted more attention to the presidential race in 2004.[10] Such behavior was unprecedented among interest groups and reflected one of the many ways in which the 2004 election broke new ground. Mark Longabaugh, senior vice president of Political Affairs for the LCV, saw it as "a historic shift from the League's almost exclusive focus on Congress. Because of the historic hostility of this administration to environmental policy, the board made a commitment to defeat George Bush."[11]

The strong feelings for and against President Bush also drove the increase in spending by groups organized under Section 527 of the Internal Revenue Service Code. Especially important in this quarter were large contributions from individuals and labor unions, which had a magnified impact because much of the money was given early.[12] Noteworthy individual donors to 527s on the Democratic side were George Soros ($23,450,000), Peter Lewis ($22,997,220), Steven Bing ($13,852,031), and Herb and Marion Sandler ($13,008,459).[13] Unions gave pro-Democratic 527s another $94 million, or "about four times as much as billionaire George Soros did."[14] Major donors to Republican-friendly 527s included Bob J. Perry ($8,095,000) and Alex Spanos and Dawn Arnall, who each gave $5 million.[15] For the most part, corporations that had been large soft money donors were not heavily involved in funding 527s in 2004.[16] Although, as we demonstrate in this book, 527s were an important part of the story in 2004, their spending fell short of the party soft money and issue advocacy spending of past cycles (see chapter 8).

Large donors were major supporters of 527 organizations and other groups long before the Bipartisan Campaign Reform Act of 2002 (BCRA) and the 2004 election. An undisclosed donor in 2000 gave the National Association for the Advancement of Colored People (NAACP) Voter Fund more than $10 million to fund election activities, including an ad that graphically reminded viewers of the dragging death of James Byrd Jr. and attacked George W. Bush for not supporting hate crimes legislation in Texas.[17] Jane Fonda contributed $11.7 million to a 527 organization in 2000, which in turn funded issue advocacy through several progressive groups.[18] The largest beneficiary of Fonda's donation was Planned Parenthood.[19]

This ample funding enabled the 527s to hire experienced professionals in 2003 and 2004, often with past experience working for the party committees. Anti-Bush 527s were more active early in the campaign, and pro-Bush and anti-Kerry 527s played a critical role in the later stages of the contest. The 527s were also important in U.S. Senate contests, although to a lesser extent, and their efforts are a possible harbinger of what may come in 2006 and beyond as individuals and groups exploit this mechanism to target unlimited resources. Kelly Patterson and Allan Cigler examine these organizations in greater detail in their respective chapters (3 and 8) of this book.

The increased emphasis on the presidency in 2004, along with defining BCRA's regulatory changes, made the federal election novel in the way money was raised, spent, and regulated. Of particular interest here are the increased emphasis both parties placed on individual contributions; the ways in which corporations, unions, special interests, and other contributors sought to influence the 2004 election; and the continued and rising importance of the ground war of voter mobilization through the mail, on the telephone, and in person. As this chapter points out, the patterns of campaign finance in the 2004 federal elections reflected change as much as continuity. Elements of continuity in the 2004 election are evident in such areas as the power of incumbency in fundraising, the importance of early money, the role of interest groups in funding campaigns, and the rising costs of campaigns.

Regulating Money and Politics in 2004

The changes in campaign financing for the 2004 election were the result of BCRA, the most important piece of regulatory legislation for campaign finance enacted in nearly three decades. BCRA built upon many provisions from the prior law, the Federal Election Campaign Act (FECA, passed in 1971 and amended in 1974), and court decisions on campaign finance. BCRA was narrowly crafted in hopes of withstanding judicial scrutiny and thus left intact many FECA provisions upheld by the Supreme Court in *Buckley* v. *Valeo*, the landmark decision on the FECA's constitutionality.[20] As Anthony Corrado discusses in some detail in chapter 2, BCRA allowed political parties to make independent expenditures, something the Court had previously ruled permissible.[21] (They were required to choose between making coordinated expenditures and independent expenditures.) However, the provision was struck down by the Supreme Court.[22] In an area reformers perceived as consistent with the FECA and the *Buckley* v. *Valeo* decision, BCRA banned soft money and in so doing banned the practice among some elected officials of raising unlimited amounts of money for the political parties from corporations, labor unions, and wealthy individuals. It was hoped this would end the undue influence those donors exercised or appeared to exercise. Soft money expenditures had reached nearly $500 million in both the 2000 and 2002 election cycles and provided a rallying point for BCRA proponents.[23]

Originally, soft money was intended to fund generic party activity and infrastructure, but eventually it became an instrument for channeling more money to particular contests. Not surprisingly, the practice of raising and spending soft money created an appearance of corruption as elected officials—including congressional leadership, the president, the vice president, and congressional candidates—solicited large soft money contributions. Corporations and unions also gave general treasury funds to party committees as soft money contributions. In 2000 soft money had come to constitute 44 percent of all the money raised by the Republican National Committee (RNC) and 42 percent of the money raised by the RNC, National Republican Senatorial Committee (NRSC), and National Republican Congressional Committee (NRCC) combined. Soft money was 52 percent of all money raised by the Democratic National Committee (DNC) in 2000 and 55 percent for the DNC, Democratic Senatorial Campaign Committee (DSCC), and Democratic Congressional Campaign Committee (DCCC) combined.[24]

The FECA had clearly proved to be ineffective at limiting and regulating the use of soft money, most of which was spent through the state parties. The large amounts raised and transferred thwarted the original intent of the FECA, which included contribution limits designed to prevent wealthy individuals or groups from exercising undue influence.

The connection between donors and elected officials soliciting large contributions was a major justification for BCRA and was frequently cited by the Supreme Court in upholding the legislation in *McConnell v. FEC*. "The interests that underlie contribution limits," the Court argued, "are interests in preventing the actual corruption threatened by large financial contributions, and the eroding of public confidence in the electoral process through the appearance of corruption."[25]

As our interviews revealed, the BCRA's ban on soft money was welcomed by at least some donors, who expressed relief that they were no longer being asked for large soft money contributions. Bill Miller at the U.S. Chamber of Commerce, for one, felt certain that corporations were happy not to have to donate as much.[26] According to Andrew Stern, president of the Service Employees International Union, the "good news" was that "the politicians can't call anymore. . . . I'm not sure in the past whether I was a union leader or an ATM."[27] BCRA thus ended the direct connection between large donors and party leaders.

Another concern of reformers was the fact that some groups or individuals included sham issue ads in their campaign strategy. These ads circumvented the FECA's contribution and disclosure limits provisions by avoiding the "magic words" of express advocacy, such as "vote for" or "support." In recent federal election cycles, the spending by soft money and issue advocacy often exceeded the candidate and party hard money spending authorized under the FECA.[28]

To address this problem, BCRA added to the express advocacy definition a new electioneering communications standard, thereby changing the ways in which groups could advertise on television or radio for or against targeted candidates. According to this new standard, "electioneering communications [encompass any] broadcast, cable or satellite advertisements that refer to a clearly identified candidate within sixty days of a general and thirty days of a primary election and are targeted to a population of 50,000 or more people in a candidate's district or state."[29] Reformers thus hoped to reduce the influence organizations, groups, or individuals sought by advertising for or against political candidates under innocuous names such as "Citizens for Better Medicare," which masked the identity of its principal funders, members of the pharmaceutical industry.[30] The new law also required more complete and timely disclosure of electioneering communications. Nonparty entities must file a disclosure report within twenty-four hours of spending $10,000 and must continue to file reports for each $10,000 spent thereafter. BCRA also retained a long-standing FECA clause prohibiting unions and corporations from using general or treasury funds for electioneering ads.

Despite the earlier ban, corporations and unions had been doing just that: contributing soft money to the parties and spending these funds on issue advocacy. In response, BCRA banned the use of general or treasury funds for broadcast electioneering communications in the last sixty days before a general election and thirty days before a primary election, a period that came to be called the "window." Groups were careful not to spend prohibited money within the window. The Media Fund, for example, spent union funds outside the window and individual contributions within the window. In five states—Pennsylvania, Iowa, New Hampshire, Wisconsin, and Florida—unions with a surplus of funds they "could not otherwise use" resorted to doing mailers within the window. Since phone calls were not affected by BCRA restrictions on union treasury funds, the Media Fund also used this medium in Missouri on two occasions to highlight the Saudi-Bush family connection.[31] With the time restriction applicable to fundraising as well, the Club for Growth divided its accounts into funds raised before the window and those raised within the window. Contributions received inside the electioneering window were channeled into the "Club for Growth.net," a 527 committee that accepted large donations ($100,000, for the most part). The resulting $4.5 million accumulated in this way could be spent with fewer restrictions within the window.[32]

Among the key FECA components that BCRA expanded upon was the disclosure of who was contributing money to candidates, political parties, and interest groups engaged in electioneering communications. As mentioned, BCRA requires disclosure of electioneering communications within twenty-four hours once $10,000 is spent and each time an additional $10,000 is spent. This disclosure must also identify the spender, all persons sharing control over communication, and donors giving $1,000 or more to the general account.[33] However, only limited disclosure is required of IRS Section 501(c)(3) groups, which are tax-exempt entities organized for charitable or other similar purposes and are prohibited by law from engaging in candidate advocacy. Such groups cannot endorse a candidate, contribute to a campaign, or establish a political action committee (PAC). They may conduct nonpartisan voter registration, turnout, or voter information activities.

IRS Section 501(c)(4) groups are social welfare organizations that must be operated for the public social welfare and not for profit but may engage in political activities so long as those activities do not become its primary purpose. Accordingly, they may engage in such activities as rating candidates on a partisan basis, sponsoring electioneering communications, and supporting voter registration and turnout efforts. Contributions to 501(c)(4) organizations are not tax-deductible. Other sections of the IRS code relating to groups that are active in federal elections include Section 501(c)(5), which concerns unions, and Section 501(c)(6), which concerns trade associations.

A single group may organize separate legal entities under more than one section of the IRS code or FECA. For example, the Sierra Club has a

501(c)(4), a PAC, and a 527. For each of these organizational forms, different disclosure rules apply. Section501(c)(3) groups are not required to disclose all donors and need only file annual reports to the IRS, with limited reporting of receipts and expenditures. Access to these reports from the groups themselves could require personal visits or written requests. However, any unincorporated Section 501(c)(3) or Section 501(c)(4) group that engages in activities subject to federal disclosure must meet those requirements. Thus, for example, any Section 501(c)(4) that finances electioneering communications totaling at least $10,000 in a calendar year must disclose these expenditures and the donors who gave $1,000 or more. While the disclosure of interest group electioneering activity in 2004 was not complete, it was more extensive than under the FECA. Anthony Corrado examines the regulations governing these groups in greater detail in chapter 2.

BCRA also revised FECA's limitations on the amount individuals, party committees, and PACs could contribute to candidates and party committees. BCRA doubled the limits for individuals contributing to candidates from $1,000 to $2,000 per primary, general, or special election. For most candidates, this means individuals "max out" when they contribute $4,000. These limits were indexed for inflation. The aggregate individual contribution limit for money given to candidates or parties was raised from $50,000 per election cycle ($25,000 a year) to $95,000 per election cycle, with no more than $37,500 to candidates and $57,500 to parties and political committees, and with adjustments for inflation. Aggregate individual contributions to national party committees increased from $20,000 per committee to $25,000 per committee, again adjusted for inflation. Individual contributions to state parties under federal law were increased from $5,000 to $10,000 per election cycle. BCRA did not change PAC contribution limits. The court upheld the constitutionality of contribution limits in *McConnell* v. *FEC,* stating that "contributions limits are grounded in the important governmental interests in preventing 'both the actual corruption threatened by large financial contributions and the eroding of public confidence in the electoral process through the appearance of corruption'" (for further discussion, see chapter 2).[34]

Yet another legacy of the FECA and *Buckley* v. *Valeo* is the ability of individuals and groups to make unlimited expenditures for and against political candidates as long as those expenditures are genuinely independent of the candidate and party. Party committees were granted this same right in a 1996 Supreme Court decision in *Colorado Republican Federal Campaign Committee* v. *FEC*.[35] As we document in this book, independent expenditures by individuals, groups, and party committees grew in 2004, and the activity by the political parties was especially important (see chapter 7).

The new law left the Federal Election Commission (FEC) intact, a development that produced serious consequences in the midst of the 2004 presidential election season. Because of its bipartisan structure, the FEC became deadlocked on the rules defining whether 527s should be treated as federal political committees under the law and thus be subject to federal contribution limits and source prohibitions. The FEC basically allowed the 527 groups to continue unimpeded by the new law. BCRA advocates vehemently contended that the lack of rulemaking by the FEC on electioneering activity circumvented the intent of the law and challenged the result in court.[36] Subsequent legislation on this matter is again before Congress.

BCRA also left the system of partial public financing of presidential elections unchanged despite widespread concern about the state-by-state spending limits in the prenomination phase and about the viability and adequacy of public funding in the general election phase. As John Green notes in chapter 4 and Anthony Corrado in chapter 5, the problems with this system only grew in 2004 as candidates Bush, Kerry, and Howard Dean all passed up the matching funds in the nomination phase of the election.[37] Bush and Kerry later accepted public funding in the general election phase while benefiting from the ability of parties and interest groups to supplement their general election campaigns.

It is noteworthy that BCRA's new definition of electioneering and express advocacy excludes political communication through the mail, on the telephone or Internet, or in person. Political analysts accurately predicted that outside groups would "look for ways around the electioneering ban, perhaps by shifting to non-broadcast communications."[38]

How the Money Was Raised

As we explore in this book, the new rules of campaign finance enacted in BCRA altered the fundraising game in important respects, particularly through its ban on soft money. In response, political parties turned their attention to federally regulated money, which was limited as to source and amount. This source has long been called *hard money,* in part because it was thought harder to raise than the unlimited soft money individuals and PACs could previously contribute to political parties.

As noted, for soft money donors it was a relief not to be courted or "shaken down" by party leaders and officeholders any longer. Indeed, there is compelling evidence that without the prodding of party leaders, some corporations reduced their overall political spending under BCRA. Some companies, reports Michael Petro of the Committee for Economic Development, even started to see a degree of risk in giving to the party, and their executives felt uncomfortable with being advised that they had to do so.[39]

By increasing the individual contribution limit, on the other hand, BCRA provided candidates for federal office with an incentive to concentrate more on raising money from individuals. Much was made in the 2000 election cycle of individual contributions to the Bush-Cheney campaign. Its hierarchal fundraising structure, which named fundraisers who bundled $100,000 in individual contributions "Pioneers," "was not a new idea, [but] Bush used this method on an unprecedented scale."[40] Presidential and congressional candidates in both parties also experienced a surge in receipts in 2004 compared with past election cycles. Most of that surge came from individuals. President Bush raised over $271 million from individuals, up from $101 million in 2000, while John Kerry more than doubled the 2000 Bush figure, raising $224 million in 2004. Kerry surpassed Gore's 2000 figure by an even greater margin, in part because Gore had accepted federal matching funds in the primary along with the spending limitations associated with them.

As another incentive for individuals to contribute to political parties, BCRA ruled that part of the aggregate individual limit, $20,000 of the $95,000 total allowance, could only go to political parties. Before, as noted earlier, individuals were allowed to donate $25,000 a year ($50,000 for the two-year election cycle), with all of that possibly going to candidates.[41] Indeed, individuals tended to give most of their contributions to candidates.[42] Under BCRA, however, individuals who want to max out in the higher aggregate limits are forced to donate at least $20,000 to parties. In 2003–04 there was a dramatic increase in the number of individuals who contributed the permitted maximum to political parties. The biggest increases were seen in the DNC and RNC. For the DNC, the maximum permitted contributions from individuals rose from more than $11 million in 2000 to more than $43 million in 2004, and for the RNC, from about $13 million in 2000 to almost $61 million in 2004.[43] The surge in individual contributions to the DNC is particularly striking as it brought "three to four times" more money than the committee's own independent expenditures director, Ellen Moran, expected.[44]

Contrary to some predictions, the soft money ban did not mean fewer overall dollars in the 2004 presidential election or spell the end of the Democratic Party: BCRA, some said, was a "suicide bill for the Democrats."[45] Others disagreed.[46] One observer predicted, almost prophetically, that under the new limits parties would actually be able to replace their lost soft money with more generous hard money contributions.[47] In court briefs for *McConnell* v. *FEC*, Donald P. Green speculated that the amount of small donations would also increase under the new rules.[48]

Individual contributions to the DNC and RNC did in fact make up for the loss of soft money in the 2004 election cycle—to a remarkable extent. Having long relied more on hard money, Republicans had an early advantage because of their established donor base. Democrats, who had been more reliant on soft money through 2002, made dramatic strides in raising hard money. The DNC raised $404 million in hard money in 2004, compared with $260 million in hard and soft money combined in 2000.[49] The RNC raised $392 million in hard money in 2004, compared with $379 million in hard and soft money combined in 2000.

The fact that the RNC and DNC were able to raise a combined $775 million without soft money indicates the parties could thrive without soft money. Clearly, both committees found new ways to raise hard money in the 2004 election cycle. For one thing, candidates and party committees put more effort into raising money from individuals in smaller increments. As table 1-1 shows, much of the improvement in individual donations to the DNC came in small (unitemized) amounts of $200 or less, as well as in larger contributions. The smaller unitemized contributions are significant because few thought that the Democratic base could be tapped for this kind of giving so quickly. In the past, the Democrats had not emphasized small donors as much as the RNC. In this cycle, however, they raised more money from small individual donors than the RNC did, turning conventional wisdom on its head. As Kelly Patterson explores in chapter 3, the surge in individual contributions in 2004 was facilitated by greater donor confidence in giving money to candidates, parties, and groups via the Internet.

As we demonstrate elsewhere in the book, individual giving to congressional candidates and congressional party committees also grew in 2004.

Table 1-1. *Sources of Receipts for National Party Committees, 2000–04*[a]
Dollars unless noted otherwise

Source	DNC 2000	DNC 2002	DNC 2004	RNC 2000	RNC 2002	RNC 2004
Total receipts	123,997,509	67,497,257	404,352,278	212,798,761	170,099,094	392,413,393
Total contributions from individuals[b]	112,157,217	55,623,021	352,550,848	193,181,420	157,825,892	350,368,907
Unitemized[c]	59,491,349	37,820,051	176,051,240	91,052,511	102,927,710	157,091,853
Unitemized as % of total from individuals	53.04	67.99	49.94	47.13	65.22	44.84
Contributions at the maximum permitted[c]	11,040,000	680,000	45,264,850	12,660,000	2,980,000	60,850,000
Maximum as % of individual total[d]	9.84	1.22	12.84	6.55	1.89	17.37
Contributions from federal candidates	1,478,662	55,113	23,916,588	56,050	160,250	26,678,514
Contributions from PACs	2,603,074	1,099,514	3,038,036	1,630,105	703,084	2,970,840
Transfers from state or other national parties	2,141,409	6,560,050	378,869	11,237,797	3,522,399	4,655,873

Source	DSCC 2000	DSCC 2002	DSCC 2004	NRSC 2000	NRSC 2002	NRSC 2004
Total receipts	40,488,666	48,391,653	88,655,573	51,475,156	59,161,387	78,980,487
Total contributions from individuals[e]	7,506,809	20,168,297	57,756,029	33,999,707	41,533,725	60,811,444
Unitemized[c]	8,408,898	9,723,282	21,179,393	19,292,125	20,231,352	29,998,982
Unitemized as % of total from individuals	48.03	48.21	36.67	56.74	48.71	49.33
Contributions at the maximum permitted[c]	1,640,000	2,020,000	12,175,000	180,000	320,000	6,125,000
Maximum as % of individual total	9.37	10.02	21.08	0.53	0.77	10.07
Contributions from federal candidates	1,133,100	1,820,984	14,637,708	2,960,305	1,621,321	3,846,670
Contributions from PACs	4,309,127	4,707,156	6,281,744	4,027,375	4,206,101	7,714,233
Transfers from state or other national parties	4,042,276	7,100,082	8,166	2,623,620	6,580,615	501,961

	DCCC			NRCC		
	2000	2002	2004	2000	2002	2004
Total receipts	48,394,476	46,436,093	93,168,931	97,314,513	123,615,586	185,719,489
Total contributions from individuals[e]	21,844,053	19,393,788	50,690,882	67,010,001	79,175,374	145,858,047
Unitemized[c]	9,932,524	11,201,482	25,141,719	34,703,962	39,673,242	49,789,260
Unitemized as % of total from individuals	45.47	57.76	49.60	51.79	50.11	34.14
Contributions at the maximum permitted[c]	1,040,000	800,000	6,675,000	480,000	180,000	3,775,000
Maximum as % of individual total	4.76	4.13	13.17	0.72	0.23	2.59
Contributions from federal candidates	11,036,046	12,131,368	23,958,309	14,664,152	14,077,114	24,247,276
Contributions from PACs	4,786,051	4,157,049	6,447,173	4,607,917	4,661,590	8,595,727
Transfers from state or other national parties	1,164,618	3,207,213	652,638	4,705,713	4,454,900	1,204,620

Source: Federal Election Commission, "Party Financial Activity Summarized for the 2004 Election Cycle," press release, March 2, 2005 (www.fec.gov/press/press2005/20050302party/Party2004final.html).

a. This table includes federal or "hard" money only.

b. Includes proceeds from Kerry Victory 2004 joint fundraising effort.

c. Unitemized contributions from individuals are those that aggregate $200 or less in a calendar year from a single person.

d. The maximum contribution from individuals was changed from $20,000 a year to $25,000 a year for the 2004 election cycle.

e. Includes both reported total plus what was reported from joint fundraising.

In this case, however, the growth in hard money contributions in 2004 did not make up for the loss of party soft money (see chapters 6 and 7).

BCRA also changed the way candidates, parties, and groups spent money in 2004, as detailed in chapter 3. It is important to remember that candidates, their parties, and allied interest groups all expend money trying to defeat or elect particular candidates. Yet most voters fail to distinguish these activities or to see that the players in the complex world of federal campaign finance are not always able to communicate with each other, despite having the same objective and targets. This creates strategic challenges for those making independent expenditures or operating Section 527 or 501(c) organizations. For example, the voter mobilization efforts of the Bush-Cheney campaign were coordinated with the work of the 72 Hour Task Force at the RNC. Because they were spending hard money, both the candidate and party shared their strategy, targets, timing, and other details. On the Democratic side, the Kerry-Edwards campaign and the DNC did the same thing. But a much larger share of the Democratic ground game was carried out by America Votes, a coalition of interest groups that could not legally communicate with the party or Kerry because their activity was funded independently of the candidate and party.

Groups have long made independent expenditures, which are unlimited but disclosed to the FEC, but that spending rose in 2004. Among interest groups, the MoveOn PAC spent the most in this fashion, and its $10 million in independent expenditures that year far exceeded the $2.4 million that the LCV or NARAL Pro-Choice America each had spent independently in 2002. MoveOn's expenditures also far surpassed the largest independent expenditures of 2000, when the LCV spent $2.1 million and the National Rifle Association (NRA) spent nearly $6.5 million.[50] For a more detailed analysis of independent expenditures by individuals, political party committees, and groups, see chapters 3, 7, and 8.

The Ground War and Voter Mobilization

The financing of the 2004 election, while conducted under new rules, was in many respects an extension of trends from 2000 and before. The importance of individual contributors to presidential candidates, bypassing federal matching funds in the nomination phase of the presidential election, and the influence of outside groups, often through negative attacks, can all be traced to earlier elections. Incumbents at the congressional level, for example, continue to enjoy substantial financial advantages, and PACs remain an important part of that advantage, thanks to earlier voter mobilization tactics and the ground war.

The 2000 election, for example, clearly set the stage for the next presidential election tactically. After losing the popular vote in 2000, the Bush campaign became convinced that it needed to do much better in voter registration and mobilization. The GOP campaign saw a model for what it hoped to accomplish in the activities of organized labor.[51] "What we saw across the country was that we were under performing and Democrats were over performing in the final 72 hours," said Blaise Hazelwood, political director at the RNC.[52] The RNC's efforts came to be known as the 72 Hour Task Force and built upon experiments and test marketing in gubernatorial elections in Virginia and New Jersey in 2001, in the 2002 midterm elections, and again in gubernatorial elections in Kentucky and Mississippi in 2003.[53]

The Democrats, who had relied more than Republicans on outside groups to mobilize voters, also elevated the importance of grassroots politics in 2004, but not to the same extent as Republicans. Anti-Bush interest groups such as America Coming Together (ACT), the LCV, and NARAL Pro-Choice America coordinated their efforts through an organization named America Votes and mounted a large scale get-out-the-vote (GOTV) campaign.

However, the renewed investment in the ground war actually started before 2004. As past research has shown, party committees and interest groups increased the amount of political mail, telephone contacting, and person-to-person electioneering in the 1998, 2000, and 2002 elections. Following the 1996 election cycle, which featured a strong emphasis on broadcast ads funded in part by soft money and interest group issue ads, the Democratic Party and especially its allied interest groups and labor unions placed greater emphasis on personal contact, mail, telephone, and GOTV efforts in 1998.[54] In 2000 and 2002 many interest groups and both parties followed suit with similar techniques in their ground war efforts.[55] In 2002 the Republican Party and its allied interest groups stepped up their efforts to match the Democrats' success in the ground war during the 1998 and 2000 elections.[56]

One such tactic employed by party committees was to target some of the money they could spend in concert with the candidates. These so-called coordinated expenditures were channeled into mail, phone banks, and GOTV drives. In the soft money era, party committees sometimes did not max out in coordinated expenditures, although they generally made full use of this means of supporting presidential candidates.[57] Coordinated expenditures in 2004 grew to $16 million at the DNC, while the RNC spent more than $16 million on coordinated expenditures, mostly on direct mail.[58]

Though often overlooked, one way of persuading and mobilizing voters occurs through communications issued by their corporate employers or unions in the workplace. Corporations, unions, trade associations, and membership organizations often communicate with their members and employees about politics. In 2000 the AFL-CIO found that internal communications with members were more effective than issue advocacy.[59] When the "primary focus" of the communication is the election, the group must report the related expenditure to the FEC; however, when electioneering is simply part of a more general communication, the FEC does not require disclosure.[60] Membership groups such as the National Education Association (NEA), National Association of Realtors (NAR), and Service Employees International Union (SEIU) engaged in more reported internal communications in 2004 than in 2000 or 2002.[61]

Groups on all sides also made greater use of the Internet to communicate with members and other interested parties. Their websites provided downloadable voter registration forms, absentee ballots, and information on early voting.[62]

The ground war efforts of both sides in 2004 were influenced by the research on voter mobilization by political scientists Donald P. Green and Alan S. Gerber.[63] Their work prompted both sides to invest in multiple personal contacts between their volunteers or paid staff and the voters they were attempting to mobilize. These efforts were far better funded than in 2000, with the Bush campaign spending approximately $125 million, or three times the expenditure in 2000, and the Democrats spending approximately $60 million, or twice the amount in 2000.

Although Kerry and the DNC spent far less than Bush and the RNC, Democratic efforts were supplemented by $100 million to $125 million from ACT's mobilization campaign. Mobilization on both sides depended on telephone contact and door-to-door canvassing, but with different participants. The Bush campaign relied heavily on volunteer workers who concentrated on contacting co-workers and friends in their respective workplaces, social circles, and exurban areas. The Kerry campaign relied more on interest groups and paid workers to bring out loyalists on election day. Both campaigns concentrated on potential voters who were strong supporters of their candidates but were infrequent voters in the past.[64]

The Republicans were more advanced in their use of voter files and targeting of individual voters, in what might be called voter profiling. With its detailed walk lists, the RNC was able to "microtarget" efforts of the ground war communications by customizing messages to voters based on demographics and their personal priorities.[65] In 2004 the committee took this strategy to a whole new level by merging numerous pieces of consumer information with voter records and mining that information so that it could be used for voter communications. Improved technology, enhanced computer storage capacity, voting history, consumer preferences, and other personal data made this possible.[66]

Evangelical Christians were among several groups targeted for increased mobilization efforts. It was said that "nobody courted the Religious Right more than Karl Rove," both on the national and the local level.[67] In the Tampa Bay area, Bush campaign officials considered churches "the largest component of the voter registration program."[68] According to Bush campaign deputy strategist Sara Taylor, "Our union is the Christian Evangelical vote."[69] The Republicans also reached conservative Christian voters through the acquisition of church directories, which they entered into their database.[70] In addition, they courted nontraditionally Republican constituencies, such as Hispanics, African Americans, women, Jews, and Catholics.[71] Most agree that the GOP did a "better job of turning out their base" in 2004.[72]

In eleven states, some conservative Christians were motivated to turn out by the appearance of initiatives banning gay marriage on the ballot. The use of controversial initiatives to activate sectors of the electorate is not a new tactic and was also used by Democratic-aligned groups in Nevada and Florida through minimum-wage initiatives on the 2004 ballot.[73] But it was the gay marriage initiatives, especially in Ohio, that apparently helped turn out conservative Christians likely to vote for the president, although it was not the most important issue for voters.[74]

In addition to mobilizing specific groups, the various campaigns targeted voters in battleground states. During the 2004 election cycle, the Center for the Study of Elections and Democracy conducted a three-wave survey of registered voters to measure the extent to which those in battleground states were exposed to more campaign communications (including personal contact, mail, telephone calls, and television or

Table 1-2. *Comparison of Political Communications Received in Battleground and Non-Battleground States*

Intensity of campaign	Late battleground[a]	Late non-battleground[b]
Voted	88.7	86.9
Voted early	9.1	7.7
Voted absentee	9.4*	14.5
Contacted about voting early[c]	36.7***	12.0
Received letter/mail from campaign	74.2***	53.5
Mean: letter or mail[d]	2.07***	1.38
Received a request to donate	23.0	21.9
Had face-to-face contact with campaign	23.0***	13.8
Received phone call from campaign	67.9***	55.3
Mean: phone calls[d]	2.04***	1.06
Received e-mail from campaign	14.6	13.6
Heard radio ad from campaign	68.7**	60.7
Saw TV ad from campaign	93.7*	90.2
N	326	1,079

Source: Brigham Young University, Center for the Study of Elections and Democracy and University of Wisconsin–Madison, Wisconsin Advertising Project, 2004 Election Panel Study, Wave 3. Electronic resources from the EPS website (http://csp.polisci.wisc.edu/BYU_UW/).

* $p < 0.05$; ** $p < 0.01$; *** $p < 0.001$.

a. Late battleground states were Florida, Iowa, Minnesota, New Hampshire, New Mexico, Nevada, Ohio, Pennsylvania, and Wisconsin.

b. Late non-battleground states were all other states, including the former battleground states of Arkansas, Arizona, Colorado, Louisiana, Maine, Michigan, Missouri, Oregon, Washington, and West Virginia.

c. Only respondents who voted early or by absentee ballot were asked this question; therefore, its N is 54 for battleground and 208 for non-battleground states.

d. Per day for the last week of the campaign.

radio ads) during the last week of the campaign than registered voters in other states (see table 1-2).[75]

The campaign environment in battleground states in 2004 was very different from that in other states. Voter feedback indicates more contacts about early or absentee voting in battleground states; more mail, face-to-face contact, and telephone calls; and more exposure to radio and TV ads. However, states did not differ significantly in the extent of solicitation for campaign contributions or in the receipt of e-mail from a campaign. This is not surprising as there is no reason to presume prospective donors or persons desiring e-mail contact with a campaign are concentrated in battleground states.

Both sides in the 2004 presidential election saw a substantial return on their ground war investment. Democrats and their allied groups exceeded their targets in turnout by about 8 million votes.[76] Republicans did even better, seeing an aggregate gain of 11.5 million votes.

Mathew Dowd, a pollster for the Bush team, estimated that the Bush campaign and the RNC were able to quadruple the number of Republican voters that could be targeted through GOTV efforts.[77] Contrary to some predictions that voter mobilization would be far more difficult to mount under BCRA, the parties achieved their largest voter registration and GOTV success ever in 2004.[78]

The greater reliance on ground war techniques in 2004 was in part the result of BCRA, which limited the kinds of money that could be spent on broadcast electioneering in the thirty days before a primary or sixty days before a general election but applied no such restriction on non-broadcast political activity. Thus some groups found themselves with funds that could not be spent on broadcast ads but could be spent on personal contact, direct mail, or telephone contact. The Media Fund, for example, spent its extra money on mail pieces in Pennsylvania, Florida, Wisconsin, Iowa, and New Hampshire, and on phone calls in Missouri.[79] Although BCRA permits state and local parties to raise limited amounts of soft money for voter registration and GOTV efforts, these funds—sometimes called Levin funds after Senator Carl Levin (Democrat of Michigan), the sponsor of the BCRA amendment concerning these funds—saw only limited use in 2004.[80]

Elections in 2004 were also affected by changes in election administration resulting from the Help America Vote Act (HAVA). Following the disputed 2000 election, Congress enacted HAVA to help update voting technology and to establish an Election Assistance Commission as a "clearinghouse and resource" for the administration of federal elections.[81] Although some states, notably Florida, were already using updated technology, the implementation of new voting equipment became a concern. In Florida, Ohio, and other states, questions also arose about voter purges, whether felons could regain the right to vote, and whether some voters had been fraudulently registered. With greater emphasis on voter mobilization by candidates, parties, and outside groups, the voting process in competitive states came under increasing scrutiny.

An Undiminished Air War

The competitive presidential race, with its early start (since Kerry in effect won the nomination in March), saw a substantial expansion of the air war as well. From extensive data on television advertising, it is clear that "the volume of advertising has not shown any noticeable decrease," and that "television advertising in 2004 clearly surpassed 2000 in overall volume of presidential ads."[82]

BCRA's new definitions of electioneering communications and limitation on how those ads could be financed within sixty days before the general election spurred some major groups to do more advertising before the sixty-day window. In 2004, ads of this kind totaled 97,554 before and 45,344 after the window, or double the number, whereas in 2000, with no time or source-of-funding constraints, issue ad totals were much the same in both periods. Furthermore, ads from interest groups as a proportion of ads from candidates and parties run within the sixty-day window dropped from 16.4 percent in 2000 to 13 percent in 2004.[83]

Overall, however, BCRA did not reduce the number of interest groups' ads run in 2004. According to Wisconsin Advertising Project scholars, interest group ads in the seventy-five largest media markets doubled between 2000 (77,607 ads) and 2004 (142,898).[84] As already noted, part of this growth came early in the cycle as groups such as the Media Fund, MoveOn.org, and the AFL-CIO ran ads against President Bush. "In fact, St. Patrick's Day [seemed] to have replaced Labor Day as the unofficial start of the general election campaign. By Labor Day 2004, more than 600,000 presidential spots had already aired in 94 of the nation's 210 media markets."[85] The number of groups running ads before the last sixty days rose from eleven in 2000 to twenty-eight in 2004. Even so, interest groups advertising in the last sixty days, such as Progress for America, provided critical support for President Bush through their effective TV advertisement.[86]

This intense interest group air war was noticeably absent in U.S. House races, where the number of ads declined from 30,411 in 2000 to 2,471 in 2004.[87] Interest group ads were more prevalent in competitive Senate races, but not as important as they had been in 1998–2002.[88]

While the presidential election took center stage in the 2004 cycle, congressional contests, especially for several U.S. Senate seats, were highly competitive and provide important insights into BCRA's broader impact. The most competitive Senate races coincided with presidential battlegrounds only in Florida, Colorado, and Pennsylvania and typically took place in "red" states such as Alaska, North Carolina, Oklahoma, and South Dakota. Senate candidates in these competitive contests exploited the higher BCRA individual contribution limits. For example,

Republican John Thune, who ran for the U.S. Senate in South Dakota in both 2002 and 2004, increased his individual contributions from $3.5 million in 2002 to over $14 million in 2004. His 2002 Democratic opponent, Tim Johnson, raised $3.3 million in individual contributions, while Senate Democratic leader Tom Daschle raised slightly more than $16 million from individuals in 2004. More generally, the proportion of candidate receipts coming from individuals in the House and Senate rose by nearly 7 percent in 2004 compared with 2002.[89]

Individual contributions to the party congressional campaign committees also increased in 2004. As previously noted, the DNC and RNC more than made up for the BCRA soft money ban with a surge in individual contributions. Although the DSCC, DCCC, NRSC, and NRCC reported substantial growth in individual contributions as well, it was not enough to make up for the loss of soft money. Total funds available to the DSCC and NRSC dropped by about 40 percent in 2004 compared with 2002 and 2000. This meant that with the exception of the race in South Dakota, party committees expended less per voter in independent expenditures in 2004 than they had in soft money transfers to state parties in the 1998–2002 period. The amount spent was still substantial, reaching an aggregate of more than $8 per voter in the 2004 Colorado Senate race, for example.[90]

Overview of the Book

To describe and assess campaign finance in the 2004 federal elections, we draw largely on data from the FEC, the Internal Revenue Service, and other agencies, as well as from various independent research projects by our authors, all experts in the subjects of their chapters. Their participation in this volume was not based on a shared view of BCRA or campaign finance reform.

In chapter 2, Anthony Corrado reviews the provisions of BCRA and how they have been applied through the rulemaking process at the FEC. In many ways, the battle over campaign finance reform was not resolved by the Supreme Court in *McConnell* v. *FEC*. Instead, the debate simply shifted from Congress and the courts to the administrative process at the FEC, where advocates and opponents of BCRA's reforms continued to wrangle over the implementation of the new law. The FEC's decisions on the meaning and application of the statutory language were highly controversial and led to new legal challenges on both sides of the BCRA debate. As a result, all parties remained uncertain about the ways the law would be put into practice and the scope of the BCRA regulations throughout this first election under the new rules. This chapter lays an important foundation for understanding what BCRA did and did not do, as well as for analyzing areas in the law most likely to be controversial.

In chapter 3, Kelly D. Patterson compares fundraising and spending in the federal elections in 2004 with recent presidential election cycles. He comments on the differences in the flow of money for presidential and congressional elections in 2004 and their long-term implications. Other topics discussed are the surge in individual donations to federal campaigns, some of the important advances in the disclosure of spending in federal elections in 2004, and the gaps that remain, particularly in the reporting of spending by Section 501(c)(3) organizations and in the money spent by corporations, groups, and trade associations on internal communications. Relying on interviews, longitudinal data, and published sources, Patterson estimates these modes of spending as well.

As in past studies, we have divided our assessment of the financing of the presidential election into the nomination and general election phases. John C. Green examines the nomination phase of 2004 in chapter 4, with important insights into the way major party candidates raised and spent money. He distinguishes between "insider" and "outsider" candidates and their fundraising strategies. Green sees the status quo as "in crisis," and he aptly conveys the extent of BRCA's failings, particularly its neglect of the public financing system for presidential elections, including the much-criticized state-by-state spending limitations. But the problems with the current campaign finance rules go well beyond these limitations, and, as Green discusses, more and more candidates are opting out of the system. He also places the 2004 experience in the context of past presidential nomination campaigns, examining the costs of the primary season, what he calls the "bridge period" between the end of the primaries and the national conventions, and then the pause between the two major party conventions. The 527s allied with the Democrats were especially important during this period.

In chapter 5, Anthony Corrado focuses on the financing of the 2004 presidential general election, that is, the ways in which candidates, party committees, and interest groups raised and spent money in the period after the nominees are determined. One factor that affected the financing was the timing of the Democratic convention, five weeks before the Republican convention, which meant that Bush could continue to raise and spend unlimited amounts during this period, while Kerry had to conserve his resources since he was already campaigning under the general election spending limit. As Corrado points out, heavy investment by the party committees and outside groups were important to both candidates, but especially to Kerry in the period after the convention. Corrado also describes the creative method the RNC devised to spend party funds in ways that were coordinated with the candidate but not limited in amount. In addition, he highlights the declining role of public money as a source of general election funding and the challenges now facing the public funding system.

In chapter 6, Paul S. Herrnson turns to the congressional elections in 2004. Before BCRA, parties and interest groups had targeted soft money and issue advocacy money on relatively few congressional races. To determine the effects of BCRA on congressional elections, Herrnson asks whether the party committees were successful in substituting hard money for soft money. How did interest groups adjust to the new restrictions on soft money? Did candidates exploit the new higher individual contribution limits? Where did the parties make independent expenditures and to what effect? Herrnson demonstrates that in many ways congressional campaign finance was business as usual. Competition continued to be concentrated in a few contests, meaning that the unprecedented hard money raised by the parties had only a few promising targets. While the activity of Section 527 organizations was more a presidential than congressional election phenomenon, there were important 527 group activities in congressional elections.

As Robin Kolodny and Diana Dwyre discuss in chapter 7, BCRA's "new rules" for financing elections affected parties even more than candidates or interest groups. Because soft money had become so central to the parties, especially in competitive states and races, they had to find ways to adapt to a world without soft money. Dwyre and Kolodny ask how well the six campaign committees that focus primarily on federal elections did so and how BCRA affected the federal campaign activities of state parties. Three other questions of interest are how parties raised money, how parties spent money, and whether BCRA diminished parties, as its opponents often argued. The analysis covers not only the post-BCRA patterns but also those of the preceding FECA-governed elections. Because the story for the party committees was different in the congressional committees, they examine the causes and implications of those differences as well.

Interest groups play multiple roles in financing American federal elections. They contribute to candidates, parties, and other interest groups; they spend money independently; and they communicate to their membership and shareholders. In chapter 8, Allan Cigler, a respected scholar of interest groups, reviews their activity before BCRA, the intent of BCRA regarding these groups, and the way they spent money on federal elections in 2004. Unions and corporations, as noted earlier, had been allowed to spend general treasury funds on issue advocacy and donate it to political parties as soft money. That practice was banned by BCRA. Cigler considers the extent to which unions or corporations found other ways of spending money to influence the 2004 election, particularly their expanded use of Section 527 and 501(c) organizations. He also discusses alliances that interest groups, 527s, and 501(c)s formed with the Democratic or Republican parties, their strategies for raising and spending money, and the extent to which they focused on the presidential election.

To conclude our analysis, Thomas E. Mann assesses how BCRA measured up against the expectations of the legislation's advocates and opponents. Mann covers the 2004 presidential and congressional elections, evaluating the central elements of BCRA such as the party soft money ban, limitations on the use of union and corporate treasury funds in broadcast electioneering, and greater disclosure requirements for 527 organizations. He also briefly discusses the impact of the Internet on campaign finance in 2004. Mann also evaluates the likely effect of legislation introduced in both houses to amend BCRA. With an eye to future elections, Mann explores what the 2004 experience taught reformers, candidates, parties, and interest groups.

Notes

1. As quoted in Glen Justice, "Bush's Side Entered October with $108 Million, Kerry's with $79 Million," *New York Times*, October 21, 2004, p. A24.

2. Commission on Presidential Debates, "September 30, 2004: The First Bush-Kerry Presidential Debate" (www.debates.org/pages/trans2004a.html [September 15, 2005]).

3. Hanna Rosin, "Billionaire against Bush," *Washington Post*, September 29, 2005, p. C1.

4. Dana Milbank and Spencer S. Hsu, "Cheney: Kerry Victory Is Risky," *Washington Post*, September 8, 2004, p. A1.

5. See www.redefeatbush.com.

6. America Votes 2004, "The Primaries: The GOP Nomination Process" (www.cnn.com/ELECTION/2004/primaries/pages/misc/gop.html [June 23, 2005]).

7. National Journal Group Inc., 2004 miscellaneous polling on George W. Bush. *Poll Track* (www.nationaljournal.com/members/polltrack/2004/national/04bushmisc.htm [June 23, 2005]).

8. Susan Page, "Bush Has 7-Point Poll Lead on Kerry," *USA Today*, September 7, 2004, p. A1.

9. Robin Toner, "A Call to Arms by Abortion Rights Groups," *New York Times*, April 22, 2004, p. A20.

10. David B. Magleby, J. Quin Monson, and Kelly D. Patterson, eds., *Dancing without Partners: How Candidates, Parties, and Interest Groups Interact in the New Campaign Finance Environment* (Brigham Young University, Center for the Study of Elections and Democracy, 2005).

11. Mark Longabaugh, LCV, interview by David B. Magleby and Joe Hadfield, Washington D.C., June 24, 2004.

12. For a discussion of the formation and development of 527s, see Steve Weissman and Ruth Hassan, "527 Groups and BCRA," in *The Election after Reform: Money Politics and the Bipartisan Campaign Reform Act,* edited by Michael J. Malbin (Lanham, Md.: Rowman and Littlefield, 2006).

13. Center for Responsive Politics, "Top Individual Contributors."

14. Weissman and Hassan, "527 Groups and BCRA."

15. Center for Responsive Politics, "Top Individual Contributors."

16. Weissman and Hassan, "527 Groups and BCRA."

17. David B. Magleby, "A High-Stakes Election," in *Financing the 2000 Election,* edited by David B. Magleby (Brookings, 2002), p. 9.

18. "Déjà vu Soft Money: Outlawed Contributions Likely to Flow to Shadowy 527 Groups that Skirt Flawed Disclosure Law" (www.citizen.org/documents/ACF8D5.PDF [January 25, 2005]), p. ii.

19. David Williams, director of Action Fund and PAC, Planned Parenthood, interview by David B. Magleby and Nicole Carlisle Squires, Washington, D.C., November 8, 2002.

20. *Buckley v. Valeo,* 424 U.S. 1 (1976).

21. *Colorado Republican Federal Campaign Committee v. FEC,* 518 U.S. 604 (1996).

22. *McConnell v. FEC,* 124 S. Ct. 619 (2003), pp. 107–44.

23. See www.opensecrets.org/payback/issue.asp?issueid=CFR&CongNo=107 &billdisplay=2&Chamber=H [October 2, 2005].

24. Federal Election Commission (FEC), "Party Fundraising Reaches $1.1 Billion in 2002 Election Cycle," press release, March 20, 2003 (www.fec.gov/press/press2003/20030320party/20030103party.html [September 15, 2005]).

25. *McConnell v. FEC.*

26. Bill Miller, vice president public affairs and national political director,

U.S. Chamber of Commerce, interview by J. Quin Monson and Betsey Gimbel, Washington, D.C., February 12, 2004.

27. Andrew Stern, president, and Jack Polidori, political director, Service Employees International Union, interview by David B. Magleby and Betsey Gimbel, Washington, D.C., June 6, 2004.

28. David B. Magleby and Jonathan W. Tanner, "Interest-Group Electioneering in the 2002 Congressional Elections," in *The Last Hurrah?* edited by David B. Magleby and J. Quin Monson (Brookings, 2004), p. 64; David B. Magleby, "The Importance of Outside Money in Competitive Congressional Campaigns," in *The Other Campaign: Soft Money and Issue Advocacy in 2000 Congressional Elections*, edited by David B. Magleby (Lanham, Md.: Rowman and Littlefield, 2003), p. 1; Marianne Holt, "The Surge in Party Money in Competitive 1998 Congressional Elections," in *Outside Money: Soft Money and Issue Advocacy in the 1998 Congressional Elections*, edited by David B. Magleby (Lanham, Md.: Rowman and Littlefield, 2000), p. 28.

29. David B. Magleby and J. Quin Monson, "The Consequences of Noncandidate Spending, with a Look to the Future," in *The Last Hurrah?* edited by Magleby and Monson, p. 277.

30. Anna Nibley Baker and David B. Magleby, "Interest Groups in the 2000 Congressional Elections," in *The Other Campaign*, edited by Magleby.

31. Erik Smith, Media Fund, interview by David B. Magleby and Kristina Gale, Washington D.C., November 10, 2004.

32. Stephen Moore, Club for Growth, interview by David B. Magleby, Washington D.C., November 5, 2004.

33. Bipartisan Campaign Reform Act, U.S. Code, vol. 2, sec. 431 (2002).

34. *McConnell v. FEC*.

35. *Colorado Republican Federal Campaign Committee v. FEC*.

36. Campaign Legal Center, "Legal Center Press Release: McCain, Feingold to Support '527 Group' Lawsuit," press release, September 14, 2004 (www.campaignlegalcenter.org/cases-166.html [January 25, 2005]).

37. Thomas B. Edsall and Dan Balz, "Kerry Says He Will Forgo Public Funding," *Washington Post*, November 15, 2003, p. A1.

38. Michael Malbin, "Thinking about Reform," in *Life after Reform: When the Bipartisan Campaign Reform Act Meets Politics*, edited by Michael Malbin (Lanham, Md.: Rowman and Littlefield, 2003), p. 16.

39. Michael Petro, vice president and director of Business and Government Policy, Committee for Economic Development, interview by David Magleby and Betsey Gimbel, Washington D.C., November 19, 2004.

40. Magleby, "A High-Stakes Election," p. 11.

41. Malbin, "Thinking about Reform," p. 11.

42. FEC, "FEC Reports Increase in Party Fundraising for 2000," Washington, May 15, 2001 (www.fec.gov/press/press2001/051501partyfund/051501party fund.html [June 29, 2005]), and "FEC Reports on Congressional Financial

Activity for 2000," Washington, May 15, 2001 (www.fec.gov/press/press2001/051501congfinact/051501congfinact.html [June 29, 2005]).

43. FEC, "Party Financial Activity Summarized for the 2004 Election Cycle," press release March 2, 2005 (www.fec.gov/press/press2005/20050302party/Party2004final.html [September 29, 2005]).

44. Ellen Moran, DNC, interview by David B. Magleby, Washington D.C., December 16, 2004.

45. Seth Gitell, "The Democratic Party Suicide Bill," *Atlantic Monthly*, July/August 2003, p. 106.

46. Thomas E. Mann and Anthony Corrado, "Despite Predictions, BCRA Has Not Been a 'Democratic Suicide Bill'" (www.brookings.edu/views/op-ed/corrado/20040726.htm [September 15, 2005]). See also Norman Ornstein and Anthony Corrado, "Hard Money Is Easy to Come By," *New York Times*, September 5, 2003, p. 19.

47. Thomas E. Mann, "Political Parties Now Facing 'Tough Love,'" *Boston Globe*, November 10, 2002, p. E11.

48. Excerpts from his brief are printed in Donald P. Green, "The Need for Federal Regulation of State Party Activity," in *Inside the Campaign Finance Battle: Court Testimony on the New Reforms*, edited by Anthony Corrado, Thomas E. Mann, and Trevor Potter (Brookings, 2003), pp. 97–115. His entire brief can be found at www.campaignlegalcenter.org.

49. FEC, "Party Financial Activity Summarized for the 2004 Cycle," press release, March 2, 2004 (www.fec.gov/press/press2004/20040302party/Party2004final.html); FEC, "FEC Reports Increase in Party Fundraising for 2000," press release, May 15, 2001 (www.fec.gov/press/press2001/051501partyfund/051501partyfund.html [March 21, 2006]).

50. Allan J. Cigler, "Interest Groups and Financing the 2000 Elections," in *Financing the 2000 Election*, edited by Magleby, p. 175.

51. "Close Election Turns on Voter Turnout," *Washington Post*, November 1, 2002, p. A1.

52. Ibid.

53. Curt Anderson, Anderson Group, and Blaise Hazelwood, RNC political director, interview by David B. Magleby and Jonathan W. Tanner, Washington, D.C., May 8, 2003; Sara Taylor and Michael Ellis, deputy to the chief strategist and research analyst, Bush/Cheney '04, interview by David Magleby and Betsey Gimbel, Arlington, Va., November 18, 2004.

54. David B. Magleby, "The Expanded Role of Interest Groups and Political Parties in Competitive U.S. Congressional Elections," in *Outside Money*, edited by Magleby, p. 4.

55. J. Quin Monson, "Get on Television vs. Get on the Van: GOTV and the Ground War in 2002," in *The Last Hurrah?* edited by Magleby and Monson, p. 101.

56. Ibid., p. 93.

57. Ibid., p.43. Also FEC (ftp://ftp.fec.gov/FEC/ [September 16, 2005].

58. Terry Nelson, political director, Bush/Cheney '04, telephone interview by David B. Magleby and J. Quin Monson, January 5, 2005.

59. Cigler, "Interest Groups and Financing the 2000 Elections," pp. 177–78.

60. David B. Magleby and Jason Richard Beal, "Independent Expenditures and Internal Communications in the 2000 Congressional Elections," in *The Other Campaign,* edited by Magleby, p. 80.

61. FEC (ftp://ftp.fec.gov/FEC/ [September 16, 2005]).

62. See www.bipac.org and www.voteforbusiness.com as examples.

63. Donald P. Green and Alan Gerber, *Get Out the Vote: How to Increase Voter Turnout* (Brookings, 2004).

64. Dan Balz and Thomas B. Edsall, "Unprecedented Efforts to Mobilize Voters Begin," *Washington Post,* November 1, 2004, p. A1.

65. Republican National Committee (RNC), "72 Hour Task Force," Preelection 2002 version, PowerPoint presentation, obtained from James Dyke, RNC press secretary, January 23, 2003. Also, Alexander Gage, president, Brent Seaborn, vice president, and Michael Myers, vice president, TargetPoint Consulting, interview by David Magleby and J. Quin Monson, Alexandria, Va., December 15, 2004.

66. Bob Bennett, NRSC, interview by Kelly D. Patterson, Washington D.C., November 5, 2004.

67. Whit Ayers, president, Ayres, McHenry, and Associates, Inc., interview by David B. Magleby and Betsey Gimbel, Washington D.C., September 16, 2004.

68. April Schiff and Nathan Hollifield, interview by David B. Magleby and Susan MacManus, July 24, 2004.

69. Taylor and Ellis, interview (see note 53).

70. Nelson, interview (see note 58).

71. Ed Gillespie, chairman, RNC, speech given at the National Press Club, November 4, 2004.

72. Kimberly Robson, deputy field director for legislative election program, People for the American Way, interview by David B. Magleby and Kristina Gale, Washington, D.C., November 5, 2004.

73. Kristina Wilfore, Ballot Initiative Strategy Center, interview by David B. Magleby, Kelly D. Patterson, and Betsey Gimbel, Washington D.C., August 18, 2004.

74. David E. Campbell and J. Quin Monson, "The Religion Card: Evangelicals, Catholics, and Gay Marriage in the 2004 Presidential Election," paper prepared for the annual meeting of the American Political Science Association, September 2, 2005, Washington, D.C.

75. For purposes of this analysis, we have defined battleground states as those characterized as competitive as of October 26 by the Cook Political

Report. Charlie Cook, "One Week Out, and One Heap of Unanswered Questions," Cook Political Report, October 26, 2004 (www.cookpolitical.com/column/2004/102604.php [September 27, 2005]).

76. "America Votes 2004" and "Election 2000" (www.cnn.com/election/2004/ and www.cnn.com/election/2000/ [September 27, 2005]).

77. Thomas B. Edsall and James V. Grimaldi, "On Nov. 2, GOP Got More Bang for Its Billion, Analysis Shows," Washington Post, December 30, 2004, p. A1.

78. See Raymond J. La Raja, "State and Local Political Parties," in Life after Reform, edited by Malbin; also Balz and Edsall, "Unprecedented Efforts to Mobilize Voters Begin," p. A1.

79. Erik Smith, interview, November 10, 2005.

80. La Raja, "State and Local Political Parties," p. 4.

81. FEC, "Election Assistance Commission: Duties and Responsibilities" (www.fec.gov/hava/eac.htm [September 14, 2005]).

82. Michael M. Franz, Joel Rivlin, and Kenneth Goldstein, "Much More of the Same: Television Advertising Pre- and Post-BCRA," in The Election after Reform, edited by Malbin, p. 13; and Joel Rivlin, deputy director, Wisconsin Advertising Project, telephone interview by David B. Magleby, J. Quin Monson, and Nisha Riggs, Provo, Utah, September 19, 2005.

83. Franz and others, "Much More of the Same," p. 10.

84. Ibid.

85. Ibid., p. 13.

86. Swift Boat Veterans for Truth's first ad aired outside the sixty-day window, between the Democratic and Republican Conventions, but their other three ads ran within the window.

87. Franz and others, "Much More of the Same," p. 11.

88. David B. Magleby and others, Electing Congress: New Rules for an Old Game (Saddle River, N.J.: Prentice-Hall, 2006, forthcoming); also Magleby, Outside Money; Magleby, The Other Campaign; Magleby and Monson, The Last Hurrah?

89. David B. Magleby, Kelly D. Patterson, and J. Quin Monson, "Introduction," in Electing Congress: New Rules for an Old Game.

90. Ibid.

TWO   *The Regulatory Environment:*
Uncertainty in the
Wake of Change

ANTHONY CORRADO

The federal elections of 2004 were the first in more than twenty years to be conducted under a major new regulatory statute: the Bipartisan Campaign Reform Act of 2002 (BCRA), which took effect after the 2002 elections. Though not a comprehensive reform, BCRA made significant changes in the rules governing the financing of federal campaigns. It barred party committees from raising and spending unregulated funds, commonly known as soft money, which had become a major source of party funding in recent elections. The law also addressed the problems associated with candidate-specific issue advocacy advertising in federal elections by explicitly defining the types of broadcast advertising that would constitute "electioneering communications" and prohibiting the use of corporate or labor union funds to pay for such advertising. It extended the scope of federal regulation by defining the types of political activity that constitute federal election campaigning and imposing new regulations on state and local parties and organized groups involved in these activities. Furthermore, it increased individual contribution limits for the first time since the adoption of the 1974 Federal Election Campaign Act (FECA). BCRA thus mandated substantial changes in both the sources and methods of financing political campaigns.

As in any case of major regulatory reform, the enactment of BCRA introduced a considerable amount of unpredictability and uncertainty

This chapter is based in part on research supported by a Colby College Social Science Grant.

into the electoral process, since the ways candidates, parties, and political groups would adapt to the new rules were yet to be seen. It was therefore difficult to anticipate how the flow of money in federal elections might change or what new practices might arise to challenge the efficacy of the statute.

Further uncertainties surrounded the implementation of the statute, which quickly evolved into a bitterly divisive process. The passage of BCRA did not bring an end—not even temporarily—to the debate on campaign finance policy that had been waged in Congress and in public for most of the preceding decade. While the advocates of reform achieved a notable success in building a winning coalition of supporters in Congress and enacting a new law, this victory merely shifted the debate from the legislative branch to the courts and administrative agencies.

Even before BCRA was signed into law, it was evident that the constitutionality of the statute would be challenged and that the case would quickly reach the Supreme Court. Many observers wondered whether its major provisions would withstand judicial scrutiny or experience a fate similar to that of the 1974 FECA, which was significantly altered as a result of the Supreme Court's ruling in *Buckley* v. *Valeo*.[1] Even if the Court did uphold the statute, the Federal Election Commission (FEC) would still have to promulgate regulations to implement the statute. How the agency would define and apply the statutory language was unknown, particularly in those instances in which Congress provided little guidance. Consequently, throughout the 2004 election cycle, either the law or the FEC's regulatory decisions implementing the law were being challenged in the courts or in administrative proceedings.

As the overview of BCRA's provisions and implementation in this chapter demonstrates, some of the debates centered on issues unique to BCRA, others on long-standing controversies renewed in its wake. In either case, the experience of putting BCRA into practice highlighted the crucial role played by the courts and the FEC in shaping campaign finance law, the consequences of judicial and administrative decisionmaking with respect to the flow of money in federal elections, and the difficulties of regulating a process as diverse and dynamic as campaign finance.

An Overview of BCRA

The principal objective of BCRA was to reduce the risk of corruption or the appearance of corruption by restoring the integrity of the regulatory framework established by the FECA.[2] The law was primarily designed to strengthen FECA restrictions on the sources and size of political contributions, as well as the requirements for public disclosure of campaign money, the efficacy of which had been seriously eroded by the growth of party soft money and unregulated issue advocacy advertising in connection with federal elections. In the 2000 elections, the parties had raised $495 million in soft money, most of it from donors of $100,000 or more and a large share from corporations and labor unions, two sources long banned from making contributions in federal elections.[3] The parties used a substantial portion of this money to pay for candidate-specific issue advocacy advertisements, which were considered outside the purview of federal regulation because they did not "expressly advocate" the election or defeat of a federal candidate by using such words as "vote for," "elect," or "defeat." Because the money used for such ads was not subject to federal contribution restrictions and strict public disclosure rules, organized groups also took advantage of the tactic, spending tens of millions of dollars on it in 2000 alone.[4] These practices essentially rendered the FECA restrictions on campaign funding meaningless.

Accordingly, BCRA was structured around two central pillars: a ban on party soft money funds and the creation of a new category of broadcast advertisements, known as electioneering communications, which were subject to disclosure requirements and funding source prohibitions (no corporate or labor union treasury funds may be used). The law made other important changes in campaign finance practices, many[5] the product of the legislative maneuvering that accompanied final passage of the bill and of advocates' efforts to anticipate likely loopholes and close off these alternatives.[6] As a result, BCRA included a number of complex and technical provisions and expanded the scope of federal regulation beyond the borders established by the FECA.

Banning Soft Money

BCRA sought to reduce the risk or appearance of corruption in the political process by severing the link between large political contributors and federal elected officials and party leaders. The law prohibits a national party committee—including any entities directly or indirectly established, financed, maintained, or controlled by a national party committee or any party official or agent acting on a committee's behalf—from soliciting, receiving, spending, transferring, or directing to another person any funds that are not subject to federal contribution limits, source prohibitions, and reporting requirements. It imposes similar restrictions on federal officeholders and candidates, or agents acting on their behalf. In short, federal elected officials, candidates, and party leaders may only raise and use "hard" money, that is, money regulated by federal law. As a general rule, they are not allowed to raise or use any funds from individuals or political committees that are not fully disclosed and subject to contribution limits. Federal law also prohibits the solicitation or use of any funds from corporation or labor union treasuries.

To safeguard against attempts to circumvent these prohibitions, BCRA regulated fundraising by federal officeholders or candidates and national party committees for nonparty organizations that are active in federal election campaigns. For example, national party committees and their officials or agents, as well as state and local party committees and their officials or agents, are barred from soliciting contributions or otherwise financially supporting tax-exempt organizations that conduct activities "in connection with" federal elections such as voter registration and turnout drives. Similarly, national and state party committees are banned from raising soft money for political organizations that operate under Section 527 of the Internal Revenue Code and seek to influence the outcome of federal elections. Party committees are not legally permitted to simply shift their soft money activities to allied organizations by raising or providing unregulated funds to interest groups or 527 committees.

BCRA's congressional sponsors recognized that a ban on soft money at the national level might encourage state or local party organizations to re-create some form of the soft money system at the state or local level. For example, state parties might solicit contributions banned under federal law (such as corporate contributions or unlimited individual contributions, which are permitted in some states) and use these funds to finance activities that would help federal candidates. To close this potential loophole, the law defined the types of state and local party activity that must be financed with federally regulated funds. Specifically, "federal election activity" includes: (1) voter registration activity within 120 days of a regularly scheduled federal election; (2) voter identification, get-out-the-vote (GOTV), or generic campaign activity conducted in connection with an election in which a federal candidate appears on the ballot; (3) any public communication, including television or radio ads, mass mailings, telephone-calling programs, or general public advertising that refers to a clearly identified federal candidate and promotes, supports, attacks, or opposes that candidate; and (4) the salary of any employee of a state, district, or local party committee who spends more than 25 percent of his or her compensated time on federal election activities. These kinds of expenses, even if incurred by a local party, must be financed with hard money.

Although it restricted the type of funding involved in national-state party transactions, BCRA did not prohibit party committees from working together in election campaigns. National party committees could continue to provide assistance to their affiliated state and local committees, but only with hard money. A national committee could still help state or local parties with their fundraising or establish a joint fundraising program with a state or local committee, or even transfer unlimited amounts of money to a state or local committee, as long as these transactions were limited to hard money. A national party committee could no longer help state and local committees raise donations that were not subject to federal contribution limits, even if the contributions were permissible under state law.

The new rules did shift the line dividing federal and nonfederal election activity, thereby bringing more state and local party activity under the rubric of federal regulation than was the case under the FECA. In protecting against a state party soft money loophole, BCRA did not simply limit federal restrictions to activities *intended* to influence federal elections or to those that *directly* benefited federal candidates (such as broadcast advertisements that featured a federal candidate) or to the salary of a state party staffer responsible for working with a federal candidate's campaign. Instead, the statutory definition encompassed activities such as partisan voter registration or GOTV programs that could reasonably be expected to have an effect on federal elections by registering and mobilizing more voters likely to vote for a federal candidate who appeared on the ballot.[7] Thus even if a state or local party mobilization drive was designed to influence a statewide election or a state legislative race, the fact that a federal candidate was also on the ballot was considered sufficient to require the use of federally regulated funds. Before the adoption of BCRA, state parties could finance such expenditures with a combination of hard and soft money, the largest share consisting of soft money.

Any state or local party activities that do not fall within the statute's definition of federal election activity are not affected by BCRA's provisions. These activities, including all communications that refer solely to a state or local candidate, can be financed with money raised under state law, including unlimited individual donations or corporate and labor gifts where allowed. In addition, state parties can continue to finance their administrative expenses with a combination of hard and soft money, just as they did before BCRA, in accordance with the FEC's allocation rules for dividing costs between federal and nonfederal funds. These allocation rules were in effect long before the passage of BCRA.[8]

BCRA's ban on soft money was far-reaching, but Congress did incorporate some limited exemptions into the law. In recognition of the varied roles that federal elected officials and candidates often fulfill, the law makes some allowances for certain types of fundraising that might occur outside of the general proscriptions. First, federal officeholders or national party officials who are candidates for state or local office may solicit contributions allowable under state law, even if prohibited under federal law, as long as they are solicited and used only for activities that refer only to a state and local candidate. A member of the House who is running for governor, for example, can solicit contributions for the gubernatorial campaign in excess of the amounts allowed under federal law as long as the contributions are permitted under state law and used only for the gubernatorial race.

Second, federal officeholders and candidates, as well as national party officials, can participate in state or local party fundraising events as a speaker or featured guest, even if the party is raising money that is not permitted under federal law. This exemption acknowledges the role of federal officials and candidates in state and local party politics and the fact that they are important members of state and local party organizations.

Third, BCRA included an exemption to ensure that federal elected officials or candidates could continue to help raise funds for tax-exempt nonprofit organizations that operate under Section 501(c) of the Internal Revenue Code, such as the American Red Cross. The law allows federal officeholders and candidates to raise money from individuals (not corporations or labor unions) in amounts up to $20,000, so long as the organization's principal purpose is not to conduct voter registration and turnout drives. A federal candidate could thus raise money for an organization like the National Association for the Advancement of Colored People (NAACP), which has conducted voter registration drives in the past, because voter registration is not the principal purpose of the organization.

Finally, Congress recognized that a ban on soft money might reduce the funds available to national party committees. During the debates on the bill, some members of Congress voiced concerns that a ban on soft money might reduce the resources available to state and local party committees for voter registration and turnout programs, since the bulk of the money for such programs in many states was raised by the national committees and sent to the state parties.[9] To address this issue, Senator Carl Levin (D-Mich.) included a provision that allows state and local committees to use a combination of hard and soft money to pay for certain voter registration, identification, and turnout activities, as well as some generic party campaign activities. This provision, known as the Levin amendment, operates as a narrow exemption to the general ban on soft money funds. Its purpose is to provide state or local parties with greater leeway in raising money for the specific purpose of financing grassroots voter participation activities.

Under the Levin amendment, state and local parties may receive contributions, known as Levin funds, in amounts of up to $10,000 per donor per calendar year, if allowed by state law. If state law permits a contribution of $10,000 or more to a party committee, which most state laws do, then any donor allowed to make a party contribution may donate up to $10,000 to a party's Levin fund. Otherwise, the amount and sources of contributions are limited to the amounts and sources allowed under state law. So if a state caps individual donations to a party committee at $5,000, the maximum Levin contribution in that state is $5,000.

Levin funds may be used to finance generic voter registration drives conducted more than 120 days before an election, as well as generic voter identification and turnout efforts that do not mention a federal candidate. However, they may only be spent in combination with federally regulated funds; the costs of the activities financed with Levin money must be divided between hard money and Levin money. The portion to be paid out of hard money is based on allocation formulas established by the FEC.

In order to ensure that the Levin exception did not become a means of undermining the ban on soft money, Congress imposed a number of restrictions on Levin funds. Only money raised by the state or local committee making the expenditures can be used in Levin funding: that includes both the hard money portion and the Levin portion. Money for activities that qualify for Levin funding cannot be transferred to a state or local committee from the national party committee or another state party. Even the hard money used to pay for the federal portion of Levin activity cannot be transferred from the national committee. In this way, the amount of money spent by a state party under this exemption is limited to the amount the state party can raise on its own. With regard to the expenditure of these funds, no Levin funds may be used to finance any voter registration or mobilization efforts that mention federal candidates. In addition, none of this money can be used to pay for broadcast, cable, or satellite communications, even when the communications are made in connection with a voter registration or turnout drive. The funds are solely to be used for generic grassroots mobilization; they are not to be used to finance television or radio advertising.

Reforming Issue Advocacy

Before the adoption of BCRA, the principal means of determining whether an advertisement or other form of political communication was a federal campaign expenditure subject to contribution limits and disclosure requirements was a standard known as the magic words doctrine. This doctrine grew out of the Supreme Court's ruling in *Buckley* v. *Valeo*. The original provisions of the 1974 FECA imposed contribution restrictions and disclosure requirements on expenditures made "relative to a clearly identified candidate" or "for the purpose of influencing" a federal election. The Court found these phrases to be too vague and broad to withstand constitutional scrutiny and held that congressional authority to regulate campaign funding was limited to expenditures that "expressly advocate" the election or defeat of a federal candidate. The Court suggested that express advocacy would encompass communications using such words as "vote for," "elect," "support," "defeat," or "Smith for Congress." These became known as the magic words that triggered federal regulation. Messages that did not include these words, even if they featured federal candidates, were cast as "issue advocacy," and any money spent on such messages was not restricted by FECA disclosure rules and contribution limits.[10] This narrow test made it easy for parties and nonparty political advertisers to avoid regulation.

The surge in candidate-specific issue advertising that began in the 1996 election cycle led advocates of campaign finance reform to focus on the problems associated with this practice and the need to craft a more inclusive standard for campaign advertising. Issue advocacy was an especially important matter because without new rules a ban of soft money would simply encourage donors, including corporations and labor unions, to shift their giving to interest groups and nonparty organizations that would be able to use unlimited funds for issue advocacy advertising targeted at specific federal candidates.

As a supplement to the magic words test, BCRA established a new category of regulated communications, known as electioneering communications. An electioneering communication is any broadcast, cable, or satellite communication that refers to a clearly identified federal candidate, is broadcast within thirty days of a primary election or sixty days of a general election, and is targeted at the constituency of the featured candidate.[11] Any ad that meets these criteria may not be paid for with corporate or labor union funds; only individual donations are permitted. The law also required disclosure of any disbursements on electioneering communications totaling $10,000 or more in a calendar year and the disclosure of any contributions of more than $1,000.[12]

BCRA therefore did not prohibit issue advocacy advertising. Instead, it regulated the sources of funding and required the disclosure of major donors who provided the funding for ads that met certain criteria. These restrictions were greater than those under previous law but still did not cover all issue advertising. The law made no changes in the regulation of issue advocacy messages that were not broadcast; and any expenditures on more grassroots-oriented forms of communication, including voter guides, mail, telephone programs, and newspaper advertisements, were not affected. Nonparty groups and political committees could still use corporate and labor funds for these methods of candidate-specific issue advocacy advertising. Furthermore, the new rules applied only to broadcast advertisements that met *all* of the law's criteria. Thus advertisements that did not feature a federal candidate were not subject to the regulations. In addition, ads broadcast by interest groups or nonparty organizations outside of the federal advertising period—that is, before the thirty-day or sixty-day windows—could still be funded with undisclosed contributions, including corporate and labor funds.

This limited approach to issue advocacy reform reflected the deference given to constitutional considerations by BCRA's congressional sponsors. Since the law expanded the realm of political communications subject to federal regulation, its effects on free political speech had to be considered. BCRA therefore incorporated safeguards to ensure that individuals or groups spending relatively small sums on advertising or engaged in grassroots politicking would not be brought into the federal regulatory process, a consequence that might serve to discourage these participants from expressing their views and thereby have a "chilling effect" on political speech. In addition, by focusing on broadcast advertising and a prohibition on corporate and labor funding, the law operated in areas where the courts had previously recognized congressional regulatory authority.[13] The law thus sought to balance the need for broader regulation and the freedom of political speech.

Consequently, BCRA's approach to issue advocacy messages was less stringent for nonparty organizations than for party committees. National parties had to finance all of their communications, including non-broadcast communications, with hard money. State parties had to use hard money for any public communications via mail, telephone calls, newspapers, or other media that promoted, supported, attacked, or opposed a federal candidate. As a practical matter, then, parties had to rely on hard money to finance all advertising that featured federal candidates. Interest groups and nonparty political committees, however, could still spend unregulated funds on certain types of communications, while the party committees could not. This difference in the rules gave interest groups an advantage in the financing of campaign messages. It also provided some advantage in the financing of television and radio advertising aired outside of the federal advertising windows.

Revising Contribution Limits

Some analysts worried that the electioneering communications regulations, combined with the ban on soft money, would leave the parties weaker than interest groups, particularly if the new rules were to reduce party funding.[14] To provide partial compensation for the loss of soft money, the statute increased some of the FECA contribution limits. These limits had not been adjusted since they were established in the 1970s, so the changes also restored some of the purchasing power lost due to inflation in the intervening years.[15]

These changes were designed to increase the role of individual contributors in federal elections and provide additional hard money resources to party committees. Accordingly, the law raised the ceilings on individual contributions to candidates and party committees but did not change the amounts that an individual could contribute to a multicandidate political action committee (PAC, $5,000 a year) or the amount a PAC could give to a candidate ($5,000 per election), a national party committee ($15,000 a year), or a state party ($5,000 a year).[16]

BCRA revised the FECA's individual contribution limits and ceiling on the aggregate amount an individual could contribute each year. The act increased the amount an individual could give to a federal candidate from $1,000 to $2,000 per election and adjusted this amount for inflation.[17] It raised the amount that could be given to a national party committee from $20,000 to $25,000 a year (adjusted for inflation) and the amount that could be given to a state party committee from $5,000 to $10,000 a year (this is the amount allowed under federal law, which is not adjusted for inflation).

Under the FECA, an individual could give a total of up to $25,000 a year ($50,000 every two years) in aggregate hard dollar contributions to candidates, parties, and PACs. BCRA raised this amount to $95,000 for each two-year election cycle and indexed it for inflation.[18] More important, the law set a sublimit of $37,500 every two years in aggregate contributions to candidates and a separate sublimit of $57,500 in aggregate contributions to parties and PACs. But of this $57,500 (which is adjusted for inflation), only $37,500 (not adjusted for inflation) can be given to committees other than national party committees. So in order to reach the aggregate ceiling, an individual would have to give at least $20,000 to national party committees. If an individual so chooses, the entire amount, $57,500, can be donated to national party committees, with no more than $25,000 a year given to any one national party committee. Finally, the new rules increased the FECA's special limit for combined contributions by the national party committee and senatorial campaign committee to a Senate candidate, which was originally set at $17,500. BCRA doubled this amount to $35,000 and adjusted it for inflation.

The Millionaires' Amendment

Perhaps the most complex component of BCRA was a provision added by the Senate, which would make it easier in certain circumstances for candidates to raise money when facing a high-spending, self-financed opponent. In a marked departure from the FECA and in response to incumbent legislators who feared the possibility of being outspent by wealthy opponents, Congress decided to allow substantial increases in contribution limits and party support for candidates running against self-funded challengers. This part of the law quickly came to be known as the millionaires' amendment.

The millionaires' amendment consists of a set of complicated financial calculations that trigger higher contribution limits or even unlimited party-coordinated spending, depending on the level of spending of a self-funded challenger. The provision takes effect when a self-funded candidate exceeds a designated threshold of personal spending on a campaign. For House races, the threshold sum is $350,000. Any amount above this threshold may trigger higher contribution limits for the candidate who is not self-funded. For Senate races, the threshold amount is $150,000 plus an amount equal to $0.04 multiplied by the voting-age population of the relevant state. A Senate candidate may qualify for higher contribution limits only after an opposing candidate's personal spending is twice the sum set by the threshold amount.

However, expenditures by a self-funded candidate, even if in excess of the threshold sum, do not automatically trigger higher contribution limits. In order to ensure that a candidate with a significant financial advantage over a self-funded challenger does not gain additional advantage from an increased contribution cap, the millionaire formulas also take into account the amounts raised by the relevant candidates. This calculation, called the opposition personal funds amount, is a measure of the amount spent by a self-funded candidate minus the amount spent by an opponent. If the self-funded candidate's opposition personal funds amount has reached 100 percent of the threshold amount in House races, higher contribution limits take effect for any non-self-funded opponent. In this instance, individual contribution limits are tripled, rising from $2,000 per election to $6,000 (in 2004), and national and state party committees are permitted to make unlimited coordinated expenditures on behalf of a non-self-funded candidate. In Senate races, higher contribution limits are put into effect once a self-financed candidate's opposition personal funds amount has reached 110 percent of the threshold sum. Depending on the amount spent by the self-funded candidate, the individual contribution limit applicable to any opponent can increase up to sixfold, rising from $2,000 to $12,000 per election (in 2004). If a self-financed challenger's spending in a Senate race reaches ten times the threshold sum, national and state parties are allowed to make unlimited coordinated expenditures in support of the non-self-funded opponent.[19]

The rules also restrict a candidate's eligibility for enhanced contributions. Candidates who qualify for higher contributions and unlimited party support may only receive such funding up to the point where they have basically matched a self-financed challenger's opposition personal funds amount.[20] These candidates must continually monitor spending to ensure that they do not accept impermissible contributions. Once they have reached the levels of equity established in the law, they may no longer accept contributions in excess of $2,000 per election, and parties may no longer make coordinated expenditures beyond the amounts established by coordinating spending limits.

Other Provisions

Three other provisions are worth noting. First, BCRA required the FEC to develop new rules on "coordination," a central concept in federal campaign finance law. Any expenditure made by a person other than a candidate or party committee is legally a "contribution" if it is coordinated with a candidate or party committee, and thus subject to the law's contribution limits and source prohibitions. For example, any expenditure by an individual in excess of $2,000 that is coordinated with a candidate would be illegal, since it exceeds the limit on individual contributions.

Like the FECA, BCRA defines coordination as a payment made in cooperation with, at the request of, or by the suggestion of a candidate or a candidate's agent, campaign, or party. The FEC had adopted regulations to implement the FECA provision, based in part on a district court decision.[21] These regulations defined the conditions in which a political communication by an interest group or nonparty political committee would be considered coordinated spending. The rules set forth a narrow definition: coordination would only be found when a party or candidate exercised control over a communication or in the case of "substantial discussion" that resulted in "formal collaboration" or "agreement."[22] Congress considered this definition insufficiently comprehensive and included a provision in BCRA that required the FEC to discard these rules and promulgate new regulations that do not rest on agreement or formal collaboration. In other words, instead of defining what constitutes coordination in the statute, Congress imposed a mandate on the FEC to come up with new rules.

Second, BCRA required a party committee to make a choice about the way it would financially support a candidate. In addition to accepting the limited coordinated spending permitted under the FECA, BCRA allowed party committees to make unlimited independent expenditures in support of candidates. This provision simply codified the Supreme Court's 1996 ruling in *Colorado Republican Federal Campaign Committee* v. *Federal Election Commission,* which recognized the right of party committees to spend money independently of candidates.[23] However, the law then went a step further in order to prevent parties from making both coordinated and independent expenditures in support of a candidate. Specifically, BCRA required parties to choose between the two methods once a candidate had received the party nomination. Furthermore, it provided that a choice made by a party at one level (for example, a state committee) would bind all affiliated party committees, including a national committee, to that option.

Third, BCRA's original provisions prohibited contributions by minors. The intent was to ensure the efficacy of contribution limits by preventing donors from circumventing limits by making contributions in the name of a child.

The Court Decides

BCRA's restrictions were designed to alter the flow of money in federal elections. In practice, the law would affect the financial activities of federal, state, and local party committees; the advertising campaigns sponsored by organized groups and ad hoc political committees; the sources of funding for voter registration and turnout drives; and the role of individual donors in the financing of federal campaigns. Not surprisingly, a legal challenge was filed as soon as the law was enacted.

Weeks before the Senate held its final vote on BCRA (known then as McCain-Feingold for its leading Senate sponsors, Arizona Republican John McCain and Wisconsin Democrat Russell Feingold), Senator Mitch McConnell (R-Ky.), the act's leading congressional opponent, announced that he was preparing a legal complaint against the proposed legislation. He filed this complaint almost immediately after the bill was signed into law.

Senator McConnell was soon joined by an array of other plaintiffs. In all, eleven separate complaints were filed against the act in the U.S. District Court for the District of Columbia, involving more than eighty plaintiffs, including the Republican National Committee, Democratic Party of California, National Rifle Association, American Civil Liberties Union, and AFL-CIO. Even liberal groups considered to be supporters of campaign finance reform filed suit, challenging the higher contribution limits. Taken as a whole, these actions challenged the constitutionality of almost every part of the law.

BCRA's congressional sponsors, in anticipation of a court challenge, had included a provision for expedited court review. Accordingly, a special three-judge panel was seated to conduct an expedited trial, with appeal directly to the U.S. Supreme Court. To promote timely review, the judicial panel consolidated the eleven cases into one case, *McConnell* v. *Federal Election Commission,* and set a strict timetable for proceeding.

The *McConnell* lawsuit generated extensive debate within the political community as to whether the law would be upheld. It thus left candidates, parties, and political consultants wondering about the financial strategies they might be able to employ in 2004. Although candidates and political committees were required to operate in accordance with the law's restrictions while the case was being litigated, they were also aware of the need to be ready to adapt to any changes mandated by the court. As FECA experience suggested, the court could produce significant changes in the rules. The *Buckley* decision, for example, dramatically altered the regulatory structure of the FECA by upholding its restrictions on contributions, but not its restraints on spending. A similar fate seemed likely for BCRA, particularly following the District Court ruling in May of 2003. In a massive 1,638-page opinion, the three-judge panel divided on a number of issues, upholding some provisions of the law while finding others unconstitutional or nonjusticiable.[24] In particular, the court supported the constitutionality of the national party soft money ban but raised questions about the constitutionality of the issue advocacy reforms. The opinion fueled the worst fear of party leaders and many advocates of reform: that the court would accept some parts of the law but not others, thereby diminishing its efficacy and creating a system in which parties were subject to much more stringent regulation than interest groups, with party soft money banned but issue advocacy advertising remaining unrestricted. However, the District Court issued a stay of the ruling soon after it was announced, pending Supreme Court review. Thus its decision had no effect on the law.

The Supreme Court quickly began a review of the case in December 2003 so that it might render an opinion before the beginning of the 2004 election year.[25] To the surprise of many observers, the Court upheld all of the major provisions of the law, albeit in some instances by the narrow margin of 5-4. In a joint opinion authored by Justices John

Paul Stevens and Sandra Day O'Connor, the Court held that the restrictions on party soft money were justified measures to address the governmental interest in preventing the actual or apparent corruption of federal candidates and officeholders. The opinion showed deference to the judgment of Congress and highlighted its reliance on the evidentiary record in the case, noting that the record was "replete with examples of national party committees' peddling access to federal candidates and officeholders in exchange for large soft money contributions." The Court was willing to extend the ban to state party committees and uphold the act's definition of federal election activity because it "concluded from the record that soft money's corrupting influence insinuates itself into the political process not only through national party committees, but also through state committees, which function as an alternate avenue for precisely the same corrupting forces." Congress was thus justified in taking steps to prevent circumvention of the law.

As for issue advocacy and the act's definition of electioneering communications, the Court concluded that ads broadcast close to an election are "the functional equivalent" of express advocacy and thus appropriately subject to federal regulation. Although plaintiffs had complained the standard was too vague and the magic words doctrine was a constitutionally mandated line, the Court argued that the express advocacy restriction is not a constitutional command, but a matter of statutory interpretation to solve vagueness problems. It further found that the electioneering communications standard was objective and easily understood and thus did not pose a constitutionally unacceptable risk to political speech.

However, the Court did strike down two provisions. One of them prohibited minors from making political contributions.[26] The Court found that this ban violated the rights of minors to express their political views. The second required parties to make a choice in the methods they would use to support candidates. The Court held that this provision placed an unconstitutional burden on the parties' right to make independent expenditures. Consequently, parties were left free to use both alternatives, as long as they took steps to ensure that independent expenditures were indeed independent.

The Implementation Controversies

Even as BCRA was being litigated in court, the FEC was at work developing new regulations to implement the legislation. As the agency responsible for administering, interpreting, and enforcing federal campaign finance laws, the FEC is charged with issuing advice and promulgating regulations to implement the laws. The adoption of BCRA required it to undertake extensive rulemaking, to bring standing regulations into conformity with the new statute and adopt rules to explain in detail the meaning and application of the statute's provisions.

To ensure that this task would be completed in a timely manner, BCRA required the FEC to issue its soft money regulations within 90 days of the statute's enactment, with the remaining regulations to be completed within 270 days. In 2002 the FEC thus undertook a "historic" number of rulemakings.[27] The process continued throughout 2003 and during most of 2004.[28] It was prolonged not only because of the number of regulations to be promulgated but also because of the unusual level of controversy surrounding them.

FEC Rulemaking

As with all federal regulatory agencies, the FEC develops and adopts regulations through a formal and open rulemaking process.[29] Members of the public and regulated entities are able to offer written comments on any proposal and, in cases of more important and controversial regulations, may testify at public hearings held by the FEC. Typically, the commission's rulemakings focus on technical legal issues and generate little public attention. Comments tend to come from the agency's "clientele," a small group of interested parties that include the regulated entities that might be affected by a change in the rules, reform organizations that monitor campaign finance law, and attorneys who specialize in this area and represent clients before the agency. The BCRA rulemakings did not follow the norm.

The two sides in the BCRA debate in Congress and the courts treated the regulatory process as another arena of conflict in which they could continue their arguments about the meaning and prospective efficacy of the law. As a result, interested parties on both sides sought to influence the content of the regulations and the commission's approach in interpreting the statute. In most instances, members of the coalitions active in the congressional debates formed the two sides in the implementation debates. Each of these coalitions included elected officials, party leaders, organized interests, and election law attorneys. One side was led by BCRA's principal congressional sponsors: Senators McCain and Feingold and Representatives Christopher Shays (R-Conn.) and Martin Meehan (D-Mass.). They were joined by reform organizations focused on defending the law, including the Campaign Legal Center, Democracy 21, and the Center for Responsive Politics. The other side consisted of representatives of organizations that would be affected by the new rules, including party committees, interest groups, labor unions, and 527 organizations. In general, advocates of the law argued for a broad reading of the statute and regulations that would not open loopholes having the potential to undermine the efficacy of the statute. Others wanted the regulations to conform to narrower interpretations, which did not impose additional restrictions on political speech or serve to expand the sphere of political activity that would fall under the rubric of the law.

A great concern of BCRA's supporters was how the regulatory process would operate under the FEC, which they found to be an ineffective and dysfunctional agency. Unlike most other federal regulatory agencies, the FEC consists of an even number of commissioners (six). No more than three may be from the same political party, so, as a practical matter, three members are Republicans and three are Democrats. Furthermore, the support of four out of the six commissioners is needed to take any action, including approval of a proposed regulation. The commission therefore tends to deadlock (voting 3-3) on issues with partisan consequences and often supports the interests of the party organizations in regulatory matters.[30] Moreover, some of the agency's past decisions have created major loopholes in the law. For example, the soft money problem arose as a result of advisory opinions and regulations passed by the FEC, and not through an action of Congress.[31]

BCRA's supporters feared that the FEC might repeat previous patterns and create loopholes in the new regulatory framework because three of the commissioners—Bradley Smith, David Mason, and Michael Toner, who were Republican appointments—favored less regulation of campaign funding and had voiced doubts about the constitutionality or potential efficacy of BCRA.[32] Accordingly, BCRA advocates diligently monitored the FEC's rulemaking process, which consisted of various tasks. In some instances, the commission simply had to modify its regulations to reflect the provisions of the statute. For example, the contribution limits noted in the regulations had to be changed to reflect the BCRA changes. In other instances, the commission had to draft regulations to govern application of the statute to specific circumstances. With respect to the ban on soft money, the commission had to clarify what it means to "solicit" funds or what activities constitute "voter identification." In the case of coordination rules, it had to draft regulations without statutory guidance as to their content.

The FEC undertook more than a dozen rulemakings in implementing BCRA. A number of regulations, particularly some of the specific rules drafted for the soft money ban, electioneering communications, and coordination, proved to be highly controversial (see table 2-1).[33]

A prime example of the differences of opinion regarding regulation and the application of the statute can be seen in the reaction to an FEC ruling pertaining to BCRA's prohibition on the soliciting and directing of soft money by federal officeholders and party officials.[34] Part of the resulting FEC regulation defined the words "solicit" and "direct" so as to make clear the type of activity that would be considered illegal. The FEC adopted the narrow meaning "to ask for" offered by its general counsel, rather than the broader definition "to request or suggest or recommend." BCRA's sponsors supported the broader definition, arguing that "to ask" was so narrow that it would allow elected officials to engage in soft money fundraising indirectly. Through "winks and nods," officials could tell donors that they could not legally accept certain contributions, but that a state party could. BCRA's supporters felt that this constituted a substantial loophole in the law. The FEC countered that broader language posed the risk of bringing large numbers of private conversations into the scope of possible federal regulation, which might have a chilling effect on political speech.

Similarly, BCRA's new rules for the financing of voter registration activity meant that the FEC had to clarify what activities constitute "voter registration." The commission concluded they were activities that *assist* in the process of registering voters, whether conducted by telephone, by individual means, or through other media. Hence their financing would include any related printing and distribution costs for voter registration materials. According to BCRA's supporters, the definition should also encompass activities designed to *encourage* individuals to register to vote, including rallies, other staged events, and meetings. Otherwise, some activities related to voter registration would escape the restrictions of the soft money ban.

In other instances, BCRA supporters found the FEC's exemptions to be too broad. The commission's definition of a "public communication," for example, did not include messages distributed via the Internet, since BCRA's legislative history did not reflect any congressional concern

Table 2-1. *FEC Rulemaking: Selected Regulatory Issues*

Subject	BCRA *provision or issue*	Final *FEC regulation*	BCRA *sponsor / reform groups' views*
Soft money	1. National party officials and federal candidates or officeholders may not "solicit" or "direct" soft money (except in very limited circumstances) for federal or nonfederal elections. But state and local parties may not raise or spend soft money, for federal elections.	Solicit or direct both mean "to ask." (In order to avoid "chilling" inquiry into the millions of innocent private political conversations that make up American politics, there must be no threat of FEC action against ambiguous requests for "support." Therefore, solicit or direct do not include "recommend" or "suggest.") §300.2 (m, n)	Should also include "recommend" or "suggest" and be applied to a series of conversations to prevent fundraising designed to evade the law. [The FEC General Counsel's draft regulations used the broader phrase "to request or suggest or recommend" based on the commission's solicitation restrictions on corporations and unions.]
	2. Federal candidates and officeholders may however attend, speak, or be featured guest at state/local party fundraising events.	There is no restriction on what the candidate or officeholder can say at such events. (This partly reflects "constitutional concerns" regarding freedom of speech.)	The candidate or officeholder should not be allowed to solicit or direct soft money (as defined in 1 above) at the event.
	3. Voter registration activity within 120 days of a federal election.	Voter registration is contacting individuals by phone or other individualized means to *assist* registration, including costs of printing and distributing information. (Does not include *encouragement of* registration, in order to avoid subjecting small local committees and grassroots groups to federal regulation.)	Should also include encouragement of voter registration such as by rallies and meetings.
Electioneering communications	1. Should communications sponsored by tax-exempt religious, educational, and charitable organizations under § 501(c)(3) of the Internal Revenue Code be exempt?	Communications paid for by 501(c)(3) organizations are exempt, because the IRS already prohibits their engagement in political campaigns, and subjecting them to regulation could discourage their participation in beneficial activities, such as grassroots advocacy. §100.29(c)(6)	*Nonprofits* supported an exemption, maintaining that the tax code already prohibits 501(c)(3)s from engaging in activities in support of or in opposition to a candidate, and feared FEC investigations under BCRA would chill the effectiveness of charitable organizations with finite resources. *Reform groups* opposed a blanket exemption, citing legislative history indicating that BCRA does not treat 501(c)(3)s and for-profit corporations differently, and saying that they saw a potential for abuse.

(Table continues)

Table 2-1. (continued)

Subject	BCRA provision or issue	Final FEC regulation	BCRA sponsor / reform groups' views
Electioneering communications (continued)	2. Should Internet communications be exempt?	Internet communications, including webcasts (unless simultaneously broadcast over the TV or radio), are exempt, because legislative history indicates that Congress did not intend to regulate electioneering communications over the Internet. While some maintain that as the Internet develops, it could come to be used like radio and television, it is premature to craft a regulation responding to unknown future advances. §100.29(c)(1)	BCRA sponsors and reform groups disagreed with a blanket exemption, stating that it did not give the FEC flexibility to restrict Internet communications, such as webcasting and videostreaming, that may someday be the functional equivalent of radio and television broadcasts. Business, civil liberties, and some nonprofit groups supported a broad exception for the Internet to ensure its unfettered growth by preventing premature regulation.
Coordination rules: Material involvement		Reflects "material" involvement (that is, important to or influencing the communication) by a candidate/party/agent in decisions regarding the communication's content, audience, method, outlet, timing, frequency, size, or duration. § 109.21(d)(2)	Reform groups thought that material involvement should extend to "discussions" as well as "decisions." They said it would be hard to prove that material involvement influenced "decisions" and argued that "discussions" of communication specifics alone would lead to de facto coordination. On the other side, business groups, a nonprofit, and unions wanted "material involvement" defined more narrowly to require control or significant influence over a communication.
Substantial discussion		Former employee or independent contractor is created, produced, or distributed after one or more "substantial discussions" about the communication between the person/agent paying for it and the candidate identified in the communication (or his party/agent), wherein information material to the communication about the candidate/party's campaign	Reform groups supported this standard as essential to prevent corrupting coordination. Business groups and a nonprofit maintained that terms such as "substantial" and "material" were vague, likely to inspire unfounded investigations, and liable to chill free speech and legitimate lobbying. Some advocated including language from the D.C. federal district court's FEC v. Christian Coalition

	plans, projects, activities, or needs is conveyed to the spender. § 109.21(d)(3)	decision, which requires that such discussions result in the candidate and the spender emerging as "partners or joint venturers."
Former employee	Is paid for by a person (or his current employer) who—during the same election cycle—was an employee (or independent contractor) of the candidate identified in the communication (or his opponent/party/agent), and who conveys or makes use of information about campaign plans, projects, activities, or needs, or used in services provided, that is material to the communication. § 109.21(d)(5)	*Reform groups* argued that when a communication is paid for by a former employee/independent contractor, coordination should be presumed unless shown otherwise, since it will be practically impossible to prove he "made use of" or "conveyed" material information. They generally favored a defined list of strategic employees/contractors similar to the list of professional services performed by common vendors (see below). On the other hand, *business groups, unions, a nonprofit, and political parties* thought terms like "made use of" and "conveyed" would chill speech, lead to burdensome investigations, and handicap those seeking employment. They also argued that the applicable time frame of a full election cycle was too long—given the short-term usefulness of political campaign strategies.
Agent: What is an "agent" of a candidate or party?	An "agent" is a person with actual authority (either express or implied) given by a candidate or party to engage in any of a list of activities closely parallel to the conduct standards. § 109.3	*Reform groups* found this "actual authority" standard too narrow (as they had previously when the FEC adopted it for the soft money regulations). They maintained that it allows candidates or parties to coordinate communications with an outside spender by using persons without formal authority to sit in on discussions and convey important information to that spender. They wanted such persons to also be treated as agents, unless they were under explicit instructions.

Source: Based on the tables prepared by the Campaign Finance Institute. Available at ww.cfinst.org/studies/ElectionAfterReform/pdf/EAR_Appendix3-5_note.pdf.

about the need to regulate Internet communications. BCRA supporters, on the other hand, feared the exemption might allow corporations or other prohibited sources of funding to provide financing for Internet sites that would be used to distribute messages or sponsor webcasts related to the election of candidates. Groups interested in ensuring unfettered communication over the Internet also became involved, supporting the FEC exemption and challenging the concerns of BCRA's advocates.

The FEC's efforts to frame practicable and enforceable guidelines on coordination were especially controversial and problematic. Since the practices deemed to signify coordinated activity can leave a donor or political committee open to charges of making expenditures held to be illegal contributions under the terms of the law, much of the implementation debate focused on coordination. Business, civil liberties, and nonprofit groups were all uneasy, since the new regulations seemed likely to affect their own political activities. Such broad concern was to be expected, given that coordination is a central concept in campaign finance law. Moreover, it had been debated at the FEC and in the courts for years and had been the subject of a number of previous FEC rulemakings and advisory opinions. In this area of the law, BCRA did not so much create a new problem as revive the debate that had been present since the adoption of the FECA but had never been resolved to the satisfaction of a number of the regulatory interests or entities. In response to Congress's directive to promulgate new coordination rules, the FEC adopted a three-part test to determine coordination.[35] It consisted of a payment standard, a set of content standards, and a set of conduct standards. A communication or expenditure is considered to be coordinated if it meets all three of these standards. The payment standard applies to the source of a payment and is used to determine whether a payment was made by someone other than a candidate. The content standard is used to determine whether a communication is reasonably related to an election. The regulations specify four content standards, any one of which establishes whether a communication is election related. The conduct standard is used to determine whether a person paying for a communication or campaign activity, or the relevant candidate, has engaged in any conduct that constitutes coordination. The regulations identify five forms of conduct that would individually satisfy the coordination test, most notably whether a communication was created or financed at the request or suggestion of a candidate, whether a candidate or his or her agent was "materially involved" in decisions about a communication or had "substantial discussions" about it, and whether common vendors or former employees were used to provide information about a candidate's plans or activities to the person or committee paying for a communication.

As this brief synopsis suggests, the regulations set forth by the FEC were complex and included terms or concepts that are not easily defined. Not surprisingly, this rulemaking engendered substantial comment and controversy. Some of the issues are noted in table 2-1.

Back to Court: Shays I

The debate over implementation of the statute continued even after the FEC promulgated the new rules, which took effect in the 2004 cycle. Although participants in the political process now had guidelines to govern their activities, the FEC's decisions did not resolve the controversy. On October 8, 2002, BCRA's principal sponsors in the House, Shays and Meehan, filed a legal complaint against the commission, charging that many of the regulations it had adopted "contravene the language" of the statute and that the rules would "frustrate the purpose and intent of . . . BCRA by allowing soft money to continue to flow into federal elections and into the federal political process."[36] The plaintiffs challenged nineteen FEC regulations and asked the court to invalidate these rules and require the FEC to redraft them.[37] More specifically, the plaintiffs challenged some of the rules on soft money, electioneering communications, and coordination, which they had also contested during the rulemaking process. The Senate sponsors, McCain and Feingold, filed an amicus curiae brief supporting the challenge.

The case, *Shays and Meehan* v. *FEC* (commonly referred to as *Shays I*), was filed in U.S. District Court for the District of Columbia and was heard by Judge Colleen Kollar-Kotelly, a member of the three-judge panel that had heard *McConnell*. The *Shays* suit on the application of the statute was thus pending even before a decision had been issued on the constitutionality of the provisions of the underlying statute. Consideration of the case was therefore delayed.[38] The judge issued her opinion on September 18, 2004, striking down fifteen separate regulations implementing BCRA.[39] The opinion also directed the FEC to conduct new rulemakings on some of the invalidated rules.

The FEC chose to appeal the court's ruling on five of the fifteen invalidated regulations. The commission appealed five key rules: the standards for coordinated communications, definitions of the terms "solicit" and "direct," the interpretation of "electioneering communications" to exclude broadcasts aired for no fee (such as public service announcements), allocation rules for state party employee salaries, and a de minimis exception from reporting requirements for Levin accounts of less than $5,000.[40] The commission also challenged the standing of the BCRA sponsors to bring the lawsuit. On July 15, 2005, the D.C. Circuit Court of Appeals affirmed the district court ruling "in all respects" and upheld the invalidation of fifteen regulations, as well as the standing of the BCRA sponsors.[41] Consequently, after the 2004 election, the FEC was still in the process of drafting regulations to implement the law.

The 527 Controversy

The most prominent—and consequential—regulatory issue in the 2004 election cycle concerned the financial activity of Section 527 organizations. Under BCRA's restraints, such organizations were encouraged to find new ways to circumvent campaign finance restrictions. While Section 527 committees had been active in federal elections before 2004, the passage of BCRA spurred a growth in this kind of involvement.[42] By the beginning of the election year, a number of political committees had been organized under Section 527 to raise and spend money in ways that were clearly designed to influence the outcome of the presidential race. These committees, initially Democratic-oriented entities for the most part and described as a "shadow Democratic party," included such prominent groups as the Media Fund, America Coming Together, the Joint Victory Fund, and MoveOn.org.[43] By March 2004, these groups had already raised tens of millions of dollars from large individual contributions, corporations, and labor unions and were beginning to spend these funds on television advertising critical of President George Bush, as well as on voter registration efforts designed to increase the Democratic vote in the general election (see chapters 4 and 8).

The activities of these organizations appeared to be an obvious violation of the rules on campaign funding. In most instances, their committees had not registered as federal political committees with the FEC, yet they were raising and spending money in ways that suggested their principal purpose was to influence a federal election. Thus complaints were filed with the FEC calling for the regulation of their activities. In January 2004 a group of BCRA's supporters filed a complaint charging three

527s with illegal use of soft money and asking the FEC to determine whether they should be registered as political committees and be subject to the restrictions of federal law.[44] A few months later, the Republican National Committee and Bush campaign committee filed a complaint alleging that Democratic-oriented 527s were illegally coordinating their activities with the Kerry for President campaign.[45]

By the time the Republicans had filed their complaint, the FEC had already initiated a rulemaking process for regulations on "political committee status." An advisory opinion issued earlier had stated that a 527 committee registered with the FEC as a federal political committee was subject to the contribution limits and disclosure requirements of federal law and must finance with hard money any public communications that "promote, support, attack or oppose" a federal candidate.[46] But that ruling did not establish the circumstances in which a 527 organization that is *not* registered as a federal committee is required to do so. One purpose of the rulemaking was to draft regulations on this issue.

Key Issues

The FECA defined a "political committee" as any committee, club, association, or other group of persons that receives aggregate contributions connected to federal elections totaling more than $1,000 during a calendar year or makes expenditures totaling more than $1,000 during an election year.[47] In *Buckley*, the Supreme Court narrowed this definition to encompass only organizations that are under the control of a candidate or whose "major purpose" is to nominate or elect a candidate.[48] The Court in *McConnell* reiterated this test.

Certain "political organizations" formed under Section 527 of the tax code have avoided the definition under federal campaign finance laws by noting that their primary purpose has been to influence elections in general, not any specific election. These groups have therefore been able to enjoy the tax advantages that accompany 527 status without having to register specifically as a federal or state political entity.[49]

How to define "political committee" for purposes of the law and apply this definition to political organizations was thus a major issue in the 527 rulemaking. It was not, however, a new issue, because the FEC had not established clear rules on this matter. The commission did initiate a rulemaking in 1990 but never drafted final rules. Almost three decades after *Buckley*, implementing regulations for the Court's construction had still not been established.

BCRA's sponsors urged the FEC to require any committee whose major purpose was to influence federal elections and that raised or spent $1,000 to register with the FEC and be subject to all federal campaign finance regulations. In their view, only 527 organizations that direct their activities entirely at nonfederal elections should be exempt from regulation.[50] A wide array of groups and organizations, including many nonprofit groups that operated under Section 501(c) of the tax code, expressed an opinion on this issue. These nonprofit groups, including Common Cause and the Brennan Center for Justice, which generally support campaign reform, believed that a rule that was too broad might encompass some of the political activities they are allowed to carry out under their particular tax status, or at least might establish a precedent for future regulation. Consequently, they initially opposed a notice of proposed rulemaking drafted by the FEC's general counsel and then mobilized supporters to submit comments on the proposed rule. The controversial nature of the regulation was reflected in the public's response. By April 1, 2004, the commission had already logged approximately 30,000 comments.[51]

Another key issue concerned the allocation rules applied to nonparty organizations. Under earlier rules adopted by the FEC, a 527 committee or other nonparty organization could finance the costs of generic nonpartisan political activities, such as voter registration drives or turnout efforts, with a combination of hard and soft money, that is, federal and nonfederal funds.[52] The allocation formula was based on the share of a committee's spending devoted to federal election activity, such as contributions made to federal candidates, or the amount of federal money raised as opposed to nonfederal money. A group like America Coming Together, which raised most of its money from nonfederal contributions and spent little on campaign contributions, could finance its voter registration activity almost entirely from soft money funds. BCRA's supporters urged the FEC to prohibit the allocation methods from becoming a major loophole in the ban on soft money.

FEC Response

On May 19, 2004, the FEC met to consider a proposed rule regarding 527 activity. One of the submissions was a bipartisan proposal offered by Commissioners Michael Toner (Republican) and Scott Thomas (Democrat) that would have required 527s that spend more than $1,000 on federal elections to register with the FEC and abide by the restrictions in federal law. The proposal also called for a change in the allocation rules, which would have required independent nonparty groups to finance voter registration and turnout efforts with a combination of federal and nonfederal funds in a 50/50 proportion. This proposal was defeated on a vote of 4-2, and other alternatives also failed to garner a majority. Consequently, the FEC chose to delay consideration of draft regulations for ninety days, thereby effectively ensuring that 527 organizations would be allowed to continue their activities through the 2004 election. These committees would end up spending hundreds of millions of dollars during the remainder of the election year.

When the FEC reconvened in August, the commission adopted a limited rule that had no effect on the 2004 election and offered little prospect of curtailing the use of unlimited funds by 527s in the future. The commission approved a 50/50 allocation rule proposed by Thomas and Toner and made it effective beginning with the 2006 election cycle. Under this rule, an interest group or organization that maintains a federal PAC, such as EMILY's List or MoveOn.org, would have to use hard money to finance half of the costs of any activities affecting both federal and nonfederal elections. But the commissioners deadlocked 3-3 on the question of whether to continue efforts to draft regulations on political committee status.[53] The FEC thus took no action to prevent 527s from using soft money in the future and increased the certainty that such activity would continue in the 2006 cycle.

To Court

The FEC's failure to adopt a broader rule to regulate the financial activities of 527 committees spurred two lawsuits against the agency. BCRA's congressional sponsors, Representatives Shays and Meehan, once again went to court to compel FEC action. President Bush's reelection campaign committee also filed a suit against the agency, asking the court to require the FEC to promulgate regulations and address the question of whether certain 527s are "political committees" for the purposes of federal campaign finance law.[54] The two suits, both filed in federal district court in the District of Columbia, were consolidated and are often referred to collectively as *Shays II*, so as to distinguish this litigation from the earlier case on BCRA regulations.[55] As of September 2005, this suit was yet to be decided.

The FEC's decision also led to a third lawsuit against the agency, this one challenging the rule the FEC did adopt. In this instance, EMILY's

List, a PAC that assists pro-choice candidates, whose founder, Ellen Malcolm, was a major fundraiser for America Coming Together, challenged the allocation rule adopted by the FEC. EMILY's List argued that enforcement of the commission's new allocation rule would inhibit some of its political activities and prohibit it from using some of the contributions it receives. This suit, *EMILY's List v. FEC*, was also pending as of September of 2005.[56]

Campaign Finance System after BCRA

BCRA made significant changes in the rules governing campaign finance and imposed federal regulations on a substantial amount of financial activity that was previously unregulated. BCRA improved the efficacy of contribution limits and disclosure requirements and established clearer guidelines for the types of political activity that had to be financed with regulated funds. But the statute also increased the complexity of federal law in certain respects, while expanding its reach. As noted in table 2-2, BCRA, when combined with the provisions of the FECA that were left unchanged, produced a patchwork of regulations on contributions and expenditures. Some contribution limits are adjusted for inflation, while others are not. Some forms of party spending are limited, while others are not. The rules governing nonparty organizations vary depending on the type of organization that is engaging in political activity. Although BCRA simplified the system by eliminating much of the unregulated funding that characterized previous elections, the system remained far from simple.

The initial implementation of BCRA through the 2004 election cycle highlighted the difficulty awaiting any reform and enforcement of campaign finance laws. Securing congressional passage of a meaningful campaign finance law in itself is not an easy task. Furthermore, it is but the first step in a process that, as a practical matter, will almost always involve judicial and administrative review. The courts and the FEC may have as much influence—if not more—on the final provisions and application of the law as does Congress. As a result, the courts and the FEC have become primary arenas for debating and deciding the rules that will eventually determine the financial activity in campaigns.

As the BCRA implementation controversies demonstrate, legal details that may at first appear to be minor technicalities or legal niceties can have a significant effect on the flow of money in federal elections. The

Table 2-2. *Federal Contribution and Spending Regulations*

			Recipient					
Donor/ spender	*Federal candidates*	*National party committees*	*State party committees (federal accounts)*	*Federal PACs*	*Coordinated expenditures (coordinated with candidate)*	*Independent expenditures/ express advocacy (not coordinated with candidate)*	*Electioneering communications*	*"Levin" accounts*
Individuals[a]	$2,000 per election[b] $37,500 per cycle[c]	$25,000 per year; $57,500 per cycle[c]	$10,000 per year; $37,500 per cycle	$5,000 per year; $37,500 per cycle	$2,000 per election (considered to be contributions subject to aggregate limit)	Unlimited, but must be disclosed to the FEC	Unlimited, but must be disclosed to the FEC	Whatever state law permits, up to $10,000
National party committees	Senate candidates $35,000 per election,[d] Presidential and House candidates $5,000 per election	Unlimited transfers of funds to other party committees	Unlimited transfers of funds to other party committees	$5,000 per year	Limited amounts based on spending formulas for types of candidates,[e] coordinated expenditures are in addition to contribution	Unlimited, but must be disclosed[f]	Unlimited, but must be disclosed	Prohibited

(Table continues)

Table 2-2. (continued)

Donor/spender	Federal candidates	National party committees	State party committees (federal accounts)	Federal PACs	Coordinated expenditures (coordinated with candidate)	Independent expenditures/ express advocacy (not coordinated with candidate)	Electioneering communications	"Levin" accounts
			Recipient					
State party committees (federal accounts)	$5,000 per election	Unlimited transfers of funds to other party committees	Unlimited transfers of funds to other party committees	$5,000 per year	Pres. candidates $5,000 per election (are considered to be contributions); limited amounts for Senate and House candidate (see formula)[e]; coordinated expenditures in addition to contribution	Unlimited, but must be disclosed	Unlimited, but must be disclosed	Prohibited
PACs (multicandidate PACs)	$5,000 per election	$15,000 per year	$5,000 per year	$5,000 per year	$5,000 per year (considered contributions)	Unlimited, but must be disclosed	Unlimited, but must be disclosed	Whatever state law permits, up to $10,000
PACs (nonmulticandidate PACs)	$2,000 per election	$25,000 per year[c]	$10,000 per year	$5,000 per year	$2,000 per election (considered contributions)	Unlimited, but must be disclosed	Unlimited, but must be disclosed	Whatever state law permits, up to $10,000

Corporations and unions	Prohibited	Prohibited	Prohibited	Prohibited (but may pay administrative costs of connected PACs)	Prohibited	Prohibited	Whatever state law permits, up to $10,000
Section 527 organizations not registered with the FEC	Prohibited	Prohibited	Prohibited	Prohibited	Prohibited	Prohibited if incorporated	Prohibited if incorporated; if not incorporated, unlimited so long as using only funds contributed by individuals and disclosed to the FEC if over $10,000	Whatever state law permits, up to $10,000
501(c)(4)s and (c)(6)s	Prohibited	Prohibited	Prohibited	Prohibited	Prohibited	Prohibited except for qualifying 501(c)(4) MCFL corporations	Prohibited except for qualifying 501(c)(4) MCFL corporations	Whatever state law permits, up to $10,000

Source: Based on Campaign Legal Center, *The Campaign Finance Guide* (Washington, D.C., 2004). Available at www.campaignfinanceguide.org.

a. Individuals are subject to a $95,000 per two-year election cycle aggregate limit. Of that limit, there is a $57,500 aggregate limit on federal noncandidate contributions, including no more than $37,500 to PACs and state/local parties' federal accounts, and a $37,500 aggregate limit on contributions to federal candidates. Foreign nationals without green cards are not allowed to make contributions in federal elections.

b. Under the "millionaires' provision," the contribution limits may be increased (tripled to $6,000 for a House candidate and up to $12,000 for a Senate candidate). Where applicable, any amount over $2,000 does not apply against the individual's aggregate contribution limit.

c. These limits are adjusted for inflation.

d. The Senate campaign committee and national committee share this limit, which equals the total amount the committees may give in combined contributions.

e. The FECA limited coordinated expenditures by a national party committee on behalf of a presidential candidate to $0.02 multiplied by the voting-age population in the United States, plus a cost-of-living adjustment. For 2004, the limit was $16.2 million. The limit on coordinated expenditures by party committees (both national and state) on behalf of a senatorial candidate was set at the greater amount of $20,000 or $0.02 multiplied by the voting-age population of the state plus a cost-of-living adjustment. For the amounts in 2004, see the state-by-state chart at www.fec.gov/pdf/record/2004/mar04.pdf. The limit for party committees (both national and state) in a House race was set at $10,000, plus a cost-of–living adjustment. In 2004 the ceiling was $37,310. The coordinated expenditure limits applicable to a Senate or House race may increase when the "millionaire's provision" is triggered.

f. A national party committee cannot make independent expenditures for its presidential candidate if a candidate formally designates the national committee to be the authorized campaign committee of the presidential candidate. In this particular instance, the party is not considered to be independent of the candidate.

definition of what constitutes a federal political committee, for example, proved to be a legal detail big enough to facilitate the flow of substantial sums of money to 527 committees. The legal meaning of "solicit," "coordination," and other statutory terms were enough to spark a federal court case and an appellate court reprimand of the FEC. Although the narrow statutory definitions adopted by the FEC did not have a significant effect on the flow of money in 2004, BCRA advocates are concerned that they will undermine the law in the future. Given the potential consequences of regulatory decisions, candidates, parties, and nonparty groups will continue to have a strong incentive to fight for reform through the regulatory process rather than the legislative process.

The debates over BCRA added an element of uncertainty and unpredictability to the 2004 election cycle that complicated the strategic decisionmaking of many political actors. For all of 2003, it was not clear whether all or any of the act's prohibitions would be upheld by the Supreme Court. Throughout most of 2004, the FEC's initial regulations were being challenged in court, with many of them ultimately invalidated by the District of Columbia Court of Appeals. What the FEC would do in response to the growth of 527s was not known until late in the election year. And at the end of the 2004 election cycle, the FEC was still busy drafting rules, some required by court direction, others required by issues that emerged during the course of the regulatory debate. By the beginning of 2005, substantial progress had been made in implementing the statute, but it remained to be seen whether additional legal challenges would force action to address the problems posed by 527s and other entities that engage in federal political activity outside the parameters of campaign finance regulation. If past is prologue, any further actions are likely to be contentious and hard fought, and the FEC may still be implementing BCRA after the 2006 election is well under way.

Notes

1. *Buckley* v. *Valeo*, 424 U.S. 1 (1976). In *Buckley*, the Supreme Court upheld the 1974 act's restrictions on contributions but struck down limits on expenditures and other provisions, including the process for constituting the Federal Election Commission. For a summary of the decision and its regulatory

consequences, see Daniel Hays Lowenstein and Richard L. Hasen, *Election Law: Cases and Materials*, 2nd ed. (Durham, N.C.: Carolina Academic Press, 2001), pp. 747–82; and Daniel R. Ortiz, "The First Amendment and the Limits of Campaign Finance Reform," in *The New Campaign Finance Sourcebook*, edited by Anthony Corrado and others (Brookings, 2005), pp. 91–122.

2. Public Law 107-155, 116 Stat. 81. For a summary and background on the provisions of BCRA, see Joseph E. Cantor and L. Paige Whitaker, *Bipartisan Campaign Reform Act of 2002: Summary and Comparison with Existing Law* (Library of Congress, Congressional Research Service, 2002); and Robert F. Bauer, *Soft Money Hard Law: A Guide to the New Campaign Finance Law* (Washington: Perkins Coie, 2002).

3. Anthony Corrado, "Party Finance in the 2000 Elections: The Federal Role of Soft Money Financing," *Arizona State Law Journal* 34 (Winter 2002): 1034–35.

4. Allan J. Cigler, "Interest Groups and Financing the 2000 Elections," in *Financing the 2000 Election*, edited by David B. Magleby (Brookings, 2002); and Craig B. Holman and Luke P. McLoughlin, *Buying Time 2000: Television Advertising in the 2000 Federal Elections* (New York: Brennan Center for Justice at New York University School of Law, 2001).

5. Documents related to the rulemakings conducted by the FEC can be found at www.fec.gov/pages/bcra/rulemakings/rulemakings_bcra.shtml. See also the documents and comments made available by the Campaign Legal Center at www.campaignlegalcenter.org/BCRA.html, as well as the discussion of the regulations in Bauer, *More Soft Money, Hard Law*, and Bauer's updated commentary offered at www.moresoftmoneyhardlaw.com.

6. For a discussion of the legislative process that led to the passage of BCRA, see Anthony Corrado, "The Legislative Odyssey of BCRA," in *Life after Reform: When the Bipartisan Campaign Reform Act Meets Politics*, edited by Michael J. Malbin (Lanham, Md.: Rowman and Littlefield, 2003), pp. 21–39.

7. Bauer, *Soft Money Hard Law*, p. 24.

8. 11 C.F.R. sec. 106.5 (2000).

9. John Cochran, "Rival Campaign Finance Bills' Prospects in House May Hinge on Allaying Black Caucus' Concerns," *Congressional Quarterly Weekly Report*, June 23, 2001, p. 1497, and Adam Clymer, "Black Caucus Members Find Themselves Courted Heavily in Soft Money Fight," *New York Times*, July 12, 2001, p. A18.

10. For a discussion of the legal concepts of express and issue advocacy, see Trevor Potter and Kirk L. Jowers, "Speech Governed by Federal Election Laws," in *The New Campaign Finance Sourcebook*, edited by Corrado and others, pp. 205–31.

11. Under BCRA, a targeted broadcast communication is one that is viewable by 50,000 persons in a candidate's constituency.

12. Under the rules, a political committee must disclose all donors of $1,000 or more. However, an organization may structure its financial accounts in a way that ensures disclosure of only those donors whose gifts are used to finance electioneering communications, as opposed to disclosing all donors to the committee or organization. If a political committee or interest group establishes a separate fund for financing electioneering communications and that fund consists exclusively of donations from individuals, only donors who give $1,000 or more to this fund need to be disclosed. Otherwise, an organization making electioneering communications must disclose all donors that give $1,000 or more to the organization, regardless of whether their gifts were used to finance electioneering communications.

13. See, for example, *Austin v. Michigan State Chamber of Commerce*, 494 U.S. 652 (1990).

14. See, among others, Sidney M. Milkis, "Parties versus Interest Groups"; and Raymond J. La Raja, "Why Soft Money Has Strengthened Parties," in *Inside the Campaign Finance Battle: Court Testimony on the New Reforms*, edited by Anthony Corrado, Thomas E. Mann, and Trevor Potter (Brookings, 2003).

15. BCRA's higher contribution limits did not fully restore the purchasing power lost due to inflation. For example, the $1,000 limit per election on an individual contribution to a federal candidate was increased to $2,000 and adjusted for inflation. If the effects of inflation since 1974 had been taken into account, the limit would have been raised to about $3,500.

16. Most PACs are multicandidate committees. To qualify for this status, a PAC must be registered with the FEC for at least six months, have received contributions from at least fifty people, and have made contributions to at least five federal candidates. In this chapter, any reference to PACs generally means a multicandidate PAC. A PAC that does not qualify as a multicandidate committee will be referred to as a non-multicandidate PAC.

17. The adjustments for inflation are based on the consumer price index and become effective at the start of an election cycle. For example, the adjustments for the 2006 election cycle became effective in January 2005.

18. A contribution is counted against the aggregate limit based on the election cycle in which it is made. So a contribution made in 2004 to a senator up for reelection in 2006 is applied to the 2004 cycle aggregate limit, not the 2006 ceiling. See 11 C.F.R. sec. 110.5(c)(1).

19. For a description of the rules applicable to the millionaire's amendment, see the FEC summary at www.fec.gov/pages/brochures/millionaire.shtml. The formulas used for calculating opposition personal funds can be found in FEC, *Record* (Washington, February 2003), pp. 2–4. For examples of how the formulas are applied, see the hypothetical examples in 68 *Federal Register* 3987–94.

20. In House races, a candidate's eligibility for higher contributions ends when the aggregate amount of contributions and party spending at the increased

limits reaches 100 percent of the opposition personal funds amount. In Senate races, eligibility ends when aggregate contributions and party spending reach 110 percent of the opposition personal funds amount.

21. *Federal Election Commission* v. *Christian Coalition*, 52 F., Supp. 2d 45 (D.D.C. 1999).

22. 11 C.F.R. secs. 109.1(b)(4) and 100.23. See Trevor Potter, "The Current State of Campaign Finance Law," in *The New Campaign Finance Sourcebook*, edited by Corrado and others, pp. 54–56.

23. 518 U.S. 640 (1996).

24. *McConnell* v. *FEC*, 251 F. Supp. 2d 176 (D.D.C. 2003).

25. *McConnell* v. *FEC*, 540 U.S. 93 (2003).

26. The Court also found some provisions to be nonjusticiable, either because the issue was not yet ripe for adjudication or because the relevant plaintiff lacked standing to bring suit. These issues included the challenge to the higher contribution limits, the millionaire's amendment, and the provision on coordination regulations.

27. FEC, *Annual Report 2002* (Washington, 2003), p. 9. An itemization of the various rulemakings completed in 2002 is included in this report.

28. For a list of the rulemakings completed in 2003 and in process for 2004, see FEC, *Annual Report 2003* (Washington, 2004), pp. 9–10.

29. The commission rulemaking process begins by drafting a proposed rule and publishing a Notice of Proposed Rulemaking (NPRM) in the *Federal Register*. In addition to presenting the proposed regulation, the NPRM requests written comments from members of the public and regulated entities. The commission reviews these comments and may additionally hold hearings where members of the public can offer their views on the proposal. The commission then often revises its proposal and votes to issue a final rule or to end or postpone the rulemaking. Once a vote is taken to issue a final rule, the text of the regulations, along with an explanation and justification of the regulations, is published in the *Federal Register*. A final rule becomes effective thirty days after publication.

30. On the problems of the FEC, see, among others, Brooks Jackson, *Broken Promise: Why the Federal Election Commission Failed* (New York: Priority Press, 1990); and Project FEC Task Force, *No Bark, No Bite, No Point: The Case for Closing the Federal Election Commission and Establishing a New System for Enforcing the Nation's Campaign Finance Laws* (Washington: Democracy 21 Education Fund, April 2002).

31. Anthony Corrado, "Party Soft Money," in *Campaign Finance Reform: A Sourcebook*, edited by Anthony Corrado and others (Brookings, 1997), pp. 171–76.

32. See Bradley A. Smith, *Unfree Speech: The Folly of Campaign Finance Reform* (Princeton University Press, 2001); David M. Mason, "Why Congress Can't Ban Soft Money," *The Heritage Foundation Backgrounder*, no. 1130, July

21, 1997, and Mason, "Campaign Finance Reform: Broad, Vague, and Unenforceable," *Heritage Lectures*, no. 732, February 13, 2002.

33. For a list of the regulations that were particularly controversial, see *The Election after Reform: Money Politics and the Bipartisan Campaign Reform Act*, edited by Michael J. Malbin (Lanham, Md.: Rowman and Littlefield, 2006), appendixes 3–5 (www.cfinst.org/studies/ElectionAfterReform/pdf/EAR_Appendix3-5_note.pdf).

34. Documents related to the rulemakings conducted by the FEC can be found at www.fec.gov/pages/bcra/rulemakings/rulemakings_bcra.shtml. See also the documents and comments made available by the Campaign Legal Center at www.campaignlegalcenter.org/BCRA.html, as well as the discussion of the regulations in Bauer, *Soft Money Hard Law*, and Bauer's updated commentary at www.moresoftmoneyhardlaw.com.

35. 11 C.F.R. secs. 109.20–37.

36. FEC, *Record* (Washington, November 2004), p. 2.

37. Case materials are available at www.campaignlegalcenter.org/cases-29.html.

38. Amy Keller, "Shays, Meehan Suit on Hold until BCRA Ruling," *Roll Call*, September 30, 2003.

39. *Shays v. FEC*, 251 F. Supp 2d 176 (2004). Regulations struck down by the courts included: "coordination" definition; coordination regulations excluding the Internet from rules; "agent" definition for purposes of coordination rules; "solicit" definition; "direct" definition; "agent" definition for purposes of the soft money rules; state party fundraising rules; "voter registration" definition as applied to state party soft money rules; "voter identification" definition as applied to state party soft money rules; "generic campaign activity" definition as applied to state party soft money rules; definition of state, district, and local employees for state party soft money rules; de minimis exemption included in Levin amendment rules; regulations excluding 501(c)(3) groups from the "electioneering communications" rules; and "electioneering communications" rules exempting broadcasts not "for a fee."

40. Kenneth P. Doyle, "FEC Votes to Ask D.C. Circuit to Back Five of 15 Overturned BCRA Regulations," *BNA Money and Politics Report*, November 1, 2004, p. 1. See also FEC, "FEC Votes on Specifics of *Shays v. FEC* Appeal," press release, October 29, 2004.

41. *Shays and Meehan v. FEC*, Civil No. 04-5352, Appeal No. 02cv01984, U.S. Court of Appeals for the District of Columbia, p. 2. Decided July 15, 2005.

42. Steve Weissman and Ruth Hassan, "BCRA and the 527 Groups," in *The Election after Reform*, edited by Malbin.

43. Dan Balz and Thomas B. Edsall, "Democrats Forming Parallel Campaign," *Washington Post*, March 10, 2004, p. A1; and Thomas B. Edsall, "GOP Complaint Cites Pro-Democratic Groups," *Washington Post*, April 1, 2004, p. A9.

44. Democracy 21 Education Fund, "FEC Complaint Filed by Three Campaign Finance Groups against '527 Organizations,'" press release, January 15, 2004.

45. Edsall, "GOP Complaint Cites Pro-Democratic Groups," p. A9; and Glen Justice, "Kerry and Democratic Groups Accused of Finance Violations," *New York Times*, April 1, 2004, p. A9.

46. FEC, Advisory Opinion 2003-37.

47. 2 U.S.C. sec. 431(4); 11 C.F.R. sec. 100.5(a).

48. *Buckley* v. *Valeo*, 424 U.S. 1, 79 (1976).

49. Potter, "The Current State of Campaign Finance Law," p. 77.

50. See the written comment offered in response to the political committee status rulemaking by McCain, Feingold, Shays, and Meehan (www.campaign legalcenter.org/FEC-36.html).

51. Kenneth P. Doyle, "FEC Receives 30,000 Public Comments Urging Hands off Political Organizations," *BNA Money and Politics Report*, April 2, 2004, p. 1.

52. 11 C.F.R. sec. 106.6(c).

53. Kenneth P. Doyle, "FEC Set to Finalize New Regulation Restricting Section 527 Organizations," *BNA Money and Politics Report*, October 15, 2004, p. 1; Glen Justice, "Panel Compromises on Soft Money Rules," *New York Times*, August 20, 2004, p. 16; and Potter, "The Current Status of Campaign Finance Law," p. 80. See also FEC, *Annual Report 2004* (Washington, 2005), pp. 18–19.

54. FEC, *Record* (Washington, November 2004), pp. 3–4.

55. *Shays* v. *FEC* and *Bush-Cheney '04, Inc.* v. *FEC*, D.D.C. nos. 04-1597 and 04-1612.

56. *EMILY's List* v. *FEC*, D.D.C. no. 05-0049.

THREE

Spending in the 2004 Election

KELLY D. PATTERSON

Nobody knew quite what to expect of federal campaign financing going into the 2004 election cycle. It was, after all, the first election conducted under the new campaign finance laws instituted by the Bipartisan Campaign Reform Act (BCRA) of 2002. Political scientists, pundits, and practitioners had their hunches, some well grounded in solid theory and past experience. Scholars, for example, looked at the interests and abilities of past campaign participants to extrapolate candidate and interest group practices in the new regulatory framework.[1] Few expected the pace of spending by presidential candidates to slacken, although with the ban on soft money, some thought party spending might diminish. Most reasoned that money would still find its way into the election process. The competitive environment and the need of consultants and candidates to innovate would make sure of that.[2]

There was less of a consensus about the role of political parties, interest groups, and individuals under the new rules. Would candidates and parties find a satisfactory replacement for the soft money banned by the new law? How aggressively would interest groups test the ban on electioneering? How important would the individual donor become as a source of campaign funds? In the aftermath of just one election cycle, it is almost impossible to answer these questions, and myriad others, definitively. Candidates, parties, and interest groups alter their practices as they learn how to navigate the law; therefore, what they did in the 2004 cycle may change in subsequent elections. Even so, it is useful to examine campaign finance in 2004 in the light of past experience. Some practices in this cycle may well be portents of what is to follow.

Overall Spending and Fundraising

Over the past twenty years, advocates of reform have consistently fretted about the amount of money spent on elections in the United States. Another concern has been that the money in the system could not be easily traced to a definitive source. For some, the amount of disclosure has been an even larger issue than the money finding its way into campaigns.[3]

The amount of money spent in elections may indeed be a cause for concern. According to one estimate, total spending reached almost $4 billion in the 2000 election cycle.[4] However, this estimate was not limited to federal election activity; it included some—but not all—of the money raised for use in nonfederal campaigns, judicial elections, and ballot initiative campaigns. With incomplete and sometimes inaccessible disclosure for campaign spending in nonfederal races, it is difficult to estimate a spending total for all campaigns.

The amount expended in federal races alone is impressive. As shown in table 3-1, the presidential candidates, congressional candidates, the national parties, state and local parties, 527 organizations, and political action committees (PACs) spent a total of $4.273 billion in the 2004 cycle. Under comparable definitions of spending, over $3.8 billion was spent in the 2000 cycle. Therefore the amount of money spent in federal races appears to have increased from the 2000 to the 2004 cycle.

The presidential candidates alone accounted for almost $1.2 billion in spending in the 2004 cycle. Parties, PACs, and other entities also spent on the candidates' behalf. Perhaps just as surprising is the large amount spent in congressional races, which almost equaled the amount spent on the presidential election. Although there were several competitive Senate races around the country, the number of competitive House races continued to dwindle. The $1.3 billion expended in congressional races seems like a rather large sum even in a cycle dominated by the presidential campaign and is $250 million more than what was spent in 2000.

Political parties also expended over $1 billion in federal campaign activity. The national parties accounted for almost $642 million of that amount. State and local parties spent $176 million. PACs spent an additional $475 million beyond their contributions to candidates on independent expenditures. One of the large stories to emerge from the 2004 cycle concerned the activity of the 527 organizations. According to analysis done by Steve Weissman at the Campaign Finance Institute (CFI), these groups spent upward of $400 million, compared with $101 million in 2001–02.

Despite overall decreases in public funding and candidate self-financing, the cycle's total rose when compared with the 2000 presidential cycle. George W. Bush chose to bypass public funds in the nomination phase of 2000, a decision criticized at the time. But in the 2004 nomination phase, Democrats John Kerry and Howard Dean joined Bush in not accepting public funds. As it turned out, Kerry benefited greatly from this decision because he was able to raise $251.6 million, whereas his spending limit would have been $50.4 million had he accepted public matching funds (see chapter 4).

The success of Bush and Kerry in nomination-phase fundraising without public funds may portend a pattern for future presidential nomination cycles. As table 3-2 shows, payouts of public funds for the presidential campaigns significantly declined from 2000 to 2004. The $28.4 million spent in total primary matching funds was less than half the amount disbursed in the 2000 presidential primaries. Moreover, the total represented the smallest amount of matching funds since 1976, the first presidential election conducted with public funds. Perhaps not too much should be made of the decline between these two election cycles since the 2000 presidential nomination campaigns featured competitive contests in both parties. Furthermore, not all candidates find it in their best interest to bypass the matching funds. Only some presidential candidates in 2004 found this to be the case in the nomination phase. Candidates such as John Edwards, Richard Gephardt, Joe Lieberman, and Wesley Clark all needed the matching funds to pursue their campaigns. However, recent cycles seem to indicate that those candidates who display a considerable fundraising prowess will likely forgo the matching funds.

Another notable feature of the 2004 presidential cycle is the significant decline in participation in the public finance system by those who file tax returns. Individuals can indicate on their tax returns if they want to earmark federal dollars to go to the presidential public finance system. The proportion of tax filers checking the option has steadily declined from a high of almost 29 percent in 1981 to approximately one in ten in 2003 (table 3-3). The lack of support has resulted in a financial crisis of sorts for the public finance system.[5] This downward trend may be due to something as obvious as the increase in electronic filings,

Table 3-1. *Overall Spending in Federal Elections, 2000 and 2004*
Millions of dollars

Spending	2000	2004
Presidential candidates	671[b]	1,230[a]
Congressional candidates	1,007[d]	1,259[c]
National parties (federal)	497[f]	642[e]
National parties (nonfederal)	498[g]	...
State and local parties (federal)	161[i]	176[h]
State and local parties (nonfederal)	330[k]	67[j]
527s	101[m]	424[l]
PACs	299[o]	475[n]
Issue advocacy	248[p]	...
Total	3,812	4,273

a. Source: www.fec.gov/press/press2005/20050203pressum/20050203pressum.html. Internal communication and electioneering communication figures updated with FEC data as of August 1, 2005. Includes all presidential election–related spending in prenomination, convention (including spending by host committees), and general election periods, plus independent expenditures (individuals, parties, groups), internal communication costs, and electioneering communications on their behalf. Candidate transfers to party committees are deducted from the total to avoid double counting.

b. See www.fec.gov/press/press2005/20050203pressum/20050203pressum.html and ftp://ftp.fec.gov/FEC/. Includes all presidential election–related spending in prenomination, convention (including spending by host committees), and general election periods, plus independent expenditures (individuals, parties, groups) and internal communication costs on their behalf. Candidate transfers to party committees are deducted from the total to avoid double counting.

c. See www.fec.gov/press/press2005/20050609candidate/20050609candidate.html. Includes all spending by congressional candidates, plus independent expenditures (individuals, parties, groups), internal communication costs, and electioneering communications on their behalf. Candidate transfers to party committees are deducted from the total to avoid double counting.

d. See www.fec.gov/press/press2001/051501congfinact/051501congfinact.html, ftp://ftp.fec.gov/FEC/; and Anne H. Bedlington and Michael J. Malbin, "The Party as an Extended Network: Members Giving to Each Other and to Their Parties," in *Life after Reform: When the Bipartisan Campaign Reform Act Meets Politics*, edited by Michael J. Malbin (Lanham, Md.: Rowman and Littlefield, 2003). Includes all spending by congressional candidates, plus independent expenditures (individuals, parties, groups), internal communication costs, and electioneering communications on their behalf. Candidate transfers to party committees are deducted from the total to avoid double counting.

e. See www.fec.gov/press/press2005/20050302party/Party2004final.html. Includes only federal (hard) activity. Includes all spending by national party committees except money contributed to candidates, and independent expenditures, coordinated expenditures, and internal communications on behalf of candidates.

f. See www.fec.gov/press/press2001/051501partyfund/051501partyfund.html. Includes all spending by national party committees except money contributed to candidates, and independent expenditures, coordinated expenditures, and internal communications on behalf of candidates.

g. See www.fec.gov/press/press2001/051501partyfund/051501partyfund.html. Transfers among committees were deducted from total.

h. See www.fec.gov/press/press2005/20050302party/Party2004final.html. Includes all spending by state and local party committees except money contributed to candidates and independent expenditures, coordinated expenditures, and internal communications on behalf of candidates. The national party transfers were deducted from the Democratic and Republican state and local party disbursements.

i. See www.fec.gov/press/press2001/051501partyfund/051501partyfund.html. Includes all spending by state and local party committees except money contributed to candidates, and independent expenditures, coordinated expenditures, and internal communications on behalf of candidates.

j. See www.fec.gov/press/press2005/20050302party/Party2004final.html. Includes nonfederal share of expenses that required some hard and some soft money in 2003–04.

k. See www.fec.gov/press/press2001/051501partyfund/051501partyfund.html. Includes nonfederal share of expenses that required some hard and some soft money in 1999–2000. They most likely spent other soft money on purely state and local races, but were not required to report it.

l. Steve Weissman and Ruth Hassan, "BCRA and the 527 Groups," in *The Election after Reform: Money, Politics, and the Bipartisan Campaign Reform Act*, edited by Michael J. Malbin (Lanham, Md.: Rowman and Littlefield, 2006). Covers all donations to groups with at least $200,000 in contributions that were either thoroughly committed to federal elections (the overwhelming majority of groups included) or were heavily involved in federal elections but also doing substantial state and local work (mainly a few labor union 527s).

m. See fecinfo.com/cgi-win/irs_ef_527.exe?DoFn=&sYR=2000. Major transfers removed. Estimate is much lower than the actual amount because 527 spending was only disclosed as of July 2000, because of the adoption of the new disclosure law.

n. See www.fec.gov/press/press2005/20050412pac/PACFinal2004.html. Includes total PAC expenditures minus PAC contributions to federal candidates and PAC independent expenditures.

o. See www.fec.gov/press/press2001/053101pacfund/053101pacfund.html. Includes total PAC expenditures minus PAC contributions to federal candidates and PAC independent expenditures.

p. Compiled from Campaign Media Analysis Group data. This money was spent on broadcast ads in the top seventy-five media markets between March 8 and November 7, 2000. This figure may include some money reported by parties, PACs, or 527s elsewhere in the table.

Table 3-2. *Payouts from the Presidential Election Campaign Fund,*
1976–2004
Millions of dollars

Year	Primary matching funds	Convention	General	Total
1976	24.8	4.1	43.6	72.6
1980	31.3	8.8	63.1	103.3
1984	36.5	16.2	80.8	133.5
1988	67.5	18.4	92.2	178.2
1992	42.9	22.1	110.5	175.4
1996	58.5	24.7	152.7	236.0
2000	62.3	29.5	147.7	239.5
2004	28.4	29.8	149.2	207.5

Source: Federal Election Commission, "2004 Presidential Campaign Financial Activity Summarized," press release, February 3, 2005 (www.fec.gov/press/press2005/20050203pressum/20050203pressum.html).

which do not have the checkoff in the default setting. Another factor is that the number of tax filings has increased at a greater rate than the number selecting the checkoff, so the decline in the percentage occurs naturally.

Whether the decline in those checking the option represents a larger crisis for the political system depends somewhat on how the evidence is viewed. Even though the number of individual donors to campaigns increased in the recent election cycle (see the discussion in the next section and in chapter 1), the number of tax filers who actually make a contribution is still considerably less than the number who check off the option on their returns. However, the decline may simply be another manifestation of the sometimes low level of confidence that citizens exhibit toward the political system or its candidates.[6]

The 2004 presidential cycle also saw fewer major party candidates pouring large amounts of their own money into their campaigns. John Kerry did put $6.4 million into his campaign at a critical phase, which he was able to quickly repay because of his very successful fundraising efforts (see chapters 4 and 5).[7] But unlike some past presidential elections, 2004 did not have candidates like Steve Forbes or Ross Perot, who spent tens of millions of dollars funding their own campaigns.[8] Only the Constitutional Party candidate, Michael Peroutka, funded his campaign primarily with his own money, spending roughly $600,000.

Congressional candidates in general spent less of their own money in 2004 than they did in 2000. A simple explanation for the change might be that despite the efforts of the political parties to recruit candidates

Table 3-3. *The Federal Income Tax Checkoff, 1973–2004*

Calendar year	Returns[a] (%)	Amount ($)	Fund balances ($)
1973[b]	0	2,427,000	2,427,000
1974[b]	0	27,591,546	27,591,546
1975	24.2	31,656,525	59,551,245
1976	25.5	33,731,945	23,805,659
1977	27.5	36,606,008	60,927,571
1978	28.6	39,246,689	100,331,986
1979	25.4	35,941,347	135,246,807
1980	27.4	38,838,417	73,752,205
1981	28.7	41,049,052	114,373,289
1982	27	39,023,882	153,454,501
1983	24.2	35,631,068	177,320,982
1984	23.7	35,036,761	92,713,782
1985	23	34,712,761	125,870,541
1986	23	35,753,837	161,680,423
1987	21.7	33,651,947	177,905,677
1988	21	33,013,987	52,462,359
1989	20.1	32,285,646	82,927,013
1990	19.8	32,462,979	115,426,713
1991	19.5	32,322,336	127,144,469
1992	17.7	29,592,735	4,061,061
1993	18.9	27,636,982	30,779,386
1994[c]	14.5	71,316,995	101,664,547
1995	13	67,860,127	146,862,732
1996	12.9[d]	66,903,797	3,657,886
1997	12.6[d]	66,347,632	69,907,162
1998	12.5[d]	63,273,081	133,194,011
1999	12.5[d]	61,089,725	165,514,977
2000	11.8	60,685,015	16,214,320
2001	11.5	59,290,251	74,959,811
2002	11	61,998,162	137,046,746
2003	11.3	59,416,489	167,279,235
2004	. . .	55,726,279	44,961,484

Source: Federal Election Commission, press release February 2005.

a. The percentages refer to the tax returns of the previous year. For example, the 17.7 percent of 1991 tax returns that indicated a checkoff of $1 or $2 directed $29,592,735 into the Presidential Election Fund in calendar year 1992.

b. The 1973 tax forms were the first to have the checkoff on the first page; in 1972 taxpayers had to file a separate form to exercise the checkoff option. To compensate for the presumed difficulty caused by the separate form, taxpayers were allowed to designate $1 for 1972 as well as 1973 on the 1973 forms. Given these circumstances, total and percentage figures for these returns would be misleading.

c. The first year in which the checkoff value was $3 was 1994 (1993 tax-year returns).

d. The participation rates for 1996–99 were taken from the Taxpayer Usage Study (TPUS), a sample-based analysis generated by the Internal Revenue Service.

who can finance their own elections, they may not always be successful.[9] The candidates recruited in the last cycle may not have had the wealth necessary to fund portions of their own campaigns, a difference that makes it difficult to compare self-financing across time. After all, not every election cycle has a candidate such as former Senator Jon

Corzine, who can "invest" $60 million in his own election. Furthermore, with a general decline in competitive races, candidates may be less likely to believe it is worthwhile to self-finance. In the future, researchers will also want to consider whether changes in the campaign finance law may have some effect on self-financing. The millionaires' amendment, for example, may deter candidates from spending their own money since it may trigger higher fundraising limits for their opponent. If past congressional races around the country are any indication, many campaign strategies are built around the likelihood that an opponent will spend personal funds. When deciding whether to spend personal funds, a candidate must weigh the potential benefit it may offer the opponent and the likelihood that by not contributing personal funds a candidate can benefit from higher fundraising limits triggered by the opponent's spending.[10]

Even with all of the changes in the campaign finance system, overall candidate spending in federal elections—for the House, the Senate, and the presidency—continues to rise (table 3-4). It is difficult to compare the spending over time in Senate races. Different states have elections every two years because of staggered senate terms. Therefore campaigning in all states is not equally expensive. However, it does seem clear that the stakes associated with wins and losses in congressional races, the increasing costs of campaign services, and the competitiveness of those who throw their hat into the ring are continuing to drive up the amount that candidates expend to pursue federal office.

When discussing the receipts and expenditures in a federal campaign cycle, it is important to keep in mind the different entities—individuals, parties, and interest groups—that can and do participate apart from the candidates. In fact, congressional and presidential candidates spent only $1.9 billion of the almost $4.2 billion spent in the 2004 cycle. The other entities can engage in electioneering through independent expenditures, although they have not all been able to do so for the same amount of time. In *Buckley* v. *Valeo,* the Supreme Court declared that expenditures made independently of the party or candidate by individuals could not be limited. In *Colorado Republican Federal Campaign Committee* v. *FEC,* arising years later, the Supreme Court expanded allowable independent expenditures to include party committee spending done independently of the candidates, declaring "that restrictions on independent expenditures significantly impair the ability of individuals and groups to engage in direct political advocacy" and "represent substantial . . .

Table 3-4. *Congressional and Presidential Campaign Expenditures, 1976–2004*

Millions of dollars

Year	House	Senate	Presidential	Total
1976	71.5	44.0	66.9	182.4
1978	109.7	85.2	. . .	194.9
1980	136.0	102.9	92.3	331.2
1982	204.0	138.4	. . .	342.4
1984	203.6	170.5	103.6	477.7
1986	239.3	211.6	. . .	450.9
1988	256.5	201.2	210.7	668.4
1990	265.8	180.4	. . .	446.2
1992	406.7	271.6	192.2	870.5
1994	406.2	319.0	. . .	725.2
1996	477.8	287.5	239.9	1,005.2
1998	452.5	287.8	. . .	740.3
2000	572.3	434.7	343.1	1,350.1
2002	613.9	322.4	. . .	936.3
2004	660.3	496.4	717.9	1,874.6

Source: Congressional data for 1972–96 from John C. Green, ed., *Financing the 1996 Election* (Armonk, N.Y.: M. E. Sharpe, 1999), p. 23; 1998 congressional data from FEC press release, April 28, 1999; 2000 congressional data from FEC press release, May 15, 2001; 2002 congressional data from FEC press release, June 18, 2003; 2004 congressional data from FEC press release, June 9, 2005; presidential data from www.opensecrets.org.

restraints on the quantity and diversity of political speech."[11] At the same time, the Court concluded that limitations on independent expenditures are less directly related to preventing corruption, since "the absence of prearrangement and coordination of an expenditure with the candidate . . . not only undermines the value of the expenditure to the candidate, but also alleviates the danger that expenditures will be given as a quid pro quo for improper commitments from the candidate."[12] Therefore political parties did not make independent expenditures until 1996, when their committees used them in selected congressional races. While such expenditures remain unlimited, they must be disclosed to the Federal Election Commission (FEC).

The *Colorado* case did not clearly sanction party independent spending in the case of a publicly financed presidential candidate. This kind of activity was not permitted until the FEC changed regulations after the passage of BCRA. Therefore, any comparison of aggregate independent expenditures over time must take into account the fact that at different points different entities account for a greater or lesser share of the total amounts.

Table 3-5. *Independent Expenditures: Presidential
and Congressional Campaigns, 1980–2004*[a]

Millions of dollars

Year	Presidential	Congressional	Total
1980	13.7	2.3	16.0
1984	17.4	6.0	23.4
1988	14.3	7.1	21.4
1992	4.4	6.6	11.0
1996	1.4	20.6	22.0
2000	14.7	18.8	33.5
2004	192.4	137.5	329.9

Source: Federal Election Commission (ftp://ftp.fec.gov/FEC/ [June 25, 2005]).

a. Data include independent expenditures by political parties, PACs, and individuals. Political parties were not permitted to make independent expenditures in congressional races until 1996; they first made independent expenditures in the presidential race in 2004.

Table 3-5 presents the total amount of independent expenditures in the last seven presidential cycles. Most of the independent expenditures listed from 1980 to 1996 reflect interest group and individual behavior because parties could not make independent expenditures until 1996. Political parties also devoted little of their resources to independent expenditures in 2000 because they could rely on issue advocacy to try to influence elections.

The aggregate trend for independent expenditures does seem to indicate some of the ways in which changes in the law affect the strategic decisions of those noncandidate entities that participate in federal campaigns. The large surge in independent expenditures in 2004 is due mainly to new rules making them possible in presidential campaigns and to greater use by the party committees on Capitol Hill. No longer able to fund issue advocacy through soft money, the Hill committees used independent expenditures to target races.

Overall, the party committees spent more than $260.6 million in independent expenditures in 2004.[13] The Democratic National Committee (DNC) spent nearly $120.5 million, the largest proportion of independent expenditures in 2004. Ellen Moran, the director of independent expenditures at the DNC, described its operation as oddly detached from the race: prohibitions against coordination with the candidate's campaign, and reluctance to inadvertently harm that campaign seemed to hamper the effectiveness of the independent expenditure operation:

"On any given day, we felt how peripheral we were despite spending vast sums of money."[14]

The Republican National Committee's (RNC's) independent expenditures were about one-fifth the size of the DNC's. Yet the RNC found other ways to expend money in the cycle and also devised a new form of spending. This 50/50 formula, as it came to be known, allowed the RNC to spend more in coordinated advertisements with President Bush as long as the ads mentioned broader messages about the political party (for more details, see chapter 5). It may be that this formula reduced the RNC's need for a larger amount of independent expenditures.[15]

Independent expenditures by the party congressional campaign committees were more evenly matched. The National Republican Senatorial Committee (NRSC) and the Democratic Senatorial Campaign Committee (DSCC) were at near parity in this regard, while the National Republican Congressional Committee (NRCC) spent only about $10 million more than the Democratic Congressional Campaign Committee (DCCC) through independent expenditures (see chapter 7). Independent expenditures by interest groups are also constitutionally protected and have been a central part of funding federal elections. Like independent spending by parties, independent spending by groups in 2004 was higher than in the 2000 cycle. Some groups—such as the National Rifle Association (NRA), National Right to Life (NRL), and the National Education Association (NEA)—have long preferred independent expenditures to issue advocacy or to setting up 527 organizations. Many of them, notably the NEA and NRA, consider campaign endorsements and involvement important to their membership. But in 2004 it was the insurgence of new groups making large expenditures that helped increase the total spent. Among interest groups in 2004, MoveOn PAC spent the most in independent expenditures. MoveOn's $10 million far exceeded the $2.4 million that the League of Conservation Voters (LCV) and NARAL Pro-Choice America each spent independently in 2002. MoveOn's expenditures also far surpassed the notable independent expenditures of interest groups in 2000, when the LCV spent $2.3 million and the NRA spent nearly $7.1 million.[16]

Interest groups making independent expenditures were more likely to favor Democratic candidates. Prominent Democratic-leaning groups included MoveOn, unions, pro-choice groups, and environmental groups. Prominent Republican-leaning groups included the NRA, the

Club for Growth, and medical, pro-life, and business organizations. Major and minor groups participated on a larger scale than ever before. The business community, for example, had "never seen more mobilization and effort" than in the 2004 election.[17] This mobilization translated into higher dollars contributed and spent. The American Medical Association (AMA) increased its spending on partisan communication in key Senate and House races dramatically, from approximately $40,000 in 2000 and $250,000 in 2002 to $500,000 in 2004.[18] The Club for Growth saw contributions climb from $4.4 million in 2000 to $8.4 million or $10.5 million in 2002, then jump to $23 million in 2004.[19] Stephen Moore, president of the Club for Growth, believed that the elimination of party soft money directly benefited his organization's activities. "Truth is, BCRA benefited us," he claimed.[20]

With individuals allowed to make independent expenditures, this activity also increased between 2000 and 2004, something predicted before the enactment of BCRA.[21] In the most visible example, George Soros, a founding investor in ACT and the Media Fund, spent $4.0 million in independent expenditures in the presidential race. Many other individuals across the country joined in the trend, spending money on newspaper ads, flyers, and billboards to communicate their opinion on the candidates. Soros spent by far the most, however, the next highest such expenditure being $50,000.[22]

How the Money Was Raised: The Return of the Individual Donor

Federal candidates raised more than $2.5 billion from individuals in the 2004 cycle. The large amount from individual donors certainly reflects the higher contribution limits put in place by BCRA. Political parties also seemed to benefit from an increase in individual donations. Together, the surge in individual contributions to candidates and political parties constitutes a major development in the 2004 election cycle.

Reformers had hoped that the new law might break the connection between the large soft money donors and party officials, spurring growth in individual contributions. To facilitate this growth, BCRA doubled the amount that individuals could contribute to federal elections. Higher contribution limits coupled with the competitiveness of the presidential election pushed individual campaign spending to a record level. The proportion of individuals reporting that they made a political contribution increased from 12 percent of the population in

Table 3-6. *Percentage of National Adult Population Making Political Contributions, 1952–2004*

Year	Polling organization	Contributed to Republican	Contributed to Democrat	Total[a]
1952	SRC	3	1	4
1956	Gallup	3	6	9
1956	SRC	5	5	10
1960	Gallup	4	4	9
1960	Gallup	n.a.		12
1960	SRC	7	4	12
1964	Gallup	6	4	12
1964	SRC	5	4	10
1968	SRC	3	3	8[b]
1972	SRC	4	5	10[c]
1974	SRC	3	3	8[d]
1976	Gallup	3	3	8[e]
1976	SRC	4	4	9[f]
1980	CPS	3	1	4
1984	CPS	2	2	4
1988	CPS	4	2	6
1992	CPS	2	2	4
1996	CPS	3	2	6
2000	CPS	6	4	12
2004	CPS	7	6	16

Sources: Survey Research Center (SRC), and later the Center for Political Studies (CPS), both at the University of Michigan; data direct from the center or from Patricia Luevano, Angus Campbell, Philip E. Converse, and Donald E. Stokes, *The American Voter* (New York: John Wiley and Sons, 1960), p. 91; 1980 data from Ruth S. Jones and Warren E. Miller, "Financing Campaigns: Macro Level Innovation and Micro Level Response," *Western Political Quarterly* 38, no. 2 (1987); 1984 data from Ruth S. Jones, "Campaign Contributions and Campaign Solicitations: 1984," paper presented at the meeting of the Southern Political Science Association, Nashville, Tenn., November 6–9, 1985; Gallup data direct or from Roper Opinion Research Center, Williams College, and from the American Institute of Political Opinion (Gallup poll).

a. The total percentage may add to a total different from the total of Democratic and Republican contributors because of individuals contributing to both major parties, or to candidates of both major parties, nonparty groups, or combinations of these.

b. Includes 0.7 percent who contributed to the American Independent Party (AIP).

c. Includes contributors to the American Independent Party.

d. Includes 0.7 percent who contributed to both parties and 0.8 percent who contributed to minor parties.

e. Includes 1 percent to another party and 1 percent to "do not know" or "no answer."

f. Republican and Democratic figures are rounded. The total includes 0.6 percent who gave to both parties, 0.4 percent to other, and 0.3 percent "do not know."

n.a. = Not available.

2000 to 16 percent in 2004 (table 3-6), the highest such proportion in a presidential election cycle since 1952, when data on this were first gathered.[23] Both parties seemed to benefit from the increase. Democrats making contributions rose from less than 2 percent in 1980 to 4 percent in 2000 and 6 percent in 2004. Over the same period, Republicans have typically been slightly more likely to give, probably as a result of income differences between party identifiers and the GOP's long-standing efforts to cultivate small individual donors.[24]

There were also subtle shifts in the underlying demographics of individual donations in 2004. For the first time, more females reported making a contribution than males. An analysis of the National Election Studies data back to 1980 shows that males are generally more likely to make a contribution to a candidate than a female. In most years the differences are not too large, reaching only 4 percent in 1980 and 1984. In subsequent cycles, however, the difference is smaller, usually about 1 percent. But 2004 reversed that trend. Females in 2004, like their male counterparts, were more likely to give to Republicans. None of the political variables, such as ideology or party identification, changes dramatically over time. Conservatives continue to be more likely to donate than liberals. Republicans are also more likely to donate than Democrats. They are all more likely to donate to candidates who come closest to their own view of the world (for example, Democrats are more likely to give to Democratic candidates).[25]

Not only did the competitiveness of the campaign motivate individuals to contribute, but the means to contribute also became easier. A major development in 2004 was the use of the Internet in fundraising by candidates, parties, and interest groups. In the 2000 election, John McCain had success using the Internet, but some questioned whether this was merely a means to collect contributions typically solicited through other methods or whether it had broader utility. The McCain campaign used the Internet not only to raise funds but also to garner favorable publicity and to contact individuals through e-mail.[26] McCain's success in this regard was a harbinger of things to come. In 2004 Howard Dean's campaign had early success using the Internet for fundraising. Before dropping out of the race, Dean raised more than $51 million, mainly over the Internet, and became the first Democratic presidential candidate ever to opt out of matching federal funds. He was so successful that in the lead-up to the primaries he had raised about $16 million more than his closest competitor.[27] The mastermind of this enterprise, Joe Trippi, gushed about the political possibilities opened up by the Internet:

> In fact, it was the opening salvo in a revolution, the sound of hundreds of thousands of Americans turning off their televisions and embracing the only form of technology that has allowed them to

be involved again, to gain control of a process that alienated them decades ago. In the coming weeks and months and years, these hundreds of thousands will be followed by millions, and this revolution will not be satisfied with overthrowing a corrupt and unresponsive political system. It won't stop at remaking politics. And it won't pay attention to national borders.[28]

Whether it was a revolution remains to be seen, but it was lucrative, and other groups recognized that fact. Tapping into constituencies similar to Dean's, MoveOn.org also did well with the medium, raising over $12.5 million during the 2004 election cycle from more than 500,000 donors recruited mainly over the Internet.[29] Most of these contributions were made with credit cards, but MoveOn also accepted checks. "Shocked at how fast it happened," the head of MoveOn, Wes Boyd, believed the phenomenon of small donations via the Internet was even more important than the proliferation of 527s (see chapter 8).[30]

Recognizing the Internet's potential, John Kerry and the Democratic Party also invested in this mode with success. They quickly discovered it to be much less expensive than fundraising through the mail and a source of immediate cash flow for campaigns. Ben Ginsberg, Republican attorney and Bush campaign general counsel for most of the election cycle, felt certain "the way the Democrats raised money will be the model for both parties in 2008."[31] Internet fundraising, the surprise star of the 2004 election, will undoubtedly increase in coming election cycles as both parties and their allies perfect the medium's political applications.

It is difficult to determine the actual number of contributors in a federal cycle, especially the number of small donors, who are typically not itemized. Of the individuals who contributed in 2003–04, over 1 million gave $200 or more, an amount large enough to be recorded by the FEC. The Republicans still received a higher proportion of the recorded contributions and a larger amount from those contributions. However, the Democrats did seem to be closing the gap. Donors who gave $200 or more to candidates, parties, or a leadership PAC were more likely to give to Republicans by a margin of 46 percent to 42 percent. The gap grew to 8 percentage points for those individuals giving only to candidates or a political party. Republicans maintained their large advantage through individuals who were able to contribute the legal limit of $95,000 for a cycle (table 3-7).

During the 2000 election cycle, individual contributions to national Democratic parties totaled $195 million and accounted for 71 percent of their receipts; for national Republican parties, contributions totaled $395 million and made up 85 percent of their receipts. During the 2004 election cycle, individual contributions to Democratic parties came to $528 and accounted for 78 percent of their receipts; Republican totals reached $655 million and accounted for 84 percent of their receipts.[32]

The surge in individual giving was also evident in the individual congressional campaign committees, but it did not make up completely for the loss of soft money. In 2004 the DCCC raised more than $93 million in hard money, compared with $56.5 million in hard money in 2002. The $93 million came close to the $103 million the DCCC raised in both hard and soft money in 2002. The DSCC fared worse in trying to make up for the lost soft money, raising about as much in 2004 as it had raised in hard and soft money in 2002: $88.7 million compared with $143 million. The Republican congressional committees also struggled to make up for the loss of soft money. The NRSC raised $79 million in 2004 compared with $125 million in 2002. The NRCC did better, raising over $185 million in 2004 compared with $193 million in 2002.[33] Overall, nearly 475,000 donors who made a contribution large enough to be itemized gave exclusively to the Republican Party, while the Democrats had almost 460,000 such donors giving exclusively to them (see table 3-7).

While the Republicans enjoyed a fundraising surge in individuals giving to the different entities within the political party, Democrats could take heart from the number of donors who gave exclusively to the candidates, organizations, or leadership PACs. In various House and Senate races, Democrats may have also done much better than expected with fundraising from individuals where the candidates made reaching out to individuals a large part of their strategy. For example, Democrat Ken Salazar raised more money from individual donors than his Republican competitor, Pete Coors. Furthermore, Salazar had already prepared a list of donors who could be tapped for more contributions when Coors tripped the millionaires' amendment. His preparation of these lists made it possible for him to solicit donations up to the $6,000 limit in this race.[34]

Parties have also been raising more money from their own candidates, both from presidential candidates giving to party committees and

Table 3-7. *Individual Campaign Contributions, 2003–04*

Contribution	Count	Total	To Dem-ocrats[a]	To Repub-licans[a]	To PACs[a]	% Dem-ocrats	% Repub-licans
> $200	1,129,221	$1,892.50	$786.50	$877.40	$258.40	42	46
> $200 only to candidates/ parties	899,491	$1,252.40	$570.30	$675.10	$0.00	46	54
> $200 only to PACs	156,206	$121.20	n.a.	n.a.	$121.20	n.a.	n.a.
$200–$1,999	874,233	$507.60	$210.40	$210.40	$86.70	41	41
>$2,000	254,988	$1,384.90	$576.10	$667.00	$171.80	42	48
>$10,000	25,442	$635.10	$277.00	$304.50	$74.90	44	48
>$95,000	362	$39.90	$14.90	$22.10	$4.40	37	55
>$1,000,000	n.a.	n.a.	n.a.	n.a.	n.a.	n.a.	n.a.
Only to Republicans[b]	474,559	$774.10	–$0.10	$733.30	$54.90	0	100
Only to Democrats[b]	458,590	$700.40	$655.60	$0.00	$53.20	100	0
To both parties[b]	37,956	$297.30	$130.90	$144.20	$35.30	44	49
Double-givers (gave at least 33% to each party)[b]	15,397	$61.40	$30.00	$30.40	$3.60	49	50

Source: Opensecrets.org.

a. In millions of dollars.

b. Figures reflect contributions to candidates, parties, and leadership PACs. The numbers in this table are based on contributions from individuals giving $200 or more.

n.a. = Not available.

from safe-seat incumbents contributing to the congressional campaign committees. In 2004 Democrats received more than $62 million from federal candidates (up from over $13 million in 2000) and Republicans received more than $54 million (up from over $17 million in 2000).[35]

One important source of funds before and after BCRA was groups who help secure individual contributions to candidate campaigns. This process, called bundling, can provide a large infusion of individual contributions into a campaign, and, because the group doing the bundling is known by the candidate, its reputation is enhanced. EMILY's List is one of the groups most identified with this process. The organization bundled contributions of $9.3 million in 2000 and $9.7 million in 2002, and that number grew to $10.6 million in 2004.[36] The Club for Growth has also become active in this regard for fiscally conservative candidates, bundling approximately $7.5 million in 2004.[37]

Interests and Innovation

The 2004 cycle also saw growth in interest group activity through 527 and 501(c) organizations (see chapter 1 for descriptions of these various groups). Although Section 527 organizations (organizations created specifically to affect the outcome of elections) received most of the media attention, a large number of 501(c) organizations also participated. Under the Internal Revenue Code, all Section 501(c)(3) organizations are absolutely prohibited from directly or indirectly participating in, or intervening in, any political campaign on behalf of or in opposition to any candidate for elective public office.[38] However, a large number of these groups expended resources for nonpartisan voter education activities or nonpartisan get-out-the-vote (GOTV) drives. Section 501(c)(4), 501(c)(5), and 501(c)(6) organizations can engage in some political activities, so long as these activities are not their primary purpose. In the 2004 cycle, several organizations developed a full range of organizations—501(c), 527, and PAC—in order to take full advantage of the many ways to educate, mobilize, and persuade the public. Others, like the Chamber of Commerce, preferred to operate only as a trade association under Section 501(c)(6) of the IRS Code. According to staffer Bill Miller, "We don't feel a need to have a 527; we can do what we need with a 501(c)(6)."[39] The amount of this type of activity seems to be increasing.

Groups also try to influence elections through communications to their members, employees, shareholders, and others about political issues, candidates, and GOTV activities. The amount spent on internal communications to help presidential candidates has steadily increased, from $2 million in 1980 to close to $24 million in 2004 (see table 3-8). Interestingly, this increase comes mostly from activity in the presidential contests. Funds spent for or against candidates in House and Senate campaigns remain relatively flat. Furthermore, in contrast to other forms of outside activity, internal communications seem to be more likely to promote a candidate than to damage another. In some cases, BCRA's new regulations may have contributed to the increase in internal communications. Some groups, wary of the legal consequences of violating BCRA's ban on coordination with candidates and parties, decided to approach the election cautiously. Ned Monroe of the Associated Builders and Contractors (ABC) says that they would only do broadcast advertising reluctantly and ended up not doing any at all. They also

Table 3-8. *Internal Communication Costs in Presidential and Congressional Campaigns, 1980–2004*

Millions of dollars

Year	Presidential candidates		House candidates		Senate candidates		Total
	For	Against	For	Against	For	Against	
1980	2.0	0.6	0.8	0.1	0.3	0.05	3.9
1984	4.7	0.05	1.0	0.06	0.6	0.0	6.4
1988	2.0	0.1	1.1	0.0	1.2	0.02	4.4
1992	4.2	0.05	2.3	0.01	1.9	0.07	8.5
1996	2.4	0.3	2.7	0.5	1.7	0.05	7.6
2000	10.9	0.6	3.6	0.2	2.3	0.1	17.7
2004	24.3	0.0	1.8	0.01	2.8	0.005	28.9

Source: Federal Election Commission (ftp://ftp.fec.gov/FEC/ [June 25, 2005]).

decided not to contribute to 527 organizations. In this instance, BCRA "meant more internal communication with [ABC] members."[40]

Under BCRA, individuals could continue to make unlimited contributions to Section 527 or 501(c) organizations, but those to 527 organizations had to be disclosed. In the past, contributions to issue advocacy groups were only voluntarily disclosed. In 2004 there was greater disclosure of 527 finances than ever before. Also, 527 expenditures that qualified as electioneering communications were disclosed under the disclosure provisions related to electioneering communications. As Al Cigler documents in chapter 8, large donors played an important role in the 2004 cycle by making direct contributions to fund Section 527 and Section 501(c) organizations or by making independent expenditures. In 2004 individuals contributed over $169.5 million to Section 527 organizations in aggregate amounts of $250,000 or more.[41] Examples of major individual donors on the left were George Soros, $23,450,000; Peter Lewis, $22,997,220; Steven Bing, $13,852,031; and Herb and Marion Sandler, $13,008,459.[42] These donors are noteworthy not only for the amounts they gave but for the visibility some sought while doing so. Thinking about the persistent media interest in his donations to Democratic organizations and the resultant Republican ire he generated, Soros quipped, "I think I may have ended up raising more money for the Republicans."[43] Large individual contributions to Republican-leaning 527s came from Bob J. Perry, who gave $8,095,000, including $4,450,000 to the Swift Boat Veterans for Truth and $3 million to

Figure 3-1. *Individual Contributions to Federal 527s, by Size of Donation, 2002 and 2004*

Percent of dollars from individual donors

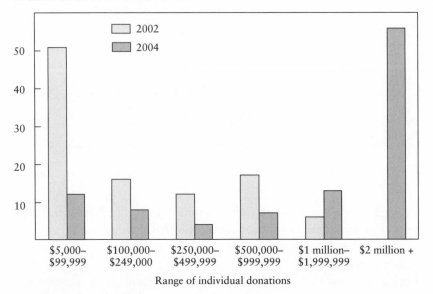

Range of individual donations

Source: Center for Public Integrity.

Progress for America. Alex Spanos gave $5 million to Progress for America, as did Dawn Arnall of Ameriquest.[44]

Clearly, the 527 organizations benefited from these large donations. Unlike the political parties and the presidential candidates that learned to rely on the small individual donor, 527 organizations raised a substantial proportion of their funds in 2004 from donations of $2 million or more. Indeed, over 50 percent of the money came from individuals who made donations larger than $2 million, whereas in 2002 more than 50 percent of the funds came from individuals donating between $5,000 and $99,999. While it is possible to debate the difference between donations of $100,000 and those of $2 million, a comparison of figures for 2002 and 2004 (figure 3-1) clearly shows that 527 organizations relied on much larger donations and that money from the largest donors still found its way into the political system in the wake of the BCRA reforms.

Table 3-9. *Proportion of Spending by National Parties, Presidential Candidates, and 527 Groups, 2003–04*

Expenditure	RNC	DNC	Bush	Kerry	R-527	D-527
Fundraising	40	14	17	8	12	10
Administrative costs	21	18	13	27	2	38
Media	20	45	54	45	81	27
Grassroots campaigning	18	20	7	7	5	21
Other[a]	1	3	9	13	—	4

Source: Dwight L. Morris & Associates, Federal Election Commission, Internal Revenue Service, Center for Public Integrity, Center for Responsive Politics, *Washington Post* staff; see graphic "The Costliest Campaign," in Thomas B. Edsall and James V. Grimaldi, "On November 2, GOP Got More Bang for Its Billion, Analysis Shows," *Washington Post*, December 30, 2004, p. A1.

a. Polling, donations to other committees and candidates, unitemized expenses.

Participants and Their Allocation Strategies

The number of participants in campaigns bewilders the average voter. The candidates usually run their own campaign organizations, complete with a set of staff separate from political parties and interest groups. Political parties participate through a variety of means, including independent expenditures and the mobilization of voters. Interest groups with allegiances to the parties also want to have some influence. Each entity has its own particular constellation of responsibilities, goals, and resources.

It is difficult to determine accurately from FEC disclosure reports the specific amounts party committees spent on various activities. Although the parties provide some information on the purpose of expenditures, it is often a general notation such as "mail" or "telephone" that does not distinguish between fundraising, grassroots communications, or GOTV activity. Even so, one analysis of party spending in the 2004 cycle has found some notable differences between candidates, parties, and the interest groups (see table 3-9). For example, the RNC devoted 40 percent of its budget to fundraising and the DNC only 14 percent. The RNC believes that a significant investment in developing donor lists and cultivating those individuals will pay off over the long term. The 527 groups loyal to Republicans spent 81 percent of their budget on the media and only 5 percent on grassroots campaigning. According to this analysis, the 527s on the Democratic side spent a considerably smaller proportion of their budget on the media and a larger share on grassroots campaigning. The Republicans decided early on to use the model of the

72 Hour Task Force to carry the burden for the ground war. Democrats, on the other hand, seemed to set up two simultaneous ground war operations: one by the Kerry campaign and the other by the Democratic 527s. The legal barrier to coordination between the two operations probably led to some inefficiency in spending.[45]

Conclusion

The trends in the 2004 data on campaign finance in federal contests hint at what lies in store for campaign spending. First, the increase in independent expenditures by parties and some groups indicates a possible future reliance on this form of electioneering. Second, the new campaign finance regime certainly seems to include the small donor. The ability of parties to raise money from the small individual donor helped ease the transition from soft money to hard money. The surge in individuals making contributions to campaigns accomplishes one of the goals of BCRA. However, it would be foolish to assume that the campaign finance system will rely entirely on individual donations. In addition, interest groups have devised different ways to participate in both the presidential and congressional campaigns. Nonparty and noncandidate electioneering activities in 2004 included several bold and expensive attempts to influence federal elections. The most visible and well funded of these—ACT, the Media Fund, America Votes, Progress for America, and Swift Boat Veterans for Truth—operated nearly exclusively on presidential battlegrounds. With the exception of ACT and the members of the America Votes coalition, they also communicated primarily through broadcast ads. In some states, such as Missouri, interest groups like ACT and the AFL-CIO continued to campaign aggressively for John Kerry even after he had ceased to run ads in the state.[46] Section 527 or 501(c) groups active in multiple Senate races in 2004 included Citizens for a Strong Senate, New Democrat Network, Americans for Job Security, and United Seniors. Some 527 organizations arose in particular contests, one example being "You're Fired, Inc.," a group that campaigned against Senator Tom Daschle (D-S.D.).[47] There is no reason to believe that more of these race-specific groups will not emerge in future election cycles.

Obviously, any future shifts in financing patterns also depend on what policymakers decide. Politicians care about the system that regulates their livelihood. In the wake of the 2004 elections, battle lines over campaign finance reform have been redrawn yet again as academics and politicians assess the effects of BCRA on the election system and determine what reforms to pursue next. Two opposing camps have emerged: those who see BCRA as a successful, yet incomplete, overhaul of the campaign finance system and those who believe BCRA has been misguided since its inception. According to BCRA supporters, led by Senators John McCain and Russell Feingold and Representatives Christopher Shays and Martin Meehan, the original sponsors of BCRA, reform now needs to focus on reining in 527 organizations and their undisclosed, unlimited spending by subjecting them to the same restrictions as other political committees registered with the FEC. For these reformers, 527s are a loophole in the original law that needs to be closed to complete the reform process started in 2002, though some have accused the reformers of partisan motivations.[48] The opposing faction, however, believes that 527 spending and its attendant effects on candidate campaigns and party activities only prove the futility of BCRA. They propose eliminating the fundraising and spending restrictions placed on political parties to allow them to compete with 527s and other groups that are less accountable and responsible. These reformers believe BCRA's regulations stifled legitimate political speech and that 527 spending was an outlet for that speech. The differing sides are largely composed of the same personalities who debated BCRA in 2002, but there have been a number of prominent defections, most notably Senator Trent Lott, who now favors regulating 527 organizations.

As policymakers decide what to do next, they confront an electoral environment that clearly bears some resemblance to the past but also includes several new features. For one thing, interested money still seeks to find its way into elections and to affect their outcomes. For another, individual donors have been playing a larger role than ever before. Furthermore, political parties have experimented with new forms of coordinating with the candidates but have also diverted more money to independent operations. Those who will decide on the policies face an almost bewildering set of choices as they seek to create a regulatory environment that meets their electoral needs, adheres to constitutional principles, and gains the confidence of the public.

Notes

1. See Michael Malbin, "Thinking about Reform," in *Life after Reform: When the Bipartisan Campaign Reform Act Meets Politics,* edited by Michael Malbin (Lanham, Md.: Rowman and Littlefield, 2003).

2. James A. Thurber and Candice J. Nelson, eds., *Campaign Warriors: Political Consultants in Elections* (Brookings, 2000).

3. Diana Dwyre and Victoria A. Farrar-Myers, *Legislative Labyrinth: Congress and Campaign Finance Reform* (Congressional Quarterly Press, 2001).

4. Candice J. Nelson, "Spending in the 2000 Elections," in *Financing the 2000 Election*, edited by David B. Magleby (Brookings, 2002), p. 24.

5. John C. Green and Anthony Corrado, "The Impact of BCRA on Presidential Campaign Finance," in *Life after Reform*, edited by Malbin, p. 182.

6. For recent scholarship on effects on trust in government and politics, see Marc J. Hetherington, *Why Trust Matters: Declining Political Trust and the Demise of American Liberalism* (Princeton University Press, 2004); and Shaun Bowler and Jeffrey A. Karp, "Politicians, Scandals, and Trust in Government," *Political Behavior* 26 (September, 2004): 271–87.

7. Glen Justice, "Kerry Takes a Mortgage of $6 Million on His House," *New York Times*, December 24, 2003, p. 16A.

8. "2004 Presidential Election" (Opensecrets.org).

9. George Will, "A Republican Senate for Some Time," *TownHall.com* (www.townhall.com/columnists/georgewill/gw20021125.shtml [September 13, 2005]).

10. Kyle Saunders and Robert Duffy, "The 2004 Colorado U.S. Senate Race," in *Dancing without Partners: How Candidates, Parties and Interest Groups Interact in the New Campaign Finance Environment*, edited by David B. Magleby, J. Quin Monson, and Kelly D. Patterson (Brigham Young University, Center for the Study of Elections and Democracy, 2005), p. 178; Robin Kolodny, Sandra Suarez, and Justin Gollob, "The Pennsylvania Thirteenth Congressional District Race," in *Dancing without Partners*, edited by Magleby and others, p. 311.

11. *Colorado Republican Federal Campaign Committee v. FEC*, 518 U.S. 604, 615 (1996).

12. *Buckley v. Valeo*, 424 U.S. 1, 19 (1976).

13. Federal Election Commission, "Party Financial Activity Summarized for the 2004 Election Cycle," press release, March 2, 2005 (www.fec.gov/press/press2005/20050302party/Party2004final.html).

14. Ellen Moran, independent expenditure director, DNC, interview by David B. Magleby and Betsey Gimbel, Washington, December 16, 2004.

15. Associated Press, "Bush Capitalizes on Huge Funding Loophole," September 22, 2004 (www.msnbc.msn.com/id/6073233/ [September 2, 2005]).

16. Allan J. Cigler, "Interest Groups and Financing the 2000 Elections," in *Financing the 2000 Election*, edited by Magleby, p. 175.

17. Tiffany Adams, vice president of public affairs, National Association of Manufacturers, interview by David Magleby and Kristina Gale, Washington, November 5, 2004.

18. Mike Cys, director, Division of Political and Legislative Grassroots,

AMA, and Jim Kwaka, regional political director, Division of Political and Legislative Grassroots, AMA, interview by David B. Magleby, December 15, 2004.

19. Stephen Moore, president, Club for Growth, interview by David B. Magleby and Richard Hawkins, Washington, November 5, 2004.

20. Ibid. Adjusted for inflation (2004 dollars) at U.S. Department of Labor, Bureau of Labor Statistics, "Consumer Price Index Home Page" (www.bls.gov/cpi/home.htm [January 25, 2005]).

21 David B. Magleby and Nicole Carlisle Squires, "Party Money in the 2002 Congressional Elections," in *The Last Hurrah? Soft Money and Issue Advocacy in the 2002 Congressional Elections,* edited by David B. Magleby and J. Quin Monson (Brookings, 2004), pp. 36–62.

22. Independent expenditure data obtained from Federal Election Commission records in Washington, January 26, 2005.

23. This paragraph is based on an analysis of the National Election Studies data back to 1980. Tables are available upon request.

24. Peter L. Francia and others, *The Financiers of Congressional Elections: Investors, Ideologues, and Intimates* (Columbia University Press, 2003).

25. This paragraph is based on an analysis of the National Election Studies data back to 1980. Tables are available upon request.

26. Andrew J. Glass, "Money Flows Online to McCain," *Atlanta Journal and Constitution,* February 4, 2000, p. 17A.

27. Marian Currinder, "Campaign Finance: Funding the Presidential and Congressional Elections," in *The Elections of 2004,* edited by Michael Nelson (Congressional Quarterly Press, 2005), p. 118.

28. "The Revolution Will Not Be Televised: Introduction," Joetrippi.com (joetrippi.com/?page_id=1379 [August 19, 2005]).

29. Wes Boyd and Joan Blades, founders, MoveOn, interview by David B. Magleby, Berkeley, California, September 10, 2004; and Center for Responsive Politics, "527 Committee Activity: Top 50 Federally Focused Organizations" (Campaign Warriors: Political Consultants in Elections; www.opensecrets.org/527s/527cmtes.asp [August 19, 2005]).

30. Boyd interview.

31. Ben Ginsberg, election lawyer, and Patton Boggs, interview by David B. Magleby, Washington, November 10, 2004.

32. Federal Election Commission, "Party Financial Activity Summarized for the 2004 Election Cycle," press release (www.fec.gov/press/press2005/20050302 party/Party2004final.html).

33. Ibid.

34. See Saunders and Duffy, "The 2004 Colorado U.S. Senate Race."

35. Federal Election Commission, "Party Financial Activity Summarized," press release, December 14, 2004 (www.fec.gov/press/press2004/20041214 party/ 20041214party.html). Note: Data from January 1, 2003, to November 22, 2004.

36. Karen White, political director, EMILY's List, interview by David B. Magleby and Richard Hawkins, Washington, November 8, 2004.

37. Moore interview.

38. Title 26, Substitute F—Income Taxes and Subtaxes, Subchapter F—Exempt Organizations, Part 1, General Rule, Sec. 504.

39. Bill Miller, vice president of public affairs and national political director, U.S. Chamber of Commerce, interview by David B. Magleby, Betsey Gimbel, and Joe Hadfield, Washington, June 24, 2004.

40. Ned Monroe, director of political affairs, Associated Builders and Contractors, interviewed by David B. Magleby and Kristina Gale, Washington, November 5, 2004.

41. Center for Responsive Politics, "Top Individual Contributors to 527 Committees 2004 Election Cycle" (www.opensecrets.org/527s/527indivs.asp?cycle=2004 [January 5, 2004]).

42. Ibid.

43. Danna Harman, "Mr. Soros Goes to Washington," *Christian Science Monitor,* August 25, 2004, p. 11.

44. Center for Responsive Politics, "Top Individual Contributors to 527 Committees 2004 Election Cycle."

45. Thomas B. Edsall and James V. Grimaldi, "On Nov. 2, GOP Got More Bang for Its Billion, Analysis Shows," *Washington Post,* December 30, 2004, p. A1.

46. E. Terrence Jones and others, "Battleground No More? The Presidential Race in Missouri," in *Dancing without Partners,* edited by Magleby and others, p. 109.

47. See Elizabeth Theiss Smith and Richard Braunstein, "The Nationalization of Local Politics: The South Dakota U.S. Senate Race," in *Dancing without Partners,* edited by Magleby and others.

48. Thomas Edsall, "Panel Backs Bill to Rein in '527' Advocacy Groups; Donations to PACs, Candidates, Political Parties Would Increase," *Washington Post,* April 28, 2005, p. A21.

FOUR   *Financing the 2004 Presidential Nomination Campaigns*

JOHN C. GREEN

The financing of the 2004 presidential nomination campaigns was extraordinary by any standard: it set a record for the total funds raised and spent by the major party nominees as well as for spending by interest groups. The reasons are not hard to find. For one thing, the 2004 campaign was a highly competitive affair, encouraging intensive and innovative fundraising. These efforts were aided by new campaign finance laws that doubled the individual contribution limits for federal candidates and encouraged the expansion of outside interest group spending, especially by 527 committees.

Of greater import, however, was the continued decay of the presidential nomination finance system. For the first time, both the Republican and Democratic presidential nominees chose to forgo matching public funds in the primaries and were free to raise unlimited funds before the national conventions. The largest portion of this money was used to influence the November 2 general election. Although the major party nominees accepted public subsidies for the national conventions and the general election campaign, their nomination finances threatened to undermine these portions of the public financing system as well, by making such funds and associated regulations less effective. Thus the public financing system now faces a crisis. Will it become increasingly irrelevant or will it be revived by timely reform? This chapter describes the financing of the 2004 nomination campaign and its implications for the future.

93

Rules, Rivals, and Resources in 2004

As in past presidential nomination campaigns, the federal campaign finance laws, the structure of competition, and the availability of resources all help account for the financial patterns in 2004. At the same time, the 2004 election was distinctive in that the rules of campaign finance were changed in 2002.

Federal Campaign Finance Laws

In 2004 presidential campaign finance was governed by the new Bipartisan Campaign Reform Act (BCRA) of 2002 and the Federal Election Campaign Act (FECA) of 1971, as amended in 1974, 1976, and 1979, interpreted by the federal courts, and implemented by the Federal Election Commission (FEC).[1] The adoption of BCRA created considerable uncertainty: not only did the new law change some rules, but the legality of some of the law's features was unclear until a U.S. Supreme Court ruling on them in November 2003 and FEC actions in the spring of 2004—well after the campaign was already under way. Despite this uncertainty, two important provisions for presidential nomination campaigns were unchanged. First, the act imposed mandatory financial regulations on all candidate committees and other political organizations. Second, it created a voluntary public financing system with additional regulations for participating candidates. This distinction between mandatory rules and voluntary regulations was critical in 2004.

Although BCRA made no direct changes to the public financing system, its alterations of the mandatory finance rules did have an important indirect impact on the system's operation (see chapters 1 and 2 on the basic rules).[2] First, BCRA doubled the maximum individual contribution limit to a federal candidate (including presidential candidates) from $1,000 to $2,000. It also raised the individual contribution limits for parties as well as the total individual contribution limits to all federal committees. Second, the new law banned "soft money" in federal elections, including the presidential election, thus providing interest groups such as 527 committees and others outside of political action committees (PACs) strong incentives to expand their activity.[3] With this possibility in mind, BCRA set new limits on electioneering communication that applied to such groups, prohibiting the use of corporate or union treasury funds to pay for broadcast advertising within thirty days of a primary or sixty days of a general election and set new disclosure requirements. However, broadcast expenditures outside of the thirty- and sixty-day windows and non-broadcast expenditures by such entities were not limited as long as they were done independently of candidates.

In 2004 the public financing system rules were as prescribed by the FECA, maintaining its voluntary character. To qualify for public funds during the primaries, a candidate must first raise $100,000 in amounts of $250 or less, with $5,000 coming from each of twenty states. Once a candidate is qualified, the first $250 of every individual contribution raised is matched dollar per dollar with public funds up to one-half of the primary spending limits for that year (PAC and party donations are not matched). Qualified candidates can receive federal funds after January 1 of the election year. They lose their qualification if they receive less than 10 percent of the vote in two successive primaries or caucuses but can requalify if they receive 20 percent in a subsequent contest.

In return for matching funds, candidates must abide by state-by-state and overall spending limits. The state limits are based on the voting-age population and are adjusted for inflation every four years. The overall limit, set in 1974, is also regularly adjusted for inflation.[4] Candidates allocate expenditures to the state contests by means of complex rules and clever strategies so state limits are not especially restrictive. However, the overall spending limit in effect determines what participating candidates can raise and spend during the nomination campaign.

In addition to the base spending limit, candidates are allowed to raise an additional 20 percent of the limit for fundraising purposes, and another 15 percent of the limit is allowed for legal and accounting expenses required to comply with the law (once a candidate withdraws from the campaign, such expenses are exempt from the limits; see chapter 5). Finally, candidates who accept matching funds are limited to giving or loaning $50,000 in personal funds to their campaigns.

In 2004 the FEC set the overall spending limit at $37.3 million, allowing an additional $7.5 million for fundraising and another $5.6 million for legal and compliance costs while a campaign is active (such costs become unlimited during the winding-down phase of an unsuccessful campaign). All things considered, the effective spending limit for an active campaign totaled $50.4 million. And a candidate could have received a maximum of $18.6 million in public matching funds.

The presidential public financing system also includes subsidies for national party nominating conventions and grants for the general election campaigns. When combined with the matching funds and the special circumstances of 2004, these rules create three financing periods (see chapter 5).

The first period is the "primary season," including the year before the primaries and the contests themselves. Because of the steady compression of the primary calendar, the year before the primaries has become very important for candidate fundraising since there is little time to do so once the contests start. Dubbed the invisible primary, this period was especially important in 2004.

The second period is the "bridge period" between the effective end of the primaries and completion of the presidential nominations at the national conventions. In 2004 both parties had clear winners of the nomination by March 2. There was also a "convention phase" in August 2004 owing to the vagaries of the political calendar: the gap between the Democratic and Republican conventions allowed the Democratic nominee to enter the general election period while the Republican nominee was still in the bridge period.

The third period is the "general election campaign," running from the conventions to Election Day. This period is defined by a candidate's acceptance of public funds and the associated prohibition on raising and spending private funds (see chapter 5 on the general election). In 2004, however, much of the eventual nominees' primary season and bridge period spending was directed at influencing the general election campaign.

With the development of these finance periods, the matching funds system has become less attractive to strong candidates.[5] The fact that the primary spending limits were indexed for inflation, while both individual contributions and matching funds were not, made accepting matching funds less attractive to the strongest candidates. The unattractiveness was reinforced by other changes in the presidential nominating system that increased the costs of competition. As a result, well-financed candidates began to forgo matching public funds and the attendant spending limits. The 2004 campaign continued this trend of strong candidates' opting out of matching funds.

Structure of Electoral Competition

Candidates' nomination campaign finances are influenced by the structure of electoral competition, which has two basic elements. The first is the mechanism by which national convention delegates are chosen in individual states. With minimal guidance from the national parties, each state sets its own means of delegate selection and the date of that caucus, convention, or primary. Thus the primary calendar varies from election to election.

The 2004 primary calendar took another step in a long-term trend toward "front-loading": clustering nomination contests early in the election year.[6] In a departure from previous years, Democratic Party leaders sought to accelerate front-loading by determining the party's nominee as quickly as possible to maximize campaign funds for the bridge period. Following custom, the 2004 contests began with the Iowa caucuses (January 19) and the New Hampshire primary (January 27), followed by eighteen contests in February and culminating in "Titanic Tuesday" (March 2) with ten delegate-rich contests. As part of this strategy, the Democrats scheduled their national convention earlier than usual (at the end of July) to give their nominee early access to the general election public funds. These plans were made on the assumption that the Democratic Party would not have the funds to assist the nominee during the bridge period because of BCRA restrictions (see chapter 5).[7]

A second significant structural element of the competition is the number of candidates in the race. Multicandidate and two-candidate races call for different financial strategies.[8] For example, with no incumbent president running in 1988, six Republicans and seven Democrats competed, whereas in 2000 only two candidates ran for the Democratic nomination. Multicandidate races encourage candidates to appeal to smaller financial constituencies, whereas two-candidate races encourage much broader appeals.

The structure of competition can be influenced by the nomination contest in the other party, especially when an incumbent president is unopposed for renomination. As with Ronald Reagan in 1984 and Bill Clinton in 1996, George W. Bush presided over a united party in 2004 and was in a position to raise and spend substantial funds, to the detriment of his eventual Democratic opponent. Indeed, the prospects of a well-financed Bush campaign had a powerful influence on the strategies of Democratic candidates, party leaders, and interest group allies as they considered how to raise the necessary campaign resources. It also meant some liberal interest groups, such as MoveOn.org, decided to spend money against Bush long before the Democratic nominee was chosen.

Campaign Resources

The campaign finance laws and the structure of competition set the basic parameters for candidates' finances. Every candidate makes a calculation of how much money he or she will need and how to acquire and spend it.

As the incumbent president, George W. Bush set the stage for the 2004 campaign. With no opponent for renomination, the Bush campaign and the Republican Party had the luxury of planning a comprehensive fundraising effort. Given the controversial nature of the president's policies, the campaign anticipated a very competitive—and expensive—general election. Because Bush had opted out of matching public funds in 2000 with considerable success, he had every incentive to do so again. Given the doubled individual contribution limit, Bush decided to set an initial goal of raising $175 million in the primary season, which he later upped to $200 million. He planned on using a substantial portion of the funds to "define" the eventual Democratic nominees in unfavorable terms.[9] The Bush strategy raised the possibility of forgoing matching public funds among the Democrats. While such an option had its costs, many observers believed that one or more of the strongest Democratic candidates would follow Bush's example. Exactly which candidate(s) would forgo public funds would depend on the results of the invisible primary in 2003.[10]

As in presidential elections, two general fundraising strategies were available to candidates during the invisible primary. The first was an "insider" strategy that concentrated on raising large individual donations early in the primary season. This approach relied on exploiting connections with networks of individual fundraisers, interest groups, and party leaders. If successful, such a strategy could drive weaker opponents from the race, secure a resource advantage in the early contests, and provide a degree of resilience if the candidate faltered in the early contests. It would also keep the option of forgoing public funds open. Governor George W. Bush had followed this strategy in the 2000 Republican primaries with obvious success. This approach was popular because of the declining real value of hard dollar contributions and matching funds. Simply put, it was more cost-effective to raise funds in larger rather than smaller amounts. BCRA's doubling of the individual contribution limits made this strategy all the more attractive in 2004.

The second, an "outsider" approach, depended on clear issue appeals, novelty, and drama to attract a large number of small donations via direct mail, telephone solicitation, and the Internet. If successful, such a strategy would undermine the credibility of "insider" opponents, generate invaluable media coverage, and produce sufficient funds to win primaries. Most observers believed that such a strategy would require matching funds to succeed, but the new donors it generated could contribute to party and interest group committees during the bridge period. Its chief drawback was the high cost of raising funds in small amounts. Indeed, conventional wisdom suggested that an outsider candidate would be at a financial disadvantage in the primary season and the bridge period, but some candidates had no alternative. In fact, the low cost of raising funds over the Internet made this alternative more attractive than conventional wisdom suggested.

While the presidential candidates pondered these alternatives, Democratic Party leaders made their own plans to cope with the bridge period, including, as noted, adjusting the primary and convention dates and raising a special hard dollar fund to spend on behalf of the presumptive nominee. The most elaborate response came from the "shadow Democratic Party," a set of 527 committees organized by political operatives, labor unions, and major donors. These committees and other groups planned special spending on behalf of the Democratic nominee during the bridge period (see chapter 8).[11]

Nomination Campaign Receipts and Disbursements in 2004

Table 4-1 lists adjusted receipts and disbursements for all presidential candidates for the primary season and bridge periods combined (January 1, 2003, to August 31, 2004).[12] A total of $675 million was raised, 192 percent more than the $352 million collected during the same period in the 2000 cycle. A total of $587 million was spent, an increase of 180 percent over the 2000 figure of $326 million. This increase was especially impressive given that the 2000 funds represented a substantial expansion over 1996.[13]

The Major Party Nominees

Much of this increase came from the two major party nominees. President Bush raised $259 million, two and one-half times more than his record-breaking nomination fundraising in 2000. Senator John Kerry did even better than the Democratic nominee in the 2000 campaign: his $241 million was more than a fourfold expansion over Al Gore's 2000 receipts.

In some respects, the 1972 presidential campaign provides a good baseline for assessing these figures, being the last "unregulated" presidential campaign before the adoption of the public financing system in 1976. In 2004 constant dollars, Richard Nixon's campaign and allied

Table 4-1. *Adjusted Presidential Nomination Receipts and Disbursements, 2003–04*

Dollars

Party	Receipts[a]	Disbursements[a]
Republican		
Bush	258,973,508	222,110,508
Primary season	158,309,938	48,483,605
Bridge period	82,163,645	159,336,458
Convention pause	18,499,925	14,290,445
Democrat		
Kerry	241,065,104	192,068,827
Primary season	40,659,599	38,190,777
Bridge period	187,999,885	141,613,627
Convention pause	12,405,620	12,264,423
Dean	51,126,685	49,949,761
Edwards	29,206,271	29,271,313
Clark	25,073,530	24,650,133
Gephardt	21,093,321	20,599,234
Lieberman	18,530,864	18,299,784
Kucinich	10,899,864	10,786,773
LaRouche[b]	9,606,641	9,601,073
Graham	4,975,253	4,975,253
Moseley-Braun	579,307	576,806
Sharpton	567,932	663,758
Reform[c]		
Nader	2,356,210	2,376,929
Libertarian		
Badnarik	537,911	503,608
Constitution		
Peroutka	348,610	350,408
Green		
Cobb	100,368	86,169

Source: Compiled from Federal Election Commission data for January 1, 2003, through August 31, 2004.

a. Adjusted by subtracting repaid loans, offsets to expenditures, and contribution refunds.

b. LaRouche is a right-wing fringe candidate who ran in the Democratic primaries 1980–2004.

c. Nader also appeared on state ballots as an independent.

committees raised and spent $280 million, more than the Bush or Kerry campaigns (by $21 million and $39 million, respectively). However, Nixon's funds covered both the nomination and the general election. If the $75 million in 2004 general election public financing is added in, then Bush spent $17 million more than Nixon in real terms and Kerry only $3 million less. Nixon's competitor, George McGovern, and his allied committees raised nearly as much as Nixon, establishing essentially the same pattern on the Democratic side.[14]

However, it is difficult to compare the Bush and Kerry nomination figures with recent presidential elections because they contain a much larger component of general election fundraising. Accordingly, table 4-1 breaks out the primary season and bridge period for each candidate. Senator Kerry raised 78 percent of his total *after* he secured the Democratic nomination in March 2004; President Bush raised 32 percent of his total after that date. Seen from another perspective, each candidate raised more private funds in the bridge period than the $75 million in public funds they received for the general election. These figures do not include the convention phase in August, when Kerry had been officially nominated and Bush had not. On balance, this period favored Bush financially because Kerry's acceptance of general election public funds limited his financial activities.

In spite of Bush's financial advantage during specific periods, Democratic fundraising was unexpectedly impressive in 2004. Not only did Kerry nearly match Bush in total funds raised, but the top two Democratic candidates, Kerry and Howard Dean, outraised Bush by some $33 million. Kerry and Dean also outraised the rest of the 2004 Democratic field by more than $170 million. Taken together, these figures dispute the conventional wisdom that Democratic presidential candidates are unable to raise large war chests.

Other Candidates

By historical standards, the nine Democratic candidates who ultimately lost the nomination to Kerry were also successful fundraisers in 2004. Together they amassed a total of $175 million, around 192 percent of Gore and Bill Bradley's combined totals in 2000. If matching public funds are excluded, the nine candidates raised $115 million, still some $24 million more than the total for the Democratic candidates in 2000. The Democratic field of candidates was unusually large in 2004; the last time it was similarly large was in 1992, when six sought the nomination to run against another President Bush. Excluding Kerry's post-primary fundraising surge, the Democratic field raised about $202 million during the primary season, more than twice the 1992 Democratic total (in 2004 constant dollars).[15]

Minor party candidates, however, raised and spent substantially less money in the 2004 nomination period than in 2000. At $3.3 million, the amount was about one-fifth of the 2000 figure. There was no effort comparable to the 2000 struggle over the Reform Party nomination (or the $13 million in public funds available to the nominee).[16] Although

Ralph Nader amassed about $1 million more in 2004 as a Reform and independent candidate than he did as a Green Party candidate in 2000, the other minor party candidates underperformed in comparison with their counterparts in 2000 at this stage of the campaign.

There are several reasons for this extraordinary increase in total funds across the board. First, Bush, Kerry, and Dean, the three major contenders, decided to forgo matching funds and were not restricted by nomination spending limits.[17] If these candidates had participated in the system, they would have been collectively limited to $150 million, $400 million less than they actually expended. Second, BCRA's doubling of the individual contribution limit from $1,000 to $2,000 dramatically increased the take from the maximum donations. For example, in 2000 the top four candidates (Bush, McCain, Gore, and Bradley) had a total of 106,953 maximum donors (then $1,000 or more) while in 2004 the top four candidates (Bush, Kerry, Dean, and Edwards) had 101,560 maximum donors (then $2,000 or more)—plus another 73,258 donors of $1,000 to $1,999.[18] Finally, the entire campaign was extremely competitive, fostering intensive and innovative fundraising, as seen in the sources of funds raised by the candidates.

Sources of Candidate Funds

Table 4-2 looks at the sources of campaign funds for Bush and the Democratic candidates during the primary season and bridge periods (for Bush and Kerry, the figures are broken out by the primary season and the bridge period). As in the past, individual donations accounted for the lion's share of all the candidates' finances, and the pattern of donations reflects the strategies employed by the candidates.[19]

The Bush Campaign

As in 2000, the Bush effort was at root an insider campaign based on an extensive network of individual fundraisers and the low cost of raising large contributions. In 2004 Bush raised $112 million in contributions of $2,000 or more for 43 percent of his total contributions, and another $34 million in donations of $1,000 to $1,999 for an additional 13 percent. Thus 56 percent of his funds came from donations of $1,000 or more. This figure was a bit less than the 65 percent he received from $1,000 donations in 2000 but represented a sum that was greater than double the 2000 campaign contributions in the largest category of gifts.

Table 4-2. *Sources of Funds: Major Party Nomination Campaigns, 2003–04*
Dollars

Party	> $2,000	$1,000–$1,999	$200–$999	> $200	Federal matching funds	Candidate and previous campaign	PACs and other committees
Republican							
Bush	112,490,380	34,484,233	30,693,159	78,413,785	0	671,100	2,878,041
Primary season	95,693,175	21,531,012	11,608,779	26,846,961	0	671,100	2,647,281
Bridge period	16,797,205	12,953,221	19,084,380	51,566,824	0	0	230,760
Democrat							
Kerry	52,585,385	41,756,545	42,749,428	78,824,097	0	16,654,000	148,385
Primary season	12,520,500	18,283,540	4,935,500	5,796,211	0	2,650,000	146,135
Bridge period	40,064,885	23,473,005	37,813,928	73,030,886	0	14,004,000	2,250
Dean	3,920,255	5,788,327	11,089,770	30,562,643	0	0	15,300
Edwards	10,421,000	4,962,786	3,516,306	2,980,567	6,647,851	962,908	2,000
Clark	5,343,617	3,179,071	3,444,136	5,395,132	7,615,360	0	45,950
Gephardt	6,436,500	3,790,185	2,289,213	1,798,881	4,104,320	2,403,521	406,462
Lieberman	6,212,500	4,273,800	2,470,710	1,208,680	4,267,797	2,000	214,320
Kucinich	388,000	495,603	1,499,910	5,481,253	3,083,963	0	16,000
Graham	2,204,333	1,006,563	858,671	412,341	0	380,000	852,250
Moseley-Braun	137,484	123,137	140,090	131,615	0	14,848	39,273
Sharpton	217,000	94,200	117,739	67,738	0	77,500	4,200

Source: Data for January 1, 2003, through August 31, 2004, from Campaign Finance Institute, "CFI's Wrap-Up Analysis of Primary Funding," press release, October 4, 2004 (www.cfinst.org/ pr/100404.html). Supplemented with Federal Election Commission data

Bush's high-dollar gifts were concentrated in the primary season, accounting for almost three-quarters of his funds.

In 2000 Bush had waged a highly successful "connections" fundraising campaign, based on an extensive network of individual fundraisers and careful monitoring of their efforts, and he pursued this strategy even more vigorously in 2004.[20] For example, he expanded his network of solicitors to 221 "Rangers" (individuals who raised at least $200,000) and 327 "Pioneers" (those who raised at least $100,000).[21] Most of this network was new to 2004, with just one-half of the 2000 Pioneers repeating as Pioneers or Rangers in 2004. Representing nearly every sector of the business community, the 2004 group was dominated by chief executive officers, with a leavening of lawyers, lobbyists, politicians, and political operatives. Once again blending accountability and competition, this system of solicitors generated at least $77 million for the campaign, or about 30 percent of Bush's total donations.

Bush increased his funds from every donor category in 2004, including those contributing less than $200, whose input jumped sevenfold (from $10 million to $78 million). In 2004 small donations made up 30 percent of Bush's total funds. Much of this success resulted from a massive direct mail program. Two-thirds of Bush's funds from small donors came during the bridge period. Although small donor funds accounted for only 17 percent of Bush donations in the primary season, they made up 51 percent after the bridge period. As a consequence, Bush contributions of $200 to $999 decreased in relative terms from 17 percent of his total in 2000 to 12 percent in 2004 but expanded in dollar amount. In sum, this comprehensive fundraising effort produced a huge expansion of Bush donors.[22] Indeed, the effort was so successful that Bush continued to raise $12 million to $14 million a month after he had completed his major fundraising events in April.

The Kerry Campaign

The Kerry campaign resembled the Bush campaign in its tiered classification of fundraisers, but it developed in a more dramatic fashion, beginning as an "insider" campaign and then expanding during the bridge period. In the nomination phase of the campaign, Kerry obtained $52.5 million in contributions of $2,000 or more, accounting for 23 percent of his total donations, and $41.7 million between $1,000 and $2,000, for 18 percent. Total funds in amounts of $1,000 or more made up 41 percent, approximately the same proportion as for Gore in 2000 (but more than five times greater in total dollars because of the increased funds raised), but substantially lower than Bush's 56 percent in 2004. Like Bush, Kerry depended mostly on large contributors early in the race. During the primary season, 70 percent of Kerry's donations came from gifts of $1,000 or more.

Kerry also raised substantial funds in small contributions. His $79 million in donations of less than $200 was about the same as Bush's and represented a slightly larger share of total donations (34 percent). This proportion was almost five times larger than Al Gore's 7 percent in 2000 and about twenty times larger in dollar amount. As with Bush, Kerry's small-dollar funds expanded dramatically after he secured the nomination: during the primary season, contributions less than $200 made up 13 percent of his total donations and during the bridge period 39 percent. Some 18 percent of Kerry's receipts came from middle-sized donations of $200 to $999, about the same as for Bush.

During the primary season, Kerry's personal wealth played a small but decisive role.[23] Because he opted out of matching funds, Kerry was able to make $6.3 million in personal loans to his campaign committee, increasing his primary season donations by about 14 percent. This amount was roughly twice the size of the matching funds he would have been eligible for on January 1, 2004. (The loans were repaid in full during the bridge period.)

During the bridge period, Kerry turned to a broader fundraising effort with the aid of the Democratic Party establishment and its allies. He quickly put together a network of high-dollar individual fundraisers, including 266 "vice chairs," who raised at least $100,000, and 298 "cochairs," who raised at least $50,000. All together these "chairs" generated at least $41.5 million for the campaign, or 18 percent of Kerry's total donations.[24] This impressive effort resembled the Bush fundraising network in many respects. Like the Bush network, Kerry's fundraisers came from a variety of business sectors, but with a larger dose of lawyers, lobbyists, politicians, and political operatives. The difference in scale between the two may simply reflect Kerry's shorter time period of operation. Kerry also benefited from joint fundraising efforts with the Democratic Party (where donations are given to the party and the candidate, and then shared between the two), which transferred $14.1 million to his campaign in the summer of 2004.

Kerry also turned aggressively to small-dollar fundraising in the bridge period, largely via the Internet, imitating and surpassing the success of the Dean campaign. In all likelihood, this expansion also reflected the ideological character of the general election campaign against Bush. Kerry obtained $79 million in donations under $200, more than twice the amount raised by Dean during the primary season ($30 million). The Kerry campaign also produced a huge expansion in the number of donors compared with the Gore campaign in 2000.[25]

Dean and the Other Democrats

Table 4-2 starkly reveals how different Dean's fundraising was from that of Bush and Kerry. Dean raised just $3.9 million in contributions of $2,000 or more, or 7 percent of total receipts, and his $1,000 to $1,999 donors accounted for $5.8 million, or 11 percent. His total from large donations of $1,000 or more was 18 percent, a figure about equal to Republican John McCain's proportion in 2000. Both Dean and McCain ran "outsider" campaigns with a greater emphasis on small donors, but Dean's funds from donors giving less than $200 were larger than McCain's, both in total dollars ($31 million versus $10 million) and in percentage of donations (58 percent versus 22 percent). Unlike Dean, McCain accepted matching funds. In terms of individual donations, the proportion of Dean's small donors was still greater than for McCain (60 percent to 40 percent). Dean's small-donor total of $30 million was about five times larger than Kerry's during the primary season ($6 million) and Gore's total from 2000 ($5.6 million). Another 21 percent of Dean's receipts came from contributions of $200 to $999. The total number of Dean donors was quite impressive. For example, in 2000 McCain had at least 97,000 small donors and Dean had at least 985,000; in contrast, McCain had 25,493 donors of $200 or more and 10,040 maximum donors, while Dean had 53,881 donors of $200 or more, but only 3,209 maximum donors.[26]

Dean's fundraising effort has been described as the "first Internet campaign" as it included meet-ups, web-video, "open source organizing," e-referenda, blogs, and extensive online fundraising.[27] The campaign made extensive use of e-mail solicitation, often cleverly pegged to news events, as well as "peer-to-peer" solicitation among the campaign's online network. As much by improvisation as design, the Dean campaign was able to use the Internet to tap a large constituency that was disenchanted with contemporary politics. In one sense, the Internet campaign forged a new kind of connections campaign—similar in some ways to the volunteer effort organized online by the Bush campaign.[28]

More important, Internet fundraising sharply lowered the cost of raising small donations.

The remaining Democratic candidates fell into two categories common in past elections. First, prominent candidates—Senators John Edwards and Joseph Lieberman, and Representative Richard Gephardt—used insider connections and matching funds to pursue the nomination. All of these candidates relied heavily on large donations, with contributions of $2,000 or more accounting for about one-half of their total receipts and contributions of $1,000 and up accounting for 70 percent or more of the individual donations. These figures are a bit higher than those for Gore's and Bradley's individual donations in 2000, whose contributions of $1,000 or more made up roughly three-fifths of total receipts. In addition, public funds made up about one-fifth of these three candidates' total receipts, a bit less than for Gore and Bradley in 2000, and donations under $200 accounted for less than one-tenth. Thus these candidates' insider strategies resembled those of the early Kerry and Bush campaigns.

The second set of candidates consisted of outsiders, three of whom represented various special constituencies: Representative Dennis Kucinich, whose quixotic campaign was largely paid for by small donations from "progressive" Democrats; former U.S. senator Carol Moseley-Braun (who sought to represent women and African Americans); and Reverend Al Sharpton (who claimed to speak for African Americans). These candidates were less successful versions of past outsiders in both parties, such as Jesse Jackson (Democrat, 1984 and 1988), Pat Buchanan (Republican, 1992), Jerry Brown (Democrat, 1992), and Alan Keyes (Republican, 2000). Like Dean, Democratic senator Bob Graham wanted to mount an insurgency, but his campaign fizzled early, much as Republican Elizabeth Dole did in 2000.

The final Democratic outsider candidate was retired General Wesley Clark, who entered the race late in the fall of 2003 but still raised $25 million. Clark had considerable balance in his funding sources; he drew more than one-quarter from donations in excess of $1,000, about one-fifth from gifts under $200, and one-quarter from matching funds. The Clark campaign is a good example of how the matching funds system can create competition in the primaries: the matching funds allowed him to enter the campaign late when doubts were being raised about other candidates, to raise funds from donors who might otherwise have been skeptical of his candidacy, and to conduct a viable campaign after

the New Hampshire primary. In this sense, Clark resembled Republican
John McCain in 2000.

Outside Money

The 2004 campaign also involved considerable outside money, funds
spent by interest group organizations and individuals for or against particular candidates. Table 4-3 reports three measures of such spending:
independent spending and communications costs for candidates (both
hard dollar funds) and "electioneering communications" reported by
527 committees in 2004 (outside the hard dollar system). The electioneering communication reports do not indicate whether the spending was
for or against a candidate, so the estimate in table 4-3 is based on the
committees' public goals.[29] As with Bush and Kerry's campaign funds,
much of this money was directed at the general election, so the table
separates the primary season, bridge period, and convention phase.
Although these figures surely understate the level of outside money, they
are nonetheless instructive.[30]

Interest groups and individuals reported a total of $23.7 million in
independent expenditures in the 2004 cycle, consisting of $21 million
"for" candidates and $2.7 million "against" them. The total was eight-
een times greater than the $1.2 million reported in 2000.[31] During the
primary season, Dean was the biggest beneficiary of positive independent
expenditures at $5.5 million, with Kerry the next closest candidate at
$200,000. Labor unions were the largest source of these funds, especially
the American Federation of State, County and Municipal Employees and
the Service Employees International Union, which both worked hard for
Dean, and the International Association of Firefighters, which supported
Kerry. Independent expenditures against a candidate were rare in the primary season, those against Bush topping the list at about $100,000.[32]

The bridge period showed a different pattern. Kerry was the beneficiary of some $10 million in positive independent expenditures, plus
another $4.7 million during the convention phase. In contrast, Bush
benefited from just $400,000 in positive expenditures during the bridge
period. Negative expenditures showed a reverse pattern: $800,000
against Kerry and $1.9 million against Bush. Kerry also benefited from
$18.9 million in favorable independent expenditures by the DNC and
$8.3 million in DNC spending against Bush during the convention phase
(not shown in the table).

Table 4-3. *Outside Money in the 2004 Nomination Contest*

Dollars

	Independent expenditures		Communication costs		Electioneering communication	
Candidate	For	Against	For	Against	Republican groups	Democratic groups
Bush	446,927	1,926,051	43,408	132,962	0	4,405,415[b]
Primary season	81,834	108,845	4,353	116,338		
Bridge period	396,910	1,292,403	4,387	15,976	1,050,391[a]	10,142,319[b]
Convention pause	18,183	524,803	34,668	648	2,853,030[a]	11,285,386[b]
Kerry	14,889,810	832,832	4,730,989	0	0	
Primary season	196,529	0	368,973	0	0	
Bridge period	10,017,677	784,504	2,646,220	0		
Convention pause	4,675,604	48,328	882,964	0	702,312[b]	
Dean	5,506,416	4,094	1,746,640	0		
Edwards	118,149	0	101,027	0		
Clark	15,531	0	0	0		
Gephardt	2,046	0	426	0		
Total	21,028,879	2,762,977	6,622,490	132,962	4,605,733	25,833,120

Source: Compiled from Federal Election Commission data.
a. Pro-Bush expenditures.
b. Anti-Bush or anti-Kerry spending.

In 2004 interest groups reported $6.7 million in internal communication costs to their members, $6.6 million for and $100,000 against candidates. Although the legal reporting requirements do not cover all of these expenditures, the reported amounts were almost twice as large as in 2000 ($3.3 million). Dean was also the chief beneficiary of such expenditures in the primary season at $1.7 million, followed by Kerry at about $400,000. In the bridge period and the convention phase, Kerry benefited from $3.5 million in favorable internal communication, with labor unions and liberal membership groups as the principal sources. The small volume of negative communication during the primary season, a little over $100,000, was directed at Bush.

The new reporting requirements for electioneering communications revealed that 527 committees chiefly concerned with the presidential race spent about $30 million in this area. Because this reporting category did not exist in 2000, there is no firm basis for a comparison over time. In all likelihood, the 2004 spending was substantially larger than in 2000.[33] More than three-quarters of this electioneering communication spending ($25 million) came from Democratic 527s, and four-fifths of it occurred during the bridge period, about evenly divided before ($10 million) and during the convention phase ($11 million). It is clear that these broadcast expenditures were overwhelmingly against Bush. The largest spender was the Media Fund, a key part of the shadow Democratic Party, reporting $17.8 million beginning in March 2004. The second largest was MoveOn.org, a liberal 527 committee, which began spending its $7.6 million in January 2004.

The Republican 527 committees were slow to develop, in part because the RNC pressured the FEC to adopt rules restricting 527s. Once this gambit failed, two prominent committees came into being. The largest was Progress for America, which spent $1 million during the bridge period and $2.9 million in the convention phase, largely in favor of Bush. The best-known Republican 527 was the Swift Boat Veterans for Truth, which spent some $700,000 during the convention phase against Kerry.

These figures do not cover all of the expenditures of the 527 committees. For instance, 527 committees operating outside of the reporting window, thirty days before a primary and sixty days before a general election, did not have to file electioneering communication reports with the FEC, although they did eventually file reports with the IRS. High-profile groups that did not file the electioneering report aired ads against Dean in December 2003: the Club for Growth, an anti-tax group, spent

$100,000 in this endeavor, and Americans for Jobs, Healthcare, and Progressive Values, a group founded by Democratic operatives and union leaders, spent $486,064. A study of the Iowa caucuses found that some unions also ran television ads before the thirty-day reporting window.[34] Not all of the 527 committee expenditures were reported under the electioneering communication rules, and some of these nonreported expenditures may have influenced the presidential race.[35] Other tax-exempt groups were also active in the 2004 nomination campaign; there are no good estimates on the magnitude of these expenditures in the nomination period, but they might well have been substantial (see chapter 8).

Taken together, the $60.8 million raised in outside money in the 2004 presidential election nomination phase is almost thee times greater than the high estimate for all outside money in 2000 ($22.5 million).[36] In contrast, Howard Dean raised $51 million in the entire cycle. The 2004 nomination phase may well have set a record for outside spending.

The Dynamics of the Campaign

What role does money play in the dynamics of the nomination campaign? Figures 4-1 and 4-2 provide an overview of the finances for the primary season and the bridge period, showing the total funds raised and cash on hand for Bush, Kerry, and Dean (the patterns for Edwards and Clark closely track Kerry's, but at a lower level). Political observers commonly use these patterns to handicap the presidential horse race.[37]

A Slow Start

In hindsight, the seeds of the nomination campaign were germinating in January 2003. Conventional wisdom assumed a battle of the insiders. The ultimate insider, President Bush, planned to once again forgo matching funds and raise an unprecedented war chest, allowing for a major assault on the Democratic nominee during the bridge period. The Democrats were well aware of this prospect and developed responses: party leaders sought to manipulate the calendar and raise special funds; interest groups allied and organized a financial rescue package via the shadow Democratic Party; and the candidates debated forgoing public funds. However, the candidates faced an additional problem: winning the nomination against a competitive field. The final decisions on matching funds were postponed until the last moment, late in 2003.[38]

On the basis of previous races, it was assumed that the insiders would compete financially in the invisible primary, each drawing on a special

Figure 4-1. *Presidential Primary Cumulative Receipts, 2003–04*

Millions of dollars

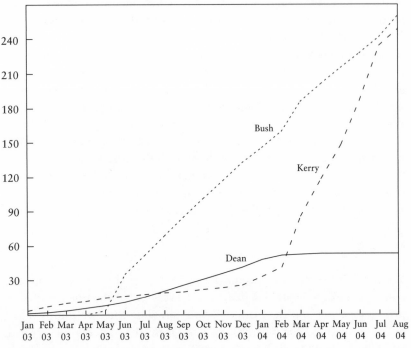

Jan Feb Mar Apr May Jun Jul Aug Sep Oct Nov Dec Jan Feb Mar Apr May Jun Jul Aug
03 03 03 03 03 03 03 03 03 03 03 03 04 04 04 04 04 04 04 04

Source: Compiled by author; based on Federal Election Commission data.

financial constituency, and the candidate that raised the most funds would then prevail in the compressed primary schedule. The top four prospects were Senator John Kerry of Massachusetts (a prominent and wealthy liberal); Senator Joseph Lieberman of Connecticut (the heir to the "New Democrat" coalition and the 2000 vice presidential nominee); Representative Richard Gephardt of Missouri (former House minority leader and close to organized labor); and Senator John Edwards of North Carolina (a Southern moderate with strong ties to trial lawyers). Two other candidates were seen as potential spoilers if the top prospects faltered: Senator Bob Graham of Florida and Governor Howard Dean of Vermont. The second-tier outsiders were expected to intensify the debate and perhaps influence the fortunes of the better-known candidates.

However, the financial race got off to a slow start, as can be seen in fig-ure 4-1. Because of the war in Iraq, Bush did not deploy his fundraising plan until the second quarter of 2003. The initial funds raised by the anointed front-runner, Kerry, failed to meet expectations. The Iraq war was a key and divisive factor among Democrats, with the insiders either strongly (Lieberman and Gephardt) or grudgingly (Kerry and Edwards) supporting the president. In this vacuum, Dean emerged as the spokesperson for an intense and growing opposition to the war. Claiming to represent the "Democratic wing of the Democratic Party," he was able to direct much of this discontent against his insider rivals. In this sense, Dean was following the well-worn path of past outsider campaigns in both parties.

A Midyear Buildup

Once the Bush connections campaign got under way, the president's war chest grew dramatically. By June he had raised $35 million and by September $85 million. Indeed, as figure 4-1 shows, the Bush fundraising maintained a steady upward growth until August 2004. Bush then began to build huge cash reserves, despite spending heavily on campaign infrastructure (figure 4-2). This part of the conventional wisdom was unfolding according to plan.

The Democratic insiders also made midyear gains as their own connections campaigns paid off. By June Kerry had raised $16 million and by September $20 million. Edwards, Gephardt, and Lieberman followed a similar trajectory. These receipts were only a little off the pace of previous insider campaigns, revealing the expected financial competition among the best-connected candidates. However, the insiders failed to build large cash balances. By September, Kerry had just $8 million in cash on hand and Edwards $5 million, with Gephardt and Lieberman even farther behind. These figures both reflected and generated dismay among some Democratic fundraisers and donors.

The plight of the insiders was exacerbated by Dean's meteoric rise in funds, based on his clear issue appeals and innovative use of the Internet. The low cost of the Internet fundraising made it possible for Dean to translate the fervor of antiwar and progressive activists into cold cash. By June Dean had raised $10 million, more than tripling his March receipts, and by September he led the field with $25 million and the most cash on hand ($10 million). A simple projection of this trajectory suggested that Dean would win the invisible primary and be well positioned to win the actual primaries in 2004. Dean's unexpected financial success seemed to validate both his insurgency and the novelty

Figure 4-2. *Presidential Primary Cash on Hand, 2003–04*

Millions of dollars

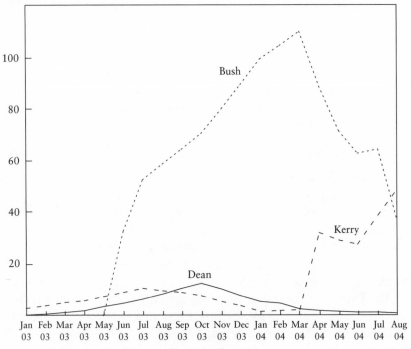

Source: Compiled by author; based on Federal Election Commission data.

of his online campaign. It appeared that he had acquired other resources as well: a new volunteer network, endorsements by key union and liberal groups, credibility with the press, and standing in the polls. By early fall, Dean was the clear front-runner.

The Race Clarifies

The Bush connections campaign kept pace in the final quarter of 2003, leaving the president with almost $90 million in cash on hand and every prospect of raising more. This figure was a powerful beacon as the Democratic field began to clarify. "People-Powered Howard" continued his torrid fundraising pace, bringing in some $30 million by October with $12 million in cash on hand. Dean's surge was accompanied by declining fundraising success among his insider rivals. By October Kerry had raised a total of $21 million, just $1 million more than in September, and worse yet, his cash reserves were falling. Given these circumstances, the Dean camp began to think beyond the primary season to the bridge period. On November 8, Dean decided to forgo public matching funds, freeing himself from primary spending limits. Although he made this decision in an unusual fashion—by means of an "e-referendum" among his supporters—he was simply following a path and timing anticipated by analysts.[39]

Dean's financial success produced several reactions. The first was Wesley Clark's entry into the race on September 17, 2003. Backed by former Clinton supporters, his was in large part a "stop Dean" campaign. Clark's initial fundraising was impressive and included an effective Internet component. He seriously considered following Dean out of the matching system but then concluded that public money would be necessary to compete in the initial primaries just weeks away. Another response was John Kerry's decision to forgo public funds, made five days after Dean's announcement. This decision allowed Kerry to make $2.8 million in personal loans to his campaign at a crucial juncture. Yet another response was a series of December television ads in Iowa and New Hampshire attacking Dean. The attacks came from a liberal group, Americans for Jobs, Healthcare, and Progressive Values, and a conservative group, the Club for Growth, who together spent $700,000 airing these ads. Finally, Dean's new front-runner status provoked sharp criticism from other Democratic candidates and invited new scrutiny by the news media.

Whatever the ultimate effect of these responses on Dean's candidacy, they did not slow his fundraising. By the end of 2003, he had raised $41 million compared with Kerry's $25 million, Edwards's $16 million, and Clark's approximately $14 million. During this period, Dean began to spend his war chest so that his cash on hand was down to $7.9 million—still considerably ahead of that of his rivals (Kerry, $3.9 million; Edwards, $1.7 million; and Clark $3.4 million). Thus at the end of 2004, Dean was the clear victor in the invisible primary and according to conventional wisdom was poised to win the actual primary contests and secure the Democratic nomination.

Six Weeks of Primaries

As 2004 began, the Democratic candidates' electoral goals had become clear: Dean was aiming for a quick victory in Iowa and New Hampshire; Gephardt, Kerry, and Edwards hoped to halt Dean's momentum in the Hawkeye State; Clark and Lieberman bypassed Iowa and hoped to stop Dean in the Granite State. Dean raised approximately $3.5 million in early January, and his rivals also improved their finances: Kerry loaned his campaign an additional $3.5 million while the payout of matching funds reinvigorated Gephardt ($3.1 million), Edwards ($3.3 million), Clark ($3.7 million), and Lieberman ($3.8 million).

The Iowa caucuses were a hard-fought affair, involving extensive spending by the candidates and interest groups. One estimate put candidates' broadcast costs at $11.5 million, which was added to by the campaigns' grassroots activities and extensive efforts by labor unions and liberal groups. Dean and Gephardt engaged in a bitter battle at the top of the polls as the caucuses approached. However, infighting and an effective campaign with shrewd appeals to veterans helped Kerry surge to a first-place finish on caucus night. Edwards came in second, immediately gaining stature. Gephardt's fourth place forced him to withdraw from the race, and Dean's disappointing third-place finish was compounded by his much-ridiculed "scream" at a post-caucus rally. The battle then shifted quickly to the New Hampshire primary, where an estimated $14 million was spent on broadcast advertising by the candidates. Here Kerry scored another victory, with Dean coming in a distant second.[40]

The Iowa and New Hampshire results established Kerry as the clear front-runner and deflated the Dean insurgency. In hindsight, it is clear that the conventional wisdom had been wrong, and that Dean's fundraising victory in the invisible primary would not translate into primary wins. It may be that the very success of Dean's Internet campaign produced a weak campaign organization—or perhaps Dean simply made major mistakes in the early contests.[41]

However, all the candidates now faced financial constraints, particularly Kerry, who had just $1.7 million in cash on hand at the end of January, behind Dean ($5.6 million), Clark ($3.4 million), and Edwards ($2.8 million). Even so, the compressed primary schedule favored Kerry's momentum, and the party leadership closed ranks behind him as the most electable of the candidates. On February 3, Kerry won five contests and did well in the two he lost (South Carolina to Edwards and Oklahoma to Clark), driving Lieberman from the race. Kerry then won the next eleven contests, leading Clark to concede. These electoral successes brought fresh funds into Kerry's coffers: by the end of February, he had raised an additional $8 million and had $2.2 million in cash on hand. During the same period, Edwards raised $7 million but spent nearly all of it. Dean's campaign continued to dwindle in February, raising only $4 million and dropping to $2.7 million in cash on hand. The final confrontation came on March 2, when Kerry won nine contests, losing only Dean's Vermont. Both Dean and Edwards then ended their campaigns.

All told, Kerry raised almost $41 million to secure the nomination, about four-fifths of the primary spending limit. If he had operated within the public financing system, he would have been limited to approximately $9 million during the bridge period. Dean had also exceeded the spending limit, and while Edwards and Clark were still below the limit, additional success might well have put them in the same fix. Thus the primary spending limits would have been devastating to the Democratic nominee in the bridge period.[42]

Bridge Period Finances

Once Kerry secured the nomination, he and the Democratic Party set about raising additional funds. A combination of money from high-dollar solicitors, well-publicized events, and Internet fundraising quickly filled his campaign coffers. In March, Kerry raised some $44 million in gross receipts and then averaged better than $35 million a month over the next four months. His cash balances began to rise as well: he had $32 million by the end of April and never dipped below $30 million through August. Kerry went from broke to flush in a few weeks.

During the primary season, Bush continued to raise funds at a steady rate, with a slight acceleration in March when Kerry clinched the Democratic nomination. His cash balance topped out at $110 million, and then he began to spend the funds as planned. A major mission was to "define" Kerry in a negative light, and to that end, Bush dedicated an initial $40 million to negative ads (about the same amount as Kerry's total spending in the primary season). Also according to plan, the 527 committees stepped up their attacks against Bush to help keep Kerry "in the race." Soon Kerry was able to finance his own response to Bush. He spent $14 million on operating expenses in March (about what he had spent in January and February combined) and then averaged $29 million for the next four months, building his cash reserves. Bush spent an average of $27 million a month in operating expenses during the same period.

The Convention Phase

Kerry was able to avoid the anticipated problems in the bridge period by forgoing public funds and receiving the assistance of allies. But by August he faced a similar problem in miniature: the Democratic national convention was scheduled a month earlier than the Republican counterpart, and once he accepted public funds for the general election, he would be unable to spend any of his preconvention funds. Given his successful fundraising, a number of advisers urged Kerry to reject the general election public funds as well.[43] In the end, Kerry accepted the public money, partly for symbolic reasons and partly because it would have been onerous to replace the $75 million in public funds during the critical final three months of the general election.

After the Democratic convention, Kerry scaled back his campaign spending and relied on others to campaign on his behalf. The DNC stepped in with some $27 million in independent expenditures, while PACs and 527 committees spent another $17 million in outside money. Meanwhile, the Bush campaign continued its efforts, spending $14 million. However, the most important expenditure during this period was one of the smallest: the $700,000 that the Swift Boat Veterans for Truth used to attack Kerry's war record. Largely a tiny "vanity buy" directed at getting the attention of the news media, this expenditure appears to have been quite effective (see chapters 5 and 8 on this point).[44]

In formal terms, the national conventions mark the end of nomination contests, but in practical terms, they are the opening events in the general election campaign. The rise of presidential primaries long ago transformed the conventions from deliberative bodies that choose presidential nominees to public relations events that showcase the party standard bearers. The major parties are well aware of the political value of such a showcase and spend lavishly on it. In 2004 the Democrats spent $64.4 million at the Boston convention and the Republicans $105.9 million in New York. Taken together, these amounts alone exceeded the general election public grants of $75 million.[45]

Both parties received a public grant of $14.9 million to help pay for each convention and obtained additional funds from local and state governments, tallying $10 million for the Democrats and $27 million for the Republicans. However, the biggest source of funding was private donations: Democrats raised nearly $40 million and the GOP $64 million. Much of this money was raised outside of the hard dollar limits.

This pattern represents a major change: the total cost for both conventions combined doubled between 2004 ($170 million) and 1992 ($77 million in 2004 constant dollars). More telling was the growth in the proportion of these funds that came from private donations, which reached nearly 61 percent in 2004 versus 14 percent in 1992. As with the nomination campaigns themselves, big money had returned to the national conventions.[46]

At the end of the nomination campaigns, both Bush and Kerry disposed of much of their remaining funds by transferring them to other committees. Bush shifted $11.2 million to national Republican committees and Kerry gave $40.4 million to party committees, including $29.5 million to national Democratic committees and $10.9 million to Democratic committees in twenty-one states. To put these figures in context, the national parties were allowed $16.2 million in coordinated expenditures in the 2004 general election. Thus Kerry more than "paid for" the costs of party-coordinated expenditures on his behalf. And the remaining funds could have been used to help his campaign via independent expenditures or GOTV efforts. The postelection reports showed Bush with $2.1 million dollars on hand, while Kerry retained $14.2 million. This Kerry figure caused consternation among some Democrats after the election.

A System in Crisis

The 2004 presidential nomination campaign finances set records beyond all expectations, both for the amounts raised and spent by the candidates under the present system. The finances of the major party candidates rivaled those in 1972, the last election before the enactment of the public financing system. The new provisions of BCRA, especially the doubling of individual contribution limits, were a major factor behind the increases in money raised. The campaign also may have set a record for outside spending. The closeness of the campaign and the intense and innovative fundraising it encouraged were also important factors. Innovations included the expansion of high-dollar fundraising networks, the growth of 527 committees, and the first full-scale Internet campaign.

However, the most important factor was the continued decay of the public financing system. In 2004 the three best-funded candidates opted out of matching funds and prospered politically, continuing a trend begun in 1996. This trend will likely continue into the future, with well-connected or popular candidates forgoing matching funds and reducing the public system to preserving impoverished and niche candidacies. In addition, the large sums of money Bush and Kerry raised in the bridge period threatened to undermine other parts of the public financing system, namely, the national convention subsidy and general election grant. In the not-too-distant future, major candidates may opt out of the general election funds as well.

What caused this decay of the public financing system? The simple answer is that the parameters of the system no longer fit the realities of the presidential nomination system.[47] The presidential primary system was just coming into being when the public financing system was enacted, and while the primaries have continued to evolve, the public financing system has not. Changes that have occurred, such as the adjusting of spending limits for inflation and the enactment of BCRA, have largely exacerbated the system's short-term problems. Both the resources available and the spending limits imposed make the system increasingly unattractive to the strongest candidates.

If present conditions continue, one might legitimately ask whether the public financing system serves a useful purpose in presidential politics. Answering this question is beyond the scope of this essay, but it is worth noting that the public financing system has been quite useful for most of its twenty-eight-year history.[48] As table 4-4 shows, it has provided a total of $1.3 billion to ninety-one candidates, divided almost equally between Democrats and Republicans (the Democrats had more candidates, but the Republicans had more successful ones). Up to 1992, it helped produce competitive primaries and general elections, enhanced the choices available to voters, and constrained the influence of the wealthy and well organized. After 1992, it fostered these things to a lesser extent, as can be seen by the declining payout for matching funds after 1996. While the absence of the best-financed candidates from the primaries has kept the system solvent, it has created a crisis. Will the public financing system become increasingly irrelevant, or will it be revived by timely reforms to encourage competition, choice, and constraint in presidential politics?

Table 4-4. *Public Subsidies in Presidential Elections, 1976–2004*[a]

Millions of dollars (unless noted otherwise)

Year	Period	Democrat	Republican	Other	Total
1976	Primary	14.7 (13)	9.0 (2)	0.0	23.7 (5)
	Conventions	2.0	1.6	0.0	3.6
	General	21.8	21.8	0.0	43.6
	Total	38.5	32.4	0.0	70.9
1980	Primary	10.5 (4)	19.1 (6)	...	29.6 (10)
	Conventions	3.7	4.4	...	8.1
	General	29.4	29.2	4.2 (1) [NU]	62.8
	Total	43.6	52.7	4.2	100.5
1984	Primary	25.7 (9)	9.7 (1)	0.2 (1) [C]	35.6 (11)
	Conventions	8.1	7.8	...	15.9
	General	40.2	40.1	...	80.3
	Total	74.0	57.6	0.2	131.8
1988	Primary	30.4 (8)	35.0 (6)	0.9 (1) [NA]	66.3 (15)
	Conventions	9.2	9.2	...	18.4
	General	45.8	46.0	...	91.8
	Total	85.4	90.2	0.9	176.5
1992	Primary	23.3 (8)	15.5 (2)	2.0 (1) [NA], 0.4 (1) [NL]	41.2 (12)
	Conventions	11.0	11.0	...	22.1
	General	55.1	55.0	...	110.1
	Total	89.4	81.5	2.4	173.3
1996	Primary	13.9 (2)	42.4 (8)	0.5 (1) [NL]	56.7 (11)
	Conventions	12.2	12.4	...	24.5
	General	61.8	61.8	29.1 [Ref]	152.7
	Total	87.9	116.6	29.6	234.0
2000	Primary	29.3 (3)	26.5 (4)	4.4 (1) [Ref], 0.7 (1) [G], 0.7 (1) [NL]	61.6 (10)
	Conventions	13.5	13.5	2.5 [Ref]	29.5
	General	67.6	67.6	12.6 [Ref]	147.8
	Total	110.4	107.5	20.8	238.8
2004	Primary	27.2 (6)	0.0	0.8 (1) [Ref, I]	28.0 (7)
	Conventions	14.9	14.9	0.0	29.8
	General	74.6	74.6	0.0	149.2
	Total	116.7	89.7	0.8	207.0
Total		645.9 (54)	623.1 (29)	58.9 (10)	1,332.8 (91)

Source: Congressional Research Service, "The Presidential Election Campaign Fund and Tax Checkoff: Background and Current Issues," March 2000. Data for 2000 and 2004 are from the Federal Election Commission.

a. Numbers in parentheses are the numbers of candidates receiving public matching funds. Totals may not add up because of rounding. D = Democrats, R = Republicans, NU = National Unity, C = Citizens, NA = National Alliance, NL = Natural Law, Ref = Reform Party, G = Green Party, I = Independent.

Notes

1. For a detailed look at federal campaign finance law, see Anthony Corrado and others, *The New Campaign Finance Reform: A Sourcebook* (Brookings, 2004).

2. See John C. Green and Anthony Corrado, "The Impact of BCRA on Presidential Campaign Finance," in *Life after Reform: When the Bipartisan Campaign Reform Act Meets Politics,* edited by Michael Malbin (Lanham, Md.: Rowman and Littlefield, 2003), pp. 175–99.

3. On the impact of BCRA, see Malbin, *Life after Reform*; and Michael J. Malbin. ed., *The Election after Reform: Money, Politics and the Bipartisan Campaign Reform Act* (Lanham, Md.: Rowman and Littlefield, 2006, forthcoming).

4. Ironically, the overall primary limit is substantially less than the sum of the state limits.

5. John C. Green and Nathan S. Bigelow, "Financing the 2000 Presidential Nomination Campaigns: The Costs of Innovation," in *Financing the 2000 Election,* edited by David B. Magleby (Brookings, 2002), pp. 49–78.

6. William G. Mayer and Andrew E. Busch, *The Frontloading Problem in Presidential Nominations* (Brookings, 2003).

7. James W. Ceaser and Andrew E. Busch, *Red over Blue: The 2004 Elections and American Politics* (Lanham, Md.: Rowman and Littlefield, 2005), pp. 75–80.

8. See John H. Aldrich, *Before the Convention: Strategies and Choices in Presidential Nominating Campaigns* (University of Chicago Press, 1980).

9. See Michael J. Malbin, "A Public Financing System in Jeopardy," in *The Election after Reform,* edited by Malbin.

10. See Green and Corrado, "The Impact of BCRA on Presidential Campaign Finance," pp. 189–95.

11. Jim Drinkard, "'Outside' Political Groups Full of Party Insiders," *USA Today,* June 28, 2004, p 7A. See also Steve Weissman and Ruth Hassan, "527 Groups and BCRA," in *The Election after Reform,* edited by Malbin; and Byron York, *The Vast Left Wing Conspiracy* (New York: Crown Forum, 2005).

12. FEC reports on receipts and disbursements were adjusted by subtracting repaid loans, offsets to expenditures, and contribution refunds. For other reports accounting for these same data, see Campaign Finance Institute, "CFI's Wrap-Up Analysis of Primary Funding," press release, October 4, 2004 (www.cfinst.org/pr/100404.html); and Marian Currinder, "Campaign Finance: Funding the Presidential and Congressional Campaigns," in *The Elections of 2004,* edited by Michael Nelson (Congressional Quarterly Press, 2005), pp. 108–32.

13. Green and Bigelow, "Financing the 2000 Presidential Nomination Campaigns." The figures in the text were adjusted to cover comparable time periods in 2000 and 2004.

14. Data on the 1972 campaign come from Hebert E. Alexander, *Financing the 1972 Election* (Lexington, Mass.: D. C. Heath, 1976), pp. 83–88. The FECA was in place in 1972, producing fairly good information on presidential finance. Of course, the extensive spending in 1972 contributed to the creation of the public financing system in 1974.

15. The 2004 figures were 1.5 times greater than in the 1988 election. The 1992 and 1988 data were compiled from FEC records.

16. See John C. Green and William Binning, "The Rise and Decline of the Reform Party, 1992–2000," in *Multiparty Politics in America*, 2nd ed., edited by Paul S. Herrnson and John C. Green (Rowman and Littlefield, 2002), pp. 99–124.

17. For additional discussion on the effects of turning down matching funds, see Christine L. Day, Charles D. Hadley, and Harold W. Stanley, "The Inevitable Unanticipated Consequences of Political Reform," in *A Defining Moment: The Presidential Election of 2004,* edited by William Crotty (Armonk, N.Y.: M. E. Sharpe, 2005), p. 80.

18. These donor figures come from the Campaign Finance Institute and were graciously provided by Michael Malbin.

19. Table 4-2 and the following discussion draw heavily on the Campaign Finance Institute, "CFI's Wrap-Up Analysis of Primary Funding," 2004. Because they are based on unadjusted contribution data, the totals do not exactly match the adjusted receipts and disbursements in table 4-1.

20. See Green and Bigelow, "Financing the 2000 Presidential Nominations Campaigns," pp. 58–61.

21. Bush also had ninety-five "Mavericks" who raised $50,000, several of whom were also Rangers or Pioneers. See Texans for Public Justice, "The Bush Pioneer-Ranger Network" (www.tpj.org [March 1, 2005]). Bush eventually designated new "Super Rangers," who helped raise at least $300,000. See Anthony Corrado, "Party Finance in the Wake of BCRA: An Overview," in *The Election after Reform,* edited by Malbin.

22. In 2000, Bush had some 94,246 donors of over $200, and in 2004 the number jumped to 189,956. Estimates from the Bush website found some 97,000 donors of less than $200 in 2000 and 1.3 million in 2004. The one partial exception to the pattern of growth was the largest donor category: in both 2000 ($1,000 plus) and 2004 ($2,000 plus), Bush had some 61,000 donors. These estimates come from the author and the Campaign Finance Institute.

23. Ceaser and Busch, *Red over Blue,* pp. 82–85; and Day and others, "The Inevitable Unanticipated Consequences of Political Reform," p. 78.

24. Public Citizen, "Kerry Campaign Bankrolled by 564 Big-Money Bundlers," press release, July 16, 2004 (www.whitehouseforsale.org/documents).

25. In 2000 Gore had some 34,609 donors of $200 or more and 19,289 maximum donors. In 2004 Kerry had 184,464 donors of $200 or more and 31,059

maximum donors. In 2000 Gore had 114,000 small donors. There are no good estimates for Kerry's small donors, but he may well have had as many as Bush. These estimates come from the author and the Campaign Finance Institute.

26. These estimates come from the author and the Campaign Finance Institute.

27. See Joe Trippi, *The Revolution Will Not Be Televised* (New York: Harper Collins, 2004); also Michael Cornfield, "The Internet and Campaign 2004: A Look Back at the Campaigners," Pew Internet and American Public Life Project (www.pew internet/pdfs/Cornfield commentary.pdf [May 2, 2005]). On Internet donors, see Institute for Politics, Democracy and the Internet in collaboration with the Campaign Finance Institute, "Small Donors and Online Giving: A Study of Givers to the 2004 Presidential Campaign" (George Washington University, 2006) (www.campaignfinanceinstitute.org/studies/IPDI_SmallDonors. pdf [March 4, 2006]).

28. Bush made extensive use of the Internet to organize his "team leader" program among grassroots volunteers. It was something of a cross between the Ranger-Pioneer network and the Dean online community. See Cornfield, "The Internet and Campaign 2004."

29. Groups included in the table made public statements that appeared to clearly favor one presidential candidate over another.

30. These data come from FEC records and were graciously made available by Robert Biersack of the FEC.

31. Here the terms "for" and "against" are from the groups' disclosure documents and were not independently verified. Thus these designations should be viewed with some caution.

32. In 2000 independent expenditures were heavily against candidates and rarely in favor; Green and Bigelow, "Financing the 2000 Presidential Nomination Campaigns," pp. 56–57

33. A careful analysis of the 2000 nomination contest by the author produced a high estimate of $5 million for this kind of activity. If this is correct, then the 2004 figures represent a sixfold increase.

34. See Arthur Sanders, "The 2004 Iowa U.S. Democratic Presidential Caucus," in *Dancing without Partners: How Candidates, Parties, and Interest Groups Interact in the New Campaign Finance Environment*, edited by David B. Magleby, J. Quin Monson, and Kelly D. Patterson (Brigham Young University, Center for the Study of Elections and Democracy, 2005), pp. 81–95.

35. For example, the Media Fund spent $38 million overall during the nomination contest, MoveOn.org $15 million, Progress for America $8 million, and the Swift Boat Veterans $7 million. For an overview of the 527 committee spending, see Weissman and Hassan, "527 Groups and BCRA."

36. This estimate of broadcast advertising comes from Kenneth Goldstein and is found in Campaign Finance Institute, "Money and Politics in the 2004

Primaries," transcript of National Press Club event, February 27, 2004 (www.CFInst.org/transcript/022894.mtml [July 1, 2005]).

37. The following narrative draws heavily on the best single account of the 2004 nomination contest: Ceaser and Busch, *Red over Blue*, pp. 69–105.

38. On the timing of these decisions, see Malbin, "A Public Financing System in Jeopardy."

39. Green and Corrado, "The Impact of BCRA on Presidential Campaign Finance," pp. 189–95.

40. Estimate from Kenneth Goldstein, found in Campaign Finance Institute, "Money and Politics in the 2004 Primaries."

41. See Caesar and Busch, *Red over Blue*, pp. 93–94.

42. However, party and interest group expenditures were far less restricted than originally anticipated. One reason is that BCRA was interpreted to allow party independent expenditures. Another reason was that the parties were able to raise more hard dollars than expected.

43. Jim Rutenberg and Glen Justice, "Some Democrats Urge Kerry to Forgo Public Campaign Financing," *New York Times*, July 9, 2004, p. 14A.

44. See Magleby and others, *Dancing without Partners*, p. 35.

45. On convention financing, see Campaign Finance Institute, "The $100 Million Exemption" (www.cfinst.org/eguide/partyconventions/financing/cfistudy.html [July 1, 2005]).

46. As with the overall finances, the 2004 convention spending can be usefully compared with 1972. See Alexander, *Financing the 1972 Election*, pp. 90–95.

47. See Green and Corrado, "The Impact of BCRA on Presidential Campaign Finance." Also Campaign Finance Institute, Task Force on Presidential Nomination Financing, *Participation, Competition, Engagement: How to Revive and Improve Public Funding for Presidential Nomination Politics* (2003).

48. For a review of reform proposals as well as its own innovative ideas, see Campaign Finance Institute, Task Force on Financing Presidential Nominations, "So the Voters May Choose . . . Reviving the Presidential Matching Fund System" (2005).

FIVE

Financing the 2004 Presidential General Election

ANTHONY CORRADO

The financing of the 2004 presidential general election effectively began when John Kerry emerged as the Democratic
Party's presumptive nominee in early March. From that point on, Kerry
and President George Bush, who was unchallenged for the Republican
nomination, were for all intents and purposes competing in a general
election contest. As a result, almost all of Kerry's spending after March
was intended to influence voting in the general election. By the time of
the nomination vote at the Democratic national convention in late July,
which under federal campaign finance law signaled the start of the formal general election period for Kerry, he had already spent more than
$140 million.[1] During the same period, Bush spent almost $160 million
and then went on to spend another $14 million in August before the
Republican convention. The combined total of this "bridge period"
spending, $314 million, was more than Bush and Al Gore had spent in
the entire 2000 primary and general elections.[2] And the formal general
election period had yet to begin.

As these figures suggest, the presidential general election campaign
was a highly competitive and well-financed contest. With most polls
indicating a tight race and with memories of the extraordinarily close
2000 election still in mind, each side sought to maximize its resources
in an effort to cede no financial advantage to the opposition. In the
period from the conventions to Election Day, the candidates and their
national committees spent more than $400 million. In addition, interest
groups and other political committees spent hundreds of millions of

dollars to influence the outcome of the race. The 2004 race was thus by far the most expensive presidential contest since the adoption of the 1974 Federal Election Campaign Act (FECA) and one of the most expensive—if not the most expensive—presidential general election in American history.

The broad financial strategies employed by the candidates and major parties were similar to those advanced in the 2000 campaign. As in 2000, both major party candidates chose to finance their general election campaigns with public funds, and the candidates and parties focused their resources on a relatively small group of electoral battleground states, which with few exceptions were the same states targeted by the candidates and parties in 2000. But the financing of the 2004 race differed from the contest waged four years earlier in important ways, most notably in the financial strategies by the party organizations, the broader scope of interest group activity, and new tactics that facilitated increased spending beyond the restrictions set forth in federal law. Some of the changes were a result of the new regulations imposed by the Bipartisan Campaign Reform Act (BCRA); others were unanticipated responses to the increasingly constraining limits of the public funding system for general elections.

The Strategic Context

Since the first publicly financed election in 1976, every eligible candidate has accepted public funding in the general election. Even though Kerry and Bush rejected public funding during the primaries, both took the $74.6 million public grant in the general campaign. Kerry decided to do so even though Democratic advisers saw many possible advantages to refusing the public money in the general campaign and instead relying on private contributions—which are free from any limits on spending. Kerry's strategy served to highlight the growing strains on the public funding system and the challenges posed by a changing financial environment.

In previous elections candidates readily accepted public funding because it eliminates the need to raise substantial amounts of money and provides the major party nominees with equal sums to spend in the general election campaign. There is also a strong financial incentive to accept its requisite spending restrictions since the amount of the grant has traditionally been greater than the amount typically raised during the primary campaign. In fact, of the major party nominees since 1976, only Bush in 2000, who refused public funding in the primaries, raised more money before the convention ($95.5 million) than the amount of the general election grant ($67.6 million).[3]

In 2004 the financial calculus used in deciding whether to accept public funds was more complicated than in the past, in part because of the unprecedented primary fundraising success of the candidates. In the general election, each candidate was eligible to receive $74.6 million of public funds.[4] This amount was equivalent to less than a third of the total amount Bush and Kerry had each collected during their respective primary campaigns. Thus for the first time since 1976 both candidates faced a realistic prospect of being able to raise substantially more money for the general election than the sum provided by the public grant. Given the high degree of partisan fervor surrounding the race, it was not unreasonable to expect that more money could be generated through private fundraising than through public funding.

For example, in the months leading up to the Democratic convention, Kerry was raising an average of more than $25 million a month, and by the time of the convention, he had amassed approximately $45 million in unspent primary money that could be spent in the general election, but only if he chose to reject the public money.[5] In other words, at the end of the nomination campaign he had about 60 percent of the amount offered by public funding in the bank, with the possibility of garnering much more. Some aides estimated that the campaign might be able to raise as much as $140 million for the general election.[6] Similarly, the Bush campaign was taking in about $12 million a month during the summer months leading up to the convention, even though the president was no longer attending fundraising events and his campaign was relying on direct mail for most of its revenue.[7] Moreover, by the time of the Republican convention, the Bush campaign had $36 million in primary funds left to spend and a base of donors of $1,000 or more who had contributed a total of $148.7 million during the primary period.[8] If only half of these donors were willing to give as much again in the general election, they alone would provide as much as the public funding grant.

Another factor that influenced the strategic thinking and incentives concerning the public funding alternative was the timing of the conventions. The Republicans would not convene until the end of August, making theirs the latest convention since 1968, when Democrats nominated Hubert Humphrey on August 29.[9] The 2004 Republican convention schedule called for President Bush to accept the party's nomination on September 2. Kerry was scheduled to accept the Democratic nomination on July 29. He would therefore have to finance fourteen weeks of general election activity with the $74.6 million in public funds, while Bush would receive the same amount to pay for only nine weeks of campaigning.[10] In addition, Bush would be able to continue to spend unlimited sums of primary money during most of August, while every dollar Kerry spent would be counted against the general election spending limit. The timing of the conventions placed Kerry at a strategic disadvantage and raised the prospect that, even if both candidates opted for public funding, Kerry might be outspent by a significant amount in key battleground states in the final weeks of the campaign.

Kerry also had to consider the implications of having to decide first. If he rejected public funding, he would be the first general election contender to do so. Given his previous record of support for public financing, he would probably be criticized for taking such a step. In doing so, he would also cede the moral high ground to Bush, who could then justify a similar decision to reject public money by citing the need to remain competitive with Kerry. Although Bush gave no indication that he would refuse the public subsidy and most observers expected that he would take it, just as he had in 2000, Kerry had to consider the possibility that Bush might reject the grant and its spending limit a few weeks after Kerry accepted. In that case, Kerry would have to stick with public funding and face the likelihood of being outspent by a substantial sum or shift his position and jump-start a fundraising effort (and repay any public funds already spent) with only two months to go in the campaign.

In addition, both candidates had to consider the likely financial activity that would form the broader context of general election financing. Even though BCRA banned soft money, which meant that candidates could not rely on the types of party soft money spending that had supported presidential candidacies in recent elections, both parties were raising record sums of hard money. The parties, which in the case of the presidential race meant principally the Republican National Committee (RNC) and Democratic National Committee (DNC), could use hard money to finance a limited amount of spending in coordination with the candidates, or, for the first time in a presidential contest, to make unlimited independent expenditures in support of the nominees. By accepting public funds, a candidate would avoid competing against his party for contributions, while still being able to help raise money for the party that could be used to support his campaign. The principal disadvantage of this approach was that it left the decision on how to spend the money to the party, rather than to the candidate and his campaign.

Given the levels of fundraising and spending by Section 527 committees throughout the bridge period leading up to the conventions, both candidates could also expect substantial interest group spending on electioneering communications, voter contact programs, or get-out-the-vote efforts throughout the general election. Each candidate therefore had to consider the financial consequences of waging a campaign that might necessitate responses to interest group electioneering, in addition to the electioneering activities of his opponent.

All the same, both candidates decided to accept the general election public funds. The financial benefit of $75 million in "free" money was still compelling enough to secure the candidates' participation in the public funding system. The grant provided the candidates with a financial "base" that allowed them to focus on campaign activities other than fundraising events. It thus saved them from having to spend time and money on fundraising and ensured that they would not be competing with their party organizations for political contributions during the general election campaign. But Kerry announced his decision only after considering tactics that might mitigate his comparative financial disadvantage.

In addition to discussing the private funding option, Kerry's advisers considered the radical step, which became public in late May, of holding the convention at the scheduled time but putting off the formal vote on the nomination until the end of August, with the vote then being conducted through ballots cast by members of the DNC.[11] In this way, Kerry's general election "clock" would be comparable to that of Bush. But this notion, which appeared to be little more than an act of political chicanery, quickly became a focal point of media attention and public criticism. Soon thereafter, Kerry's campaign cast the idea as a "distraction" that was shifting focus from the election's core issues and dismissed it as a viable option.[12] Kerry was thus left with a comparative financial disadvantage in the early part of the formal general election period.

One other notable difference between the strategic context of the 2004 and 2000 campaigns was the lack of a significant third-party candidacy. In 2000 Al Gore had to be concerned about the presidential bid of Ralph Nader, who ran as the Green Party nominee. Although Nader attracted votes from both sides of the political aisle, his liberal platform was particularly appealing to voters who were likely to vote Democratic, and his candidacy was widely regarded as a threat to Democratic prospects. Indeed, after the election, some observers charged that Nader had cost Gore the election since the Nader vote in a few states, most importantly in Florida, was far greater than Bush's margin of victory in those states.[13]

Nader ran again in 2004, this time as an independent. He did not receive the Green Party nomination (and thereby access to its ballot line in twenty-three states) but did receive the endorsements of both the Reform and Populist Parties.[14] His candidacy never matched even the minor level of interest and support that it had achieved in 2000, when he captured 2.7 percent of the general election vote.[15] As soon as Nader announced his decision to run, the Democrats quickly cast his role as that of a spoiler who was likely to enable Bush's reelection. With the electorate deeply divided in its assessments of the president's performance and the Democrats more unified behind their nominee than they were in 2000, few voters were open to the alternative of a third-party candidate. The Democrats and a coalition of liberal advocacy groups, known as United Progressives for Victory, also mounted legal challenges in a dozen states to prevent Nader from qualifying for the general election ballot. These efforts helped keep Nader off the ballot in such crucial states as Ohio and Pennsylvania and forced his campaign to spend substantial time and money on ballot access activities in other states, including Florida, Wisconsin, Illinois, and Michigan.[16] In part as a result of these tactics, Nader appeared on the ballot in only thirty-four states in 2004, compared with forty-three in 2000.[17]

Nader raised $3.4 million in the entire 2004 election cycle, down from $5.1 million in the 2000 cycle. His 2004 finances included $865,000 in public matching funds earned before the start of the general election campaign. Nader spent most of his money ($2.3 million) before the end of August. This left only about $1 million for general election campaigning. Overall, Nader's biggest expenditures were the costs related to ballot access activities, which amounted to at least $674,000, and payroll expenses, which totaled $472,000.[18] Given his meager resources and dearth of public support, Nader was never a significant influence in the 2004 race and garnered less than 1 percent of the vote.

Candidate Finances

Bush and Kerry each supplemented the $74.6 million of public funding with private contributions that were raised to pay general election legal and accounting compliance costs, also known as GELAC funds. This money, which is exempt from the general election spending ceiling but subject to federal contribution limits ($2,000 per individual donor), can only be used to cover the costs incurred to comply with the law and must be deposited in a separate account established for this purpose. Such compliance costs include legal and accounting services, as well as no more than 10 percent of a campaign's payroll and overhead expenses.[19] In 2004 the candidates raised a combined $21.1 million in GELAC funds, with Bush raising $12.2 million and Kerry $8.9 million. The total was slightly more than the $20.5 million raised by the candidates in 2000. In that election cycle, Bush collected $9 million and Gore $11.5 million.[20] When combined with the public funds, the total amount available to the Bush campaign was $86.8 million, compared with $83.5 million for Kerry.

Both candidates also held in reserve some of their leftover primary money. These funds could not be spent on general election campaign activities, but they could be transferred to an account that could be used after the election to pay any costs associated with a recount or other legal challenges. Given the experience in 2000 and the expectation that some challenges were likely to be filed in the eventuality of another close contest, the candidates, particularly Kerry, kept some of this money in the bank so that it would be available if needed. Most of the leftover funds, however, were transferred to the national party committees for use during the general election.

Federal Election Commission (FEC) regulations allow federal candidates to transfer unlimited sums from their campaign accounts to party committees. Kerry and Bush both took advantage of this option. Kerry was the first to take this action, eventually transferring $23.6 million to the DNC and $3 million each to the Democratic Congressional and Senatorial Campaign Committees. Kerry also transferred $10.8 million to Democratic state party committees in targeted general election states, including $1.7 million to Pennsylvania, $1.6 million to Michigan, and $1.4 million to Florida.[21] After making these transfers, he still had more than $15 million remaining in his primary account.[22] In mid-October, Bush followed Kerry's lead and transferred most of his remaining primary funds to the party committees, sending $26.5 million to the RNC and $1 million each to the National Republican Senatorial and Congressional Committees.[23]

The candidates spent the major portion of their general election public funds on media advertising, with most of the expenditures focused on a small number of states. Before the convention, Kerry and the Democratic Party broadcast ads in up to twenty-one states in an effort to expand the number of "battleground" states that might be in play in the general election. Most notably, Kerry and the Democrats spent about $20 million and made twenty-five visits to Arizona, Arkansas, Colorado, Louisiana, Missouri, North Carolina, and Virginia in hopes of making at least some of these states competitive in the fall.[24] But by the beginning of September, opinion polls indicated that all of these states were leaning toward Bush, and the race narrowed to ten highly competitive states where the candidates concentrated their resources (Florida, Ohio, Pennsylvania, Iowa, Minnesota, Nevada, New Hampshire, New Mexico, West Virginia, and Wisconsin) and four others that were largely a target of party spending (Maine, Michigan, Oregon, and Washington).[25]

The target states were very similar to those in the 2000 race and included nine states won by Gore, three of them by margins of less than 10,000 votes.[26] Kerry therefore had a greater number of states to defend than Bush and had to extend his public funds over a longer period of time. Kerry made a strategic decision at the start of the general election campaign to conserve his public resources early in the race in order to avoid being outspent in key states in the final weeks of the contest. In other words, he sought to avoid the problem Gore faced in 2000: because Gore spent large sums early, he was short of funds in the final weeks of the election and had to choose between spending money in Ohio or Florida in the final days of the campaign.[27]

Kerry's strategy had one major drawback: it left him vulnerable in August. In order to save funds for the crucial final weeks of the campaign, the candidate had to refrain from spending large sums in August. From the end of the convention through August 20, Kerry spent no money on television advertising.[28] During this period, a 527 committee called Swift Boat Veterans for Truth (SBVT) attacked Kerry's service record in Vietnam by launching a relatively small wave of advertising in seven media markets, including markets in Ohio, Wisconsin, and West Virginia.[29] While the DNC and Democratically oriented 527 committees were financing substantial media campaigns, their advertisements were focused on attacking Bush, rather than promoting Kerry or responding directly to SBVT's attacks on Kerry. Kerry finally responded to these attacks in late August, spending about $400,000 on ads against SBVT. But by this time the damage was done, and media coverage of the SBVT's charges had amplified the attacks and undermined the image of Kerry's military service (see chapter 8).[30]

However, Kerry did remain competitive with Bush in terms of total media spending. According to one analysis of the information contained in FEC disclosure reports, Bush allocated $52 million, or almost 70 percent of his public money, to media expenditures. Kerry allocated $49.8 million to media expenditures, or almost 66 percent of his public funds.[31] Kerry was also financially competitive throughout the final weeks of the campaign. In mid-October, Kerry reported $24.5 million in public money left to spend, compared with $22.4 million for Bush.[32] Much of the media spending in those final weeks was focused on Florida, Ohio, and Pennsylvania (because both campaigns recognized that the winner of two of these three was likely to be elected), as well as Wisconsin, Iowa, Nevada, New Hampshire, and New Mexico.[33]

Besides media, other major candidate expenditures included travel and personnel costs, as is the case in every general election campaign. One notable difference in the candidates' allocations was Bush's $5.2 million expenditure on "message phone calls."[34] This disbursement reflected the Bush campaign's emphasis on direct contact with base voters as a supplement to media spending. Bush also used $820,552 of his public funds to pay for survey research.[35] Kerry spent $1.6 million on polling but financed these costs through the party, using coordinated expenditures.

Candidate spending patterns thus indicate that the general election largely followed the spending patterns established before the conventions. The candidates concentrated their spending on advertising and left much of the work of field organizing and voter contact to the parties and partisan allies. This allowed them to maximize the share of their limited public funding that could be devoted to media in a select group of targeted states.

Party Financing

The public funds provided to candidates represented a minor share of the total amount expended in the presidential general election. Given the stakes in the race, party committees and interest groups had strong incentives to provide assistance to their favorite candidate and did so to an unprecedented extent. The spending by the national party committees was especially noteworthy. Although BCRA banned soft money, thereby prohibiting parties from soliciting the types of unlimited contributions that were responsible for $495 million of the receipts in the 2000 cycle, the DNC and RNC more than made up for their loss of soft money by raising hard dollar contributions.[36] Supplied with ample coffers, both parties spent funds in a variety of ways to provide as much assistance as possible to their respective nominees. Consequently, the parties outspent the candidates by significant amounts, in part by taking advantage of new regulations and in part by employing a new tactic—"hybrid spending"—that increased the candidates' ability to stretch their public dollars and exercise some control over large amounts of party money.

Coordinated Expenditures

Under the provisions of the FECA, each national party committee is allowed to spend a limited amount of money in coordination with its presidential nominee. In 2004 the amount each committee could spend in this manner was set at $16.2 million. In making coordinated expenditures, the party committees may consult with the candidates or their campaign staffs to determine how the money will be spent. The candidates therefore have some control over how it is allocated.

In 2004 the RNC and DNC each spent about $16 million in coordination with the candidates. In 2000 their coordinated expenditures came to $27.2 million, with about $21.2 million of this amount devoted to broadcast advertising.[37] But in 2004 they pursued dramatically different spending strategies.

As in 2000, the Democrats allocated much of their coordinated spending to media advertising, but the portion was smaller than in 2000. In 2004 the party spent $6.5 million on media and production expenses, which represented about 40 percent of its total coordinated spending, whereas in 2000, 70 percent went to advertising.[38] Other major expenditures in 2004 included $3.4 million to pay the travel expenses of campaign surrogates and staff, $1.9 million for expenses incurred in staging campaign events, and $1.6 million for polling.

In contrast, the Republicans spent a relatively small amount of money on media advertising. Of the $16.1 million spent in coordination with the candidate, only $1.8 million was allocated to advertising. Instead, the Republicans emphasized targeted methods of voter contact, primarily mail. Most of the party's coordinated spending, about $13.4 million, was used to finance mailings to prospective voters. The party also spent about $843,000 on telephone contact programs. As with the spending of the Bush campaign committee, the party spending indicates that the Republicans placed greater emphasis on grassroots voter contact than did the Democrats.

Independent Expenditures

Another reason that coordinated funding for media advertising declined in 2004 was the availability of alternative means of financing this activity. In fact, both parties mounted more intensive advertising campaigns than in previous elections. These efforts were made possible by the new BCRA regulations.

Before the adoption of BCRA, federal campaign finance law sought to limit the amount of direct assistance parties could provide to their publicly funded presidential nominees by establishing a coordinated spending limit and prohibiting the national committees from disbursing additional money independently in support of a presidential candidate. This restriction was predicated on the assumption that the parties were so closely linked to their presidential nominees that they could not act independently of the candidate. Thus, for regulatory purposes, any party spending on behalf of a candidate was considered to be coordinated with the candidate.

In 1996 and 2000 the parties were able to circumvent this restriction on independent expenditures by relying on "issue advocacy" advertising and other types of spending funded largely with soft money that were not "expressly advocating" the election or defeat of a candidate. Thus these outlays were not legally considered "independent expenditures in support of a candidate." BCRA eliminated the party "issue advocacy" option by banning soft money outright and specifying that any party advertising that supports, promotes, attacks, or opposes a federal candidate constitutes a campaign expenditure that has to be financed with federally regulated funds. But it also included a provision that allowed party committees to spend unlimited amounts of hard money independently of a candidate. This provision acknowledged the Supreme Court's 1996 ruling in *Colorado Republican Federal Campaign Committee v. FEC* (known as *Colorado I*), which held that parties could spend money independently of a candidate.[39] As adopted, the provision required the party organizations to decide at the time of a candidate's nomination whether to opt for limited coordinated expenditures or unlimited independent expenditures. The Supreme Court struck down this requirement in *McConnell v. FEC*, however, and the FEC accordingly drafted new regulations that, for the first time, allowed the party to spend unlimited amounts of money independently in support of its presidential nominee, in addition to spending a limited amount in coordination with a candidate.[40]

Both parties capitalized on the new rule, although the Democrats made greater use of the independent spending strategy (see chapter 7). The DNC and RNC spent a combined $138.5 million in this way in connection with the presidential race, with the DNC spending $120.3 million and the RNC $18.2 million.[41] Indeed, from the time of Kerry's nomination at the end of July, the DNC maintained a relatively steady stream of presidential advertising, which averaged about $9 million a week. In August alone, the DNC spent $35.3 million independently in support of Kerry to pay for advertising that criticized Bush and thus to offset Bush's superior financial position in the period between the two party conventions.[42] The DNC also financed a substantial wave of advertising in the final two weeks of the campaign, spending $41 million from October 14 through Election Day.

The RNC did not come close to matching the DNC's independent spending. Furthermore, in contrast to the DNC, the Republicans waited until the end of the campaign before making all of their independent expenditures, disbursing all of their $18.2 million in independent expenditures after October 13. Of this amount, $3.9 million was spent on postage and mail and most of the balance on advertising.[43] As in the case of coordinated spending, the Republicans allocated more of their independent expenditures to direct means of voter contact than did the Democrats.

Hybrid or "Allocated" Expenditures

The Republicans also relied on a wholly innovative funding tactic that had not been anticipated by the presidential public funding rules or BCRA. It consisted of campaign advertisements jointly funded by the RNC and Bush campaign in an "allocated" or "hybrid" manner. The underlying assumption was that advertising or other campaign expenses could be funded in accordance with FEC allocation rules still in place after the adoption of BCRA that permitted cost sharing between a candidate and the party in certain circumstances.[44] While the parties could no longer make expenditures using hard and soft money as they had with issue advocacy advertising in previous campaigns, the Republicans believed that they could still share some of the costs of communications with the candidate if the advertising included a generic party message. Accordingly, the costs of advertisements that featured the president but included a general message of support for the Republican Party were divided between the RNC and the presidential campaign.

Whether the FEC accepted this interpretation of the regulations was not made clear at the time since neither the party nor the presidential campaign committee sought a formal advisory opinion from the FEC. Instead, the RNC simply proceeded to implement the tactic.

This hybrid approach offered a number of advantages over the independent expenditure. It allowed the presidential campaign to exercise more control over the content of the advertising message since the party did not have to act independently of the presidential campaign in this instance. Further, the RNC reasoned that its share of allocated expenditures would not count against the party's coordinated spending limit or constitute a contribution to a publicly funded candidate. This was a creative way of reducing the severity of the spending caps imposed on a publicly funded presidential candidate. In effect, the practice allowed the presidential campaign to stretch its limited public resources by allowing the candidate to pay for only a portion of an advertising expense, rather than bear the entire cost. It also allowed the party to spend more in coordination with its nominee than the amount allowed under the coordinated spending limit.

The initial advertisements financed in this manner were broadcast in September; they featured President Bush, mentioned the Republican "leaders in Congress," and presented a generic message about the Republican Party's agenda. Once the practice became evident, the DNC soon followed suit, producing a number of advertisements jointly financed with the Kerry campaign.[45] In all, the RNC reported $45.6 million in generic hybrid expenditures to the FEC. The DNC did not specify its hybrid spending in its FEC reports. However, an analysis conducted by the FEC did note that the DNC spent $24 million on media production and consulting that was not included in the independent or coordinated expenditure totals reported by the committee.[46] So the parties disbursed as much as a combined $69.6 million on this new form of

campaign funding. In doing so, they established a means of circumventing the restrictions of the public funding regulations that is likely to
become a model for future general election contests.

Generic Expenditures

In addition, parties relied on indirect, or generic, means of support to
advance the prospects of their respective nominees, the most important
being voter registration drives and voter turnout programs. BCRA prohibited the national parties from paying for voter mobilization efforts
with soft money funds, as they had in the past, but they could still use
hard money to pay for partisan voter registration efforts during the general election period, as well as partisan get-out-the-vote campaigns. The
law placed no limit on expenditures for generic voter mobilization
designed to identify their supporters and get them out to the polls.

In light of the outcome of the 2000 race, both parties made such programs a priority and financed extensive voter contact and turnout operations. Although spending on these types of activities was not itemized
in FEC reports, both parties made major commitments in these areas.
Overall, the DNC reported expenditures of $80 million on field organiz-
ing efforts, or more than twice the amount the party spent in 2000.[47]
The Republicans spent even more, with a budget of about $125 million,
or three times the amount budgeted in 2000.[48] While these efforts were
not solely oriented to the presidential contest, the race for the White
House was certainly the principal focal point of almost all of this party
spending.

Interest Group Spending

Organized groups or other nonparty political committees are also
allowed to finance presidential electioneering activities in a variety of
ways, so long as they do not coordinate their activities with a candidate,
which would make their expenditures a contribution to the candidate
(see chapter 8). Interest groups and political committees can make independent expenditures in support of a presidential candidate, just as
party committees can, but, as in the case of parties, they may only use
funds raised in accordance with federal contribution limits for this purpose. Typically, these expenditures are paid from money raised by an
organization's federal political action committee (PAC). Under BCRA,
political committees, including section 527 organizations, are also

allowed to support candidates through electioneering communications, which are broadcast communications that feature a presidential candidate and are aired within sixty days of the general election. BCRA states that these communications may not be financed with money received from corporate or labor union treasuries, but it does not specifically prohibit the use of unlimited individual contributions, which were a principal source of revenue for a number of the largest 527 groups in 2004. Labor unions and corporations may also spend funds communicating with their members, which can include expenses to advocate the election or defeat of a presidential candidate. A labor union or corporation, however, must disclose to the FEC any expense in excess of $2,000 that advocates the election or defeat of a federal candidate.[49]

A wide array of interest groups spent money on advertising in the presidential race, with the largest sums disbursed in the form of electioneering communications. In all, political groups and organizations reported $54.8 million in electioneering communications, with expenditures in support of Bush (or against Kerry) reaching $36.8 million and those in support of Kerry (or against Bush) $18 million, thus differing by a margin of two to one.[50] The major spenders were the section 527 committees focused on the presidential race (see chapter 8). On the Republican side, the top spenders were the Progress for America Voters Fund, SBVT, and Club for Growth.net, a subsidiary of the well-established conservative antitax group, Club for Growth. On the Democratic side, the leaders were the same organizations that had already spent millions of dollars against Bush before the start of the sixty-day electioneering communications window: the Media Fund and MoveOn.org Voter Fund.

Interest groups also spent significant amounts on independent expenditures. In almost all cases, these activities were financed from PAC money and involved groups that did not report significant spending on electioneering communications, with the major exception of MoveOn.org, which used its PAC, as opposed to its 527 committee, to finance some of its independent expenditures against Bush. In total, political groups other than the parties reported spending about $42.8 million independently in the presidential contest, with the vast majority of this amount, $35.2 million, spent in support of Kerry, either in the form of communications advocating Kerry or opposing Bush. About one-fifth of this amount, $7.6 million, was spent in support of Bush (or in opposition to Kerry).[51]

This disparity in favor of Kerry was largely due to the activities of MoveOn.org and labor unions.[52] In addition to its electioneering communications, MoveOn disbursed $10.4 million from its PAC to finance $7.8 million of advertising in support of Kerry and $2.6 million against Bush. The other top spenders on the Democratic side, the labor unions, included the United Auto Workers ($4.8 million), American Federation of State, County and Municipal Employees ($3.4 million), and Service Employees International Union ($2.4 million). Other liberal groups that spent substantial amounts included the League of Conservation Voters ($2.7 million), National Education Association ($1.3 million), and NARAL Pro-Choice America ($1.2 million). Another notable source was the financier George Soros, who was not only one of the top donors to Democratically oriented 527 groups but also spent $4 million out of his own pocket in the weeks before the election to buy anti-Bush ads in major newspapers.

On the Republican side, Bush's largest supporter was the National Rifle Association, which spent a total of $3.3 million, including almost $2.4 million on communications opposing Kerry. Only two other committees reported substantial disbursements in support of the president: the National Right to Life Committee, which reported a total of $1.1 million, and the Florida State Republican Party, which spent $1 million in independent expenditures.

Labor unions also spent substantial sums communicating with their members and their families. While the exact amount spent is uncertain, since only expenditures of more than $2,000 have to be reported, disclosure reports filed with the FEC clearly indicate that this kind of spending was significantly higher than in 2000. In 2004, membership organizations reported total communications costs of $24.3 million, which was more than double the $11.5 million reported in 2000.[53] The vast majority of these expenditures represented labor union communications designed to persuade members to turn out and vote against Bush, with $23 million spent in support of Kerry and only $1.3 million in support of Bush. Thus largely through the efforts of unions and liberal groups, interest group spending—at least the types of spending disclosed to the FEC—favored Kerry by a sizable margin.

Conclusion

Although both major party nominees opted for public funding in the general election, this source functioned as more of a floor rather than a ceiling on spending in the presidential race. Despite the limitations on the amounts directly spent by the candidates, their parties and allied groups were able to supplement these resources in significant ways. In addition to the $21.2 million that they raised in GELAC contributions, the candidates were able to exercise some control over other funds, specifically the coordinated and hybrid expenditures of the national party committees, which totaled $101.9 million, or about three times as much as the total amount permitted ($32.4 million) under the coordinated spending limit.

The public funds received by the candidates constituted less than a third of the money spent to influence the outcome of the presidential race. In all, FEC disclosure filings by the candidates, party committees, and interest groups show a combined $532.6 million in general election spending, with $320 million reported by Kerry and his Democratic allies and $212.6 million by Bush and his supporters (see table 5-1). This total does not even include the tens of millions of dollars spent by the party committees on partisan voter identification and turnout programs, nor the tens of millions spent by interest groups and section 527 committees on voter identification and turnout, as well as non-broadcast communications not defined as "electioneering communications," such as mail, telephone messages, and Internet activities. If these expenditures were to be included, the estimate for total spending in connection with the presidential general election would exceed $700 million.

One notable aspect of the financing of the 2004 presidential race was the prominent role played by the parties. Though some observers feared that the ban on soft money would diminish party efforts, the parties pressed on and more than compensated for the revenue loss through their remarkable success in raising hard money (see chapter 7). Free to spend unlimited sums of money independently of the candidates, the parties spent more in direct support of their respective nominees than ever before. Indeed, the $240.4 million total for party-coordinated, independent, and hybrid spending ($160.3 million for the Democrats and $80.1 million for the Republicans) was more than double the combined amount spent in 2000 on coordinated expenditures and soft money–funded issue advocacy advertising.[54]

The direction of spending in 2004 is also noteworthy. The candidates and parties on both sides devoted most of their resources to broadcast advertising in a small cluster of targeted states, but differed in their financing of more direct methods of voter outreach. President Bush and the RNC allocated more money to telephone and mail than either Kerry or the DNC, perhaps in response to the extensive voter mobilization

Table 5-1. *Presidential General Election Spending, 2004*
Millions of dollars

Expenditure	Kerry	Bush
Candidate		
Public	74.6	74.6
GELAC[a]	8.9	12.2
Subtotal	83.5	86.8
Party		
Coordinated	16.0	16.1
Independent[b]	120.3	18.2
Hybrid	24.0	45.8
Subtotal	160.3	80.1
Interest groups and political committees		
Electioneering communications[c]	18.0	36.8
Independent[d]	35.2	7.6
Communication costs[e]	23.0	1.3
Subtotal	76.2	45.7
Total	320.0	212.6

Source: Based on FEC data as of August 15, 2005.

a. Includes funds reported as of December 31, 2004. See FEC, "2004 Presidential Campaign Activities Summarized," press release, February 3, 2005.

b. Kerry total includes expenditures made in support of Kerry or against Bush. Bush total includes expenditures made in support of Bush or against Kerry.

c. Figures include electioneering communications reported to FEC as of August 1, 2005.

d. Kerry total includes expenditures made in support of Kerry or against Bush. Bush total includes expenditures made in support of Bush or against Kerry.

e. Figures may include some expenditures made before the start of the formal general election period.

programs being financed by a number of Democratically oriented 527 groups. Whether this difference had any meaningful effect on the final outcome is hard to determine, but the Republican approach was certainly in accord with recent research demonstrating that more direct and personal methods of voter contact are more effective in mobilizing individuals to vote than broadcast advertising.[55]

Above all, the presidential general election campaign, like the prenomination campaigns, raised important questions about the equity and adequacy of the public funding program. In 2004 the incentives to participate in public funding were still strong enough to persuade both candidates to accept the general election grant. But whether these incentives will continue to encourage candidate participation is uncertain. Future nominees will look at public funding with the lessons of 2004 in mind. That is, they will have to consider whether the expenditure limit provides enough spending capacity to meet the strategic needs in a campaign that is likely to feature greater spending by party organizations and interest groups. They will also have to judge the potential consequences of any resource inequities created by the relative timing of the conventions. And, unlike most of their predecessors, they may have to gauge whether they can raise substantially more money on their own than the amount provided by the public grant. The decision to accept public funding is no longer a simple choice. The public funding system has reached its tipping point. In future elections, candidates will view private financing as a realistic alternative to the public funding option.

Notes

1. For a discussion of the presidential nomination campaign and the amounts spent by candidates during various periods in the primary season, see chapter 4.

2. In 2000 Gore and Bush spent a combined $131.6 million in the prenomination period and a combined $165 million in the general election, for a total of $296.6 million. See John C. Green, "The 2000 Presidential Nominations," in *Financing the 2000 Election*, edited by David B. Magleby (Brookings, 2002), p. 55; and Anthony Corrado, "Financing the 2000 Presidential General Election," in *Financing the 2000 Election*, edited by Magleby, p. 89.

3. FEC, "2004 Presidential Campaign Financial Activity Summarized," press release, February 3, 2005 (www.fec.gov/press/press2005/20050203pressum.html).

4. The limits for 2004 are noted at www.fec.gov/pages/brochures/pubfund_limits_2004.shtml (July 25, 2005).

5. Ron Fournier, "Kerry to Give Dems Leftover Campaign Cash," Associated Press news release, November 18, 2004, p. 1; and Jim Rutenberg and Glen Justice, "Political Memo: Some Democrats Urge Kerry to Forgo Public Campaign Financing," *New York Times*, July 9, 2004, p. A14.

6. Thomas B. Edsall and Jim VandeHei, "Kerry Aims to Accept Federal Funding," *Washington Post*, July 13, 2004, p. A9. See also Klaus Marre, "Kerry Could Spurn Public Cash: Fundraisers Insist He Can Raise More than $75 Million," *The Hill*, July 7, 2004 (www.thehill.com/news/070704/cash.aspx [July 8, 2004]).

7. David Morgan, "Record-Setting Bush Fundraising Drive Nears Climax," Reuters news release, March 31, 2004; and Scott Lindlaw, "Bush Collects $1.5M at D.C. Fund-Raiser," Associated Press news release, March 31, 2004.

8. Campaign Finance Institute, Task Force on Financing Presidential Nominations, *So the Voters May Choose: Reviving the Presidential Matching Fund System* (Washington, 2005), p. 12.

9. Richard C. Bain and Judith H. Parris, *Convention Decisions and Voting Records*, 2nd ed. (Brookings, 1973), p. 323.

10. Stuart Rothenberg, "Campaigning: In White House Race, Kerry's $75M Won't Equal Bush's $75M," *Roll Call*, March 11, 2004, p. 7.

11. See Edsall and VandeHei, "Kerry Aims to Accept Federal Funding," p. A9; Dan Balz and Thomas B. Edsall, "Kerry Ponders Delay in Party Nod," *Washington Post*, May 22, 2004, p. A1; and Dan Balz and Jim VandeHei, "Kerry Weighs the Value of Delaying Nomination," *Washington Post*, May 26, 2004, p. A10.

12. Robin Toner and Glen Justice, "Kerry Abandons Plan to Delay Accepting Nomination," *New York Times*, May 27, 2004, p. A20.

13. Gerald M. Pomper, "The Presidential Election," in *The Election of 2000*, edited by Gerald M. Pomper and others (Chatham, N.J.: Chatham House, 2001), pp. 133– 35.

14. Brian Faler, "A Lighter Shade of Green?" *Washington Post*, May 22, 2004, p. A6; and Brian Faler, "Nader Scrambles to Collect Thousands of Signatures," *Washington Post*, April 3, 2004, p. A6.

15. Pomper, "The Presidential Election," p. 133.

16. James W. Ceasar and Andrew E. Busch, *Red over Blue: The 2004 Elections and American Politics* (Lanham, Md.: Rowman and Littlefield, 2005), p. 172; Katharine Q. Seelye, "Convictions Intact, Nader Soldiers On," *New York Times*, August 2, 2004, p. A14; Matt O'Connor, "Backers Sue to Keep Nader on Fall Ballot," *Chicago Tribune*, July 28, 2004, p. A6.

17. Ceasar and Busch, *Red over Blue*, p. 172.

18. Financial data based on FEC filings for Nader for President 2004. Figures for expenditures based on disbursements disclosed on Nader's FEC reports as compiled by PoliticalMoneyLine and as posted in the presidential campaign summary at www.politicalmoneyline.com. Ballot access expenses include outside services and contractors for ballot access and signature gathering. Payroll expenses include disbursements for payroll and employee taxes.

19. For a discussion of the regulations governing GELAC funds, see Anthony Corrado, "Public Funding of Presidential Campaigns," in Anthony Corrado and others, *The New Campaign Finance Sourcebook* (Brookings, 2005), pp. 195–97.

20. FEC, "2004 Presidential Campaign Financial Activity Summarized."

21. Ibid.

22. Fournier, "Kerry to Give Dems Leftover Campaign Cash."

23. FEC, "Party Financial Activity Summarized for the 2004 Election Cycle," press release, March 2, 2005 (www.fec.gov/press/press2005/20050302party/Party2004final.html).

24. Ron Fournier and Liz Sidoti, "Democrats Limit Advertising to 14 States," Associated Press news release, September 9, 2004.

25. Ibid.; and Dan Balz, "Size of Battleground May Be Smaller than Expected," *Washington Post*, September 12, 2004, p. A4.

26. Fournier and Sidoti, "Democrats Limit Advertising."

27. Balz, "Size of Battleground May Be Smaller," p. A4. Balz cites Tad Devine, senior strategist for the Kerry-Edwards campaign, who observed: "We did not want to be in the situation that the Democratic nominee was in four years ago of having to choose between Ohio and Florida." In 2000 Gore did not advertise in Ohio during the final two weeks of the campaign in an effort to compete with Bush's advertising in Florida. In the final two weeks of the 2000 election, Bush and the RNC spent $4.9 million on advertising in Florida markets, while Gore and the DNC spent $3.6 million. Data on 2000 advertising expenditures provided by Tad Devine.

28. Neilsen Monitor-Plus and the University of Wisconsin Advertising Project, "Over Half a Million TV Spots Have Been Aired in the 2004 Presidential Race," press release, August 27, 2004, p. 2 (www.polisci.wisc.edu/tvadvertising/Press%20Releases.htm).

29. Ibid., p. 1.

30. Center for the Study of Elections and Democracy, "527s Had a Substantial Impact on the Ground and Air Wars in 2004, Will Return," press release, December 16, 2004.

31. Totals based on an analysis of FEC disclosure reports conducted by PoliticalMoneyLine.com. See the presidential campaign summary for the 2004 election cycle (www.politicalmoneyline.com [August 1, 2005]).

32. Kenneth P. Doyle, "Bush, Kerry Camps Roughly Even in Money at about $100 Million in Race's Final Days," *BNA Money and Politics Report*, October 25, 2004, p. 1.

33. "Eight States, 99 Electoral Votes Draw Focus from Bush, Kerry," *USA Today*, October 16, 2004 (www.usatoday.com/news/politicselections/nation/2004-10-16-electoral-votes_x.htm [August 20, 2005]).

34. Totals based on an analysis of FEC disclosure reports conducted by PoliticalMoneyLine.com. See the presidential campaign summary for the 2004 election cycle (www.politicalmoneyline.com [August 1, 2005]).

35. Ibid.

36. For a discussion of party money in the 2004 cycle, see chapter 6, and Anthony Corrado, "Party Finance in the Wake of BCRA: An Overview," in *The Election after Reform: Money, Politics and the Bipartisan Campaign Reform Act*, edited by Michael J. Malbin (Lanham, Md.: Rowman and Littlefield, 2006, forthcoming).

37. FEC, "2004 Presidential Campaign Financial Activity Summarized"; and Corrado, "Financing the 2000 Presidential General Election," p. 94.

38. Anthony Corrado, "Party Finance in the 2000 Elections: The Federal Role of Soft Money Financing," *Arizona State Law Journal* 34 (Winter 2002): 1046.

39. *Colorado Republican Federal Campaign Committee* v. *FEC*, 518 U.S. 604 (1996).

40. *McConnell* v. *FEC*, 540 U.S. 93, 199-205 (2003); and 69 *Fed. Reg.* 63919 (November 3, 2004).

41. FEC, "2004 Presidential Campaign Financial Activity Summarized."

42. The $35.3 million total includes $8 million in media ads purchased on July 28 that is reported in the DNC's August monthly disclosure and $27.3 million for August noted in the DNC's September monthly report. On the focus and negative tone of the DNC advertising, see Neilsen Monitor-Plus and the University of Wisconsin Advertising Project, "Presidential TV Advertising Battle Narrows to Just Ten Battleground States," press release, October 12, 2004, p. 3 (www.polisci.wisc.edu/tvadvertising/Press%20Releases.htm).

43. Totals based on the amounts reported in the pre–general election and post–general election itemized disclosure reports filed by the RNC.

44. See 11 C.F.R. sec. 106.

45. Liz Sidoti, "Bush Team Orchestrates Larger Ad Campaign," Associated Press news release, September 22, 2004; Sidoti, "Kerry Campaign, DNC to Run Joint Ads," Associated Press news release, September 24, 2004.

46. FEC, "Party Financial Activity Summarized." Tracking data maintained by the Kerry campaign show a total of $37.2 million in hybrid expenditures. If half of this amount was allocated to the party, the total would have been $18.6 million. The FEC analysis suggests that the costs may have been allocated on a 60 percent to 40 percent basis, with the party paying the larger portion. Kerry tracking figures provided by Tad Devine, senior strategist, Kerry for President, in a telephone interview, January 11, 2005. A copy of the summary data was also provided.

47. Democratic National Committee, "Democratic News: 2004 Progress Report," electronic newsletter, December 10, 2004; Jackson Dunn, National Finance Director, Democratic National Committee, transcript of remarks delivered at the Campaign Finance Institute Campaign Finance Reform Forum, National Press Club, Washington, January 14, 2005, p. 16 (www.cfinst.org/events/ElectionAfterReform.html [August 16, 2005]); and Dan Balz and Thomas B. Edsall, "Unprecedented Efforts to Mobilize Voters Begins," *Washington Post*, November 1, 2004, p. A6.

48. Balz and Edsall, "Unprecedented Efforts to Mobilize Voters Begins."

49. See 2 U.S.C. sec. 441b and 11 C.F.R. sec. 114.3.

50. Based on FEC data as of August 20, 2005.

51. Based on FEC data as of August 20, 2005, which showed independent expenditures, including those of the national party committees, totaling $63.2 million for Kerry, $92.0 million against Bush, $14.3 million for Bush, and $11.5 million against Kerry. Figures reported in text exclude the independent expenditures reported by the national party committees.

52. Figures on group spending in this section are based on the itemized independent expenditures reported in FEC press releases on independent expenditures.

These releases can be found at www.fec.gov/press/press2004/20041029indexp.
html.

53. FEC data as of August 20, 2005. Also FEC, "2004 Presidential Campaign Financial Activity Summarized."

54. In 2000, the national party committees spent $27.2 million on coordinated expenditures in the presidential race and according to the best available estimates, about $60 million on issue advocacy advertising. See Corrado, "Party Finance in the 2000 Elections," pp. 1041–48.

55. For a thorough discussion of recent research on various methods of voter contact, see Donald P. Green and Alan S. Gerber, *Get Out the Vote!* (Brookings, 2004).

SIX   *Financing the 2004*
           Congressional Elections

PAUL S. HERRNSON

The 2004 congressional elections occurred in the shadow of a hotly contested presidential race. Despite the attention on President George W. Bush and Senator John Kerry, several congressional elections offered their fair share of drama. Some Democrats believed they could make significant inroads into the Republican majority in the House of Representatives and even win control of the Senate; many Republicans hoped to increase their seats in both chambers and perhaps win enough seats in the Senate to make it harder for the Democrats to use the filibuster to obstruct the GOP's policy agenda. To add to the pressures, candidates, political parties, and interest groups of all stripes had to learn to operate within the confines of a new federal campaign finance law, the Bipartisan Campaign Reform Act (BCRA) of 2002.

The financing of the 2004 congressional elections cannot be understood without examining the new setting in which campaign contributors and fundraisers operated. Some other important considerations are the contributions of parties, political action committees (PACs), and individuals; their impact on the resources available to different types of candidates; the independent, parallel, and coordinated campaigns mounted by party organizations and interest groups; and the effect of money on the outcomes of selected 2004 congressional elections.

The Strategic Context

The setting for the 2004 elections posed several challenges for congressional candidates, political parties, interest groups, and individuals who contribute and spend money in elections. Perhaps the most daunting was learning to operate under BCRA, which was designed to close some of the loopholes of the Federal Election Campaign Act (FECA) and thereby prevent candidates and political parties from circumventing federal contribution limits, expenditure ceilings, and disclosure requirements. It also aimed to reduce corruption and the appearance of corruption associated with federal candidates' raising unlimited donations from wealthy interests for political parties.

All the same, the enactment of BCRA injected some unpredictability into the financing of congressional elections. The exact meaning of some provisions was open to interpretation by the Federal Election Commission, which was charged with translating the legislation into regulatory and enforcement procedures (see chapter 2). There was also a strong possibility that key provisions could be overturned in the courts. In addition, questions arose about the ability of candidates, party committees, interest groups, and individual donors to adapt to the new regulatory framework.

Another significant aspect of the setting for the 2004 elections was the concentration of competition in a small number of races. Members of Congress have enjoyed very high reelection rates over the past few decades. Most senators have easily reclaimed their party's nomination and gone on to win the general election. House members have been even more successful in holding on to their seats. Reelection rates for members of the lower chamber have exceeded 90 percent for decades. Good constituent relations, accurate representation of constituents' policy preferences, skillful use of the perks of office, superior fundraising, and relatively weak opposition are among the major explanations for the high reelection rates in the Senate and the House.

Redistricting has recently become important in stifling competition in House elections. Before the 2002 election cycle, the redistricting process sparked an increase in the number of competitive House contests in the election immediately following, although this number gradually declined as the next redistricting period approached (see figure 6-1).[1] However, the redistricting before the 2002 elections produced only a few competitive contests. Among the more important reasons for this change is an increase in the number of divided state governments, which meant that both Democrats and Republicans influenced the redrawing of congressional boundaries in many states. Second, improved technology enabled district mapmakers to estimate the numbers of Democratic, Republican,

Figure 6-1. *Competitive House Elections, 1982–2004*[a]

Number of elections

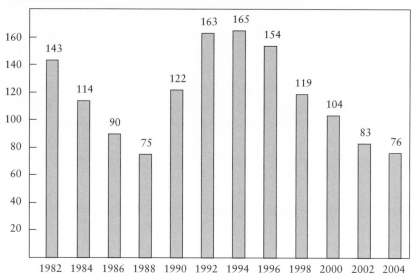

Source: Data compiled by author.
a. Competitive races are those decided by a margin of 20 percent or less or in which a challenger defeated an incumbent by more than 20 percent of the vote.

and independent voters with tremendous precision. Third, House incumbents and their allies participating in the states' redistricting seemed unusually risk averse when redrawing district lines, preferring to carve out extremely safe seats for themselves instead of sacrificing a little political security to create competitive seats that would improve the chances of increasing their party's House membership. The successful efforts of House majority leader Tom DeLay (R-Tex.) to engineer the redrawing of congressional seats in Texas before the 2004 elections further reduced the number of competitive seats.

The concentration of competition in congressional elections had significant implications for candidates and those who finance their campaigns. As discussed later, amassing the resources needed to mount a competitive campaign is rarely a problem for congressional incumbents or most contesting an open seat. Challengers, however, are another story. Few House challengers succeed in raising the funds needed to wage a competitive bid for office. Many Senate challengers are similarly underfunded. With a limited number of close congressional races, political parties, groups, and individuals who contribute or spend money in congressional elections have few opportunities to influence the outcomes of elections and thereby alter the composition of Congress.

Going into the 2004 elections, the Republicans controlled 227 House seats, the Democrats 205, and an independent 1 seat, while 2 seats were vacant. House Republicans needed to defend 19 open seats, and their Democratic counterparts needed to defend 15. Since both parties desired to increase their membership in the lower chamber as much as possible, they had strong incentives to commit most of their resources to the relatively few House elections that seemed competitive and to limit the flow to most other contests.[2]

Control of the Senate was more uncertain. The GOP held fifty-one seats, the Democrats forty-eight, and an independent one. Thus, a one-seat shift to the Democrats accompanied by a Democratic presidential victory would have given them procedural control because a Democratic vice president would be in place to cast the deciding vote. Given that the Democrats had to defend nineteen of the thirty-four seats up for election, including five open seats in the increasingly conservative South, the prospects for a Democratic takeover were not all that strong. However, leaders of both parties understood that if the cards fell a certain way it was within the realm of possibility, and they recognized the value of increasing the number of seats occupied by fellow party members. Like their House counterparts, Senate party leaders had strong incentives to focus their resources in a small number of unpredictable races.

Many ideologically oriented advocacy groups and individual contributors found themselves in similar situations. With relatively few congressional races falling into the potentially competitive category early in the election season, and even fewer belonging to this bracket later on, these donors had limited opportunities to invest their money where it could change the outcome of a race. Only access-oriented contributors, those donors who were more concerned with forging and maintaining good relationships with incumbents than electing legislators that shared their views on issues, had both the incentives and opportunities to contribute to larger numbers of House candidates.[3]

With control over the levers of power, party leaders and other politicians could influence the flow of money in elections. Republican control over the presidency, the House, and the Senate gave the GOP a leg up in the fundraising process. President George Bush, Vice President Richard

Cheney, and other members of the administration invested substantial amounts of time and effort to help Republican congressional candidates raise money and win votes. Nevertheless, the high degree of partisan polarization in Washington and among the political elites on both the left and right, who account for most political donations, to some degree helped counteract Republican leaders' fundraising efforts. Both Democratic and Republican candidates raised substantial sums in 2004.

Campaign Contributors

Individual and institutional motivations to donate money are of major consequence to congressional campaigns. Political parties, interest groups, and individuals contribute and spend money in elections for a variety of reasons. Democratic and Republican Party committees and some PACs and individuals contribute to influence the outcomes of elections, whereas others invest to gain access to influential members of Congress. Some donors give for both reasons. And some individuals contribute because they enjoy socializing with politicians and participating with other individuals in the political process.

Political Parties

The current polarization of voters and politicians withstanding, American political parties act more pragmatically than ideologically. First and foremost, party leaders want to win control of political institutions. This goal strongly outweighs considerations of restructuring society in accordance with some grand vision.[4] For the most part, candidates develop and run campaigns that appeal to their local constituencies. Even as party constituencies have become more ideologically cohesive locally and nationally, local conditions and concerns tend to dominate congressional candidates' strategies and tactics. Because both national parties seek to win as many House and Senate seats as possible, they become heavily involved in competitive elections where they know their efforts have the potential to make the difference between victory and defeat and virtually ignore contests where the outcome seems a foregone conclusion.

The Democratic Congressional Campaign Committee (DCCC) and the National Republican Congressional Committee (NRCC) play the lead role in devising the parties' national strategies in House elections. They advise House candidates on campaign strategy and assist in hiring campaign consultants, raising money, conducting issue and opposition research, and encouraging contributions from PACs and individuals. The congressional campaign committees are particularly helpful in assisting with the fundraising of freshman lawmakers, incumbents in jeopardy of losing their seats, and nonincumbents in competitive elections. In recent years, they have played a critical role in redistributing the wealth from party leaders and other safe incumbents to candidates involved in races that are too close to call. The Democratic Senatorial Campaign Committee (DSCC) and the National Republican Senatorial Committee (NRSC) perform similar roles in Senate elections. The Democratic National Committee (DNC) and the Republican National Committee (RNC) are much less involved in congressional elections, but their voter registration and mobilization efforts can influence the outcomes of these contests.[5]

Although some prognosticators warned that BCRA's ban on unregulated soft money would do irreparable harm to the parties, national party organizations were able to offset their losses in soft money to some degree by raising record amounts in federally regulated hard dollars.[6] Under BCRA, the national, congressional, and state party committees can each contribute $5,000 to a House candidate in the general election; the parties' national and senatorial campaign committees can contribute a combined total of $35,000 in direct contributions to a Senate candidate; and state party committees can contribute an additional $5,000 to candidates for the House and Senate.[7] Parties also provide additional assistance to candidates through coordinated expenditures. These transactions, which offer both parties and candidates the opportunity for input, routinely pay for public opinion polls, television and radio ads, issue and opposition research, fundraising, and other campaign activities. The limits for national party coordinated expenditures are indexed for inflation. In 2004 national parties could make a total of $37,310 in coordinated expenditures in House elections and between $74,620 and $1,944,896 in Senate elections, depending on the size of the state's voting-age population.[8] State party committees are authorized to spend the same amounts in coordinated expenditures in House and Senate elections as the parties' national organizations. As discussed later, parties also can spend unlimited amounts on independent expenditures.

In 2004 the national parties vigorously pursued funds to sustain these various activities. Lacking the significant fundraising advantages derived from having a party member occupy the White House, or even the lesser benefits gained from having majorities in one or both houses of Congress, the Democrats turned to DNC chair Terry McAuliffe and prominent congressional leaders to raise badly needed cash. The DNC, DCCC, and DSCC all improved their direct mail donor bases and introduced other fundraising operations. The net result was that all three committees set new fundraising records. The DNC raised $394.4 million in hard money for the 2004 election cycle, over three times more than it raised in hard money in 2000 and almost six times the amount it raised in 2002. The DCCC took in $93.2 million, roughly twice the amounts it raised in 2000 and 2002. The DSCC amassed almost $88.7 million, which amounted to 83 percent and 118 percent increases over the previous two election cycles. Democratic state and local committees raised $171.2 million (including funds transferred from the national committees), or about one-third and one-seventh more than in the previous cycles.

Republicans typically enjoy a fundraising advantage because they have a deeper pool of wealthy and upper-middle-class donors and are usually a step or two ahead of the Democrats when it comes to harnessing technology for fundraising and other purposes—although both parties capitalized on the Internet for fundraising in 2004. Using the fundraising prowess of President Bush to maximize these advantages, the RNC raised $392.4 million, 84 percent more than it had collected in hard money in the previous presidential contest and 131 percent more than in the 2002 midterm elections. The NRCC raised over $185.7 million, 91 percent more than it had raised in 2000 and 50 percent more than in 2002. The NRSC, which experienced the least financial growth of Washington's Republican organizations, raised just under $79 million, 53 percent more than it raised in 2000 and one-third more than in 2002. State and local Republican Party committees collected $182.9 million (including funds transferred from the national committees), thus increasing their respective takes by 33 percent and 4 percent over previous election cycles. Encouraged by BCRA's ban on soft money, the 2004 elections dramatically accelerated the existing trend of growth in party hard money receipts for both the Democrats and the Republicans.

During the 2004 elections, Democratic Party organizations used hard money to directly contribute about $806,000 to their party's House candidates and spent almost $2.9 million in coordinated expenditures on their behalf. The Democrats also contributed almost $1.1 million directly to their Senate candidates and spent over $10.2 million on coordinated expenditures.[9] Parties prefer to distribute more in coordinated expenditures than direct contributions because the limits for coordinated expenditures are substantially higher and because coordinated expenditures enable the party to exercise more influence on a candidate's campaign. During the period between 1998 and 2002, the national parties pared back their hard money contributions and coordinated expenditures, choosing instead to channel their hard money to party committees in those states hosting extremely close congressional races so the funds could be used to the advantage of candidates competing in those contests. The parties did this because federal regulations required them to match their soft money expenditures in a given state with a specific level of hard dollars. Thus by transferring hard money to certain states rather than spreading these funds to more candidates, the parties could increase the total funds they spent in very tight races. The BCRA's prohibitions against national party soft money contributions put an end to this spending strategy and freed the parties to make coordinated independent expenditures in more congressional elections.

Reflecting their greater wealth, Republican House and Senate party committees spent more hard money in 2004 than the Democrats. The GOP distributed almost $4.7 million to its House candidates; this included almost $1.2 million in contributions and more than $3.2 million in coordinated expenditures. The Republican Party also contributed almost $1.9 million to Senate candidates and made $9.3 million in coordinated expenditures. Although Republican candidates traditionally receive more party support than Democratic candidates, the gap has narrowed over the last few election cycles.

The parties targeted their money strategically in the 2004 House races. Both parties distributed most of their funds to candidates in competitive contests.[10] Table 6-1 displays the percentages of contributions and coordinated expenditures distributed to general election candidates involved in typical two-party contested races.[11] The Democrats distributed 80 percent of their funds to candidates in competitive races. The Republicans delivered 81 percent of their funds to GOP candidates in these same contests. Democratic Party spending favored House incumbents, who received roughly 51 percent of all party contributions. Ironically, the Republicans, who controlled the House and had more incumbents in the House to defend, committed fewer resources to incumbent retention—only 43 percent of their total—than the Democrats. Indeed,

Table 6-1. *Distribution of Party Contributions and Coordinated Expenditures in the 2004 House and Senate Elections*[a]

Election	House		Senate	
	Democrats	Republicans	Democrats	Republicans
Competitive				
Incumbents	41	31	10	16
	(27)	(38)	(4)	(4)
Challengers	19	32	7	14
	(38)	(27)	(4)	(4)
Open seats	20	18	49	57
	(15)	(15)	(7)	(7)
Uncompetitive				
Incumbents	10	12	35	3
	(135)	(136)	(10)	(7)
Challengers	10	7	0.01	10
	(136)	(135)	(7)	(10)
Open seats	1	0.3	. . .	. . .
	(15)	(15)	. . .	. . .
Total (thousands of dollars)	3,468	4,200	11,055	10,375
N	(366)	(366)	(32)	(32)

Source: Compiled from Federal Election Commission data.

a. Incumbents in competitive elections lost or won by 20 percent or less of the two-party vote. Challengers in competitive elections won or lost by 20 percent or less of the two-party vote. Open-seat candidates in competitive elections won or lost by 20 percent of the two-party vote. Incumbents in uncompetitive elections won by more than 20 percent of the two-party vote. Challengers in uncompetitive elections lost by more than 20 percent of the two-party vote. Open-seat candidates in uncompetitive elections won or lost by more than 20 percent of the two-party vote. Figures include contributions and coordinated expenditures by all party committees for general election candidates in major party–contested races, excluding a small number of atypical elections, including incumbent-versus-incumbent contests and elections in which one of the candidates did not complete the campaign. Some columns may not add to 100 percent because of rounding.

the GOP devoted 39 percent of its contributions and coordinated expenditures to Republican challengers who sought to defeat Democratic House incumbents, whereas the Democrats invested only 29 percent in defeating Republican House members. Both parties dedicated about one-fifth of their funds to capturing open seats.

The parties also committed significant resources to some of the unusual races that took place in 2004. In Texas, for instance, redistricting resulted in two incumbent-versus-incumbent match-ups. The Democrats spent $82,611 in contributions and coordinated expenditures to help Charles Stenholm in the state's 19th district and $94,522 to help Martin Frost in the 32nd district. The GOP also invested heavily in these contests, delivering $82,802 in contributions and coordinated expenditures to Stenholm's opponent, Randy Neugebauer, and $82,725 to Pete Sessions, who was running against Frost.

In the Senate races, the unusually unstable political environment created challenges for party strategists. In Illinois, Republican candidate Jack Ryan decided to abandon his bid for junior state senator in late June, after embarrassing and politically harmful allegations about his personal life became the center of a media feeding frenzy. This turned what was expected to be a competitive election into a lopsided contest won by Democrat Barack Obama, then an Illinois state senator. The contest between Senator James Bunning (R-Ky.) and Democratic challenger state senator Daniel Mongiardo, first predicted by political analysts to be an easy home run for the incumbent, became a nail-biter that was not decided until the last inning because Bunning, a member of the Baseball Hall of Fame, began to exhibit erratic behavior. First, he compared Mongiardo to one of Saddam Hussein's sons. Then he failed to show up in Kentucky for a debate, instead telecasting his participation from the RNC's television studio in Washington, where he read his opening and closing statements from a teleprompter in violation of the debate's rules.[12] Although Bunning's wild pitches did not cost him the election, his margin of victory was a mere 2 percentage points—far fewer than anyone had anticipated early in the election season.

The uncertainties surrounding the 2004 Senate elections had implications for the distribution of party resources. Nevertheless, the parties spent well over a majority of their funds in competitive races. The Republicans' targeting was superior in this regard. Republican candidates in typical two-party competitive elections received 87 percent of the party's funds, with most of those resources going to candidates for open seats and challengers facing vulnerable Democrats. Republican candidates in lopsided races received a mere 13 percent. The Democratic Party did not distribute its resources as effectively. Democrats in competitive contests received only 65 percent of the party's resources, as considerable funds were spent to protect incumbents in lopsided races. Most of these funds (more than $3.1 million) were spent to protect California Senator Barbara Boxer, who defeated challenger Bill Jones by 21 points. As the distribution of party contributions and coordinated expenditures in the elections for the Senate and the House demonstrates, parties can and do act strategically, but pressures from nervous incumbents, the usual rise and fall in the competitiveness of some elections, and unpredictable events can lead them to spend limited resources ineffectively.

There were a few close elections for both chambers where hindsight suggests one party or the other should have spent more money and some lopsided contests where one or both of the parties should have spent less.

Political Action Committees

Interest groups were heavily involved in the 2004 elections, providing direct contributions to specific congressional candidates, disseminating advertisements both for and against candidates, and mobilizing voters. PACs contributed $289.1 million to congressional candidates in 2004.[13] Business interests—such as corporations, corporations without stock, cooperatives, and trade, membership, and health associations—sponsored 59 percent of all PACs. Labor PACs accounted for less than 7 percent of the PAC community, and nonconnected PACs, including ideological PACs and PACs associated with federal candidates, made up the remaining 34 percent.

A relatively small group of organizations accounted for most of the PAC contributions. Less than 14 percent of all PACs made almost 82 percent of all contributions to congressional candidates in 2004. PACs associated with business interests contributed more money than any other group; in fact, corporate PACs accounted for more than one of every three PAC dollars, trade association PACs accounted for another 27 percent, and PACs sponsored by corporations without stock and cooperatives accounted for another 2 percent. Labor PACs contributed less than 17 percent of all PAC dollars, substantially less than their pro-business rivals.

Most PACs use ideological, access-oriented, or mixed strategies when contributing to House and Senate candidates.[14] Ideological PACs are similar to political parties in that their primary goal is to influence the political process through elections. Most contribute to maximize the number of House members in office who share their policy views, often on such salient issues as abortion rights and the environment. These PACs distribute most of their resources to candidates in competitive contests but occasionally make contributions to encourage the careers of promising politicians. Rarely interested in gaining access to legislators, they concentrate on advancing issues linked to fundamental values that officeholders are seldom willing to compromise. Planned Parenthood and the Right to Life are two prominent examples of this type of PAC.

Access-oriented PACs view elections pragmatically. Their main goal is to gain access to members of Congress who are in a position to influence regulations, appropriations, or treaties that affect the environment in which their industry or workforce operates. These groups consider campaign contributions an important tool for reaffirming or strengthening their relationships with influential lawmakers. They recognize that contributions can arouse goodwill in representatives and senators, making it easier for the group's lobbyists to influence the legislative process.

PACs that follow access strategies are likely to contribute most of their money to incumbents, especially to members of the House and Senate who occupy party leadership posts, who chair or are members of important committees or subcommittees, or who are recognized leaders in specific policy areas. Because these PACs are interested in influencing congressional policy decisions more than election outcomes, they are not too concerned about the competitive aspect of elections. In fact, some recipients of PAC dollars do not even have opponents. Corporations and other businesses with dealings before Congress, such as AT&T and Microsoft, make up the largest share of this group.

PACs in the last group, mostly trade associations and labor unions, follow mixed strategies. They make some contributions to candidates who share their views and some to incumbents with whom they wish to maintain access. In the first case, most of the contributions go to candidates in close races, and in the second case to powerful incumbents. In elections where PAC decisionmakers are under cross-pressures because the incumbent is in a position to influence the group's legislative priorities while the challenger is more supportive of the group's interests, most PACs that follow mixed strategies contribute solely to the incumbent, but a few also contribute to the challenger. The National Association of Realtors' PAC is the largest such group, followed by the PAC sponsored by the National Automobile Dealers' Association.

PAC contributions and expenditures held true to form in the 2004 elections. Corporate and trade association PACs gave about two-thirds of their respective House donations to Republican candidates (see table 6-2). Similarly, nonconnected PACs gave nearly 64 percent of their House donations to Republicans. Labor union PACs gave 87 percent of their House funds to Democrats. The overall distribution of PAC money favored members of the House majority, with Republicans receiving 56 percent of the total funding and Democrats collecting the remainder.

Many PACs began to favor Republican candidates over Democrats following the GOP takeover of Congress in 1995, but they did not wholly abandon the Democrats, nor did they abandon their previous

Table 6-2. *Distribution of PAC Contributions in the 2004 House Elections*[a]

Percent unless noted otherwise

Election	Corporate	Trade, member-ship, and health	Labor	Non-connected	Cooperative	Corporation without stock
Competitive						
Incumbents						
Democrats	6	8	16	8	12	9
Republicans	18	16	2	21	11	16
Challengers						
Democrats	—	1	9	5	—	1
Republicans	1	2	—	8	—	3
Open seats						
Democrats	1	2	7	4	3	1
Republicans	3	3	—	11	1	2
Uncompetitive						
Incumbents						
Democrats	24	25	49	12	31	25
Republicans	45	40	10	23	38	40
Challengers						
Democrats	—	—	4	2	1	—
Republicans	—	1	—	3	—	1
Open seats						
Democrats	—	1	2	—	1	—
Republicans	2	2	—	3	1	1
Total (thousands of dollars)	65,643	52,158	36,216	29,306	1,837	2,380

Source: Compiled from Federal Election Commission data.

a. Dash (—) means less than 0.5 percent. See Table 6-1 for cell *N*'s and other information.

contribution strategies. During the 2004 elections, corporate PACs continued to support House incumbents with the vast majority of their funds, with 93 percent going to incumbents, 6 percent to open-seat candidates, and a mere 1 percent to challengers. Whether a race was close seemed of little concern as 63 percent of their House contributions went to incumbents of both parties who won with more than 20 percent of the two-party vote. Trade association PACs followed a similar pattern, except that they committed slightly more of their funds to challenger and open-seat candidates.

Labor PAC contributions to 2004 House candidates continued to reflect their inclination to follow mixed strategies. They donated the vast majority of their money to Democrats because of shared ideological goals. However, they gave 65 percent of their contributions to Democratic House incumbents, who because of their high reelection rates would be best positioned to influence legislation important to the labor movement. Indeed, incumbents in uncompetitive elections received more labor dollars than any other group of Democratic candidates. Labor PACs even allocated 12 percent to Republican incumbents, up from 8 percent in 2002. Labor PACs' mixed strategy may have enabled them to maintain good relations with some friendly or powerful Republican incumbents, including moderate representatives such as Sherwood Boehlert of New York, who received well over $200,000 in labor PAC funds, and Speaker Dennis Hastert of Illinois, who raised about $114,000 from labor.

Nonconnected PACs also followed their usual pattern, giving most of their House contributions to candidates in close elections. They contributed 17 percent of their funds to Democratic general election candidates in competitive contests and 40 percent to Republicans in similar races. These PACs distributed 36 percent of their House contributions to challengers and candidates in open-seat contests.

PAC contributions to Senate candidates followed predictable patterns and bear similarities to PAC activity in House elections (see table 6-3). Corporate and trade PACs invested significant sums in pursuit of access, giving substantial portions of their funds to safe and endangered incumbents. Both sets of PACs were more generous to candidates from the majority party. The only advantage enjoyed by the Democrats came from labor PACs, which supported Democratic candidates, with 93 percent of their Senate contributions, down from 95 percent in 2002. This may not seem like very much change, but coupled with the shift in labor money in House races, it may portend a further decline in organized labor's support for Democratic candidates, especially where union interests are satisfied with the quality of representation from congressional Republicans, which could be one reason for the trickling away. Dissatisfaction with the representation they receive from some Democrats could be a second. A third reason might be that labor lobbyists need access to Republican members of Congress in order to protect their policy interests.

PAC donations thus underscore the differences in the two parties' constituencies. Labor has been a faithful ally of the Democratic Party for more than five decades, including ten years marked by near-continuous Republican congressional majorities. Meanwhile, the Republican Party

Table 6-3. *Distribution of PAC Contributions in the 2004 Senate Elections*[a]

Percent unless noted otherwise

Election	Corporate	Trade, membership, and health	Labor	Nonconnected	Cooperative	Corporation without stock
Competitive						
Incumbents						
Democrats	12	13	19	10	22	15
Republicans	18	16	5	14	10	13
Challengers						
Democrats	—	1	11	6	3	1
Republicans	4	5	—	8	—	4
Open Seats						
Democrats	5	5	26	3	8	6
Republicans	19	19	—	22	8	16
Uncompetitive						
Incumbents						
Democrats	19	19	33	15	29	25
Republicans	23	20	4	11	16	18
Challengers						
Democrats	—	—	2	—	—	—
Republicans	1	1	—	2	4	2
Open seats						
Democrats	2	1	2	2	1	2
Republicans	1	1	—	3	—	2
Total (thousands of dollars)	23,164	13,952	6,991	13,533	395	877

Source: Compiled from Federal Election Commission data.

a. Dash (—) means less than 0.5 percent. See Table 6-1 for cell N's and other information.

has been able to draw substantial support from corporations and trade association PACs, even before 1995, when in the legislative minority. Both parties have strong supporters among nonconnected PACs, most of which contribute the vast majority of their funds to only one party's candidates.

Individuals

Individuals constitute the largest source of campaign money in congressional elections. In 2004 individual donors gave approximately $720.8 million dollars to all primary and general election candidates for the House and the Senate. Individual contributions differ from those of parties and PACs in that they are rarely the product of well-researched or systematic decisionmaking in pursuit of organizational objectives. Some large contributors are plugged into political organizations and may consider the network's communications when selecting candidates for contributions, but most individual donors give small amounts to a few candidates. Indeed, 36 percent of all donors who give $200 or more in an election cycle contribute to only one candidate, another 56 percent contribute to two to five candidates, and only 8 percent contribute to more than five.[15] Moreover, most individual contributions to congressional candidates do not travel very far: three-fourths of all contributions were made to a candidate in the donor's state, and in the case of House races, 70 percent went to a candidate in the donor's district or a neighboring district.[16]

BCRA, as noted in chapter 2, raised the ceilings for contributions to congressional candidates, so for the first time an individual could contribute more than $1,000 to a candidate in each stage of the election (primary, general, and runoff if one is held). This law also substantially raised the aggregate limit an individual can contribute to federal candidates, party committees, and PACs. Thus BCRA created new opportunities for wealthy individuals to contribute to congressional candidates. A significant number of donors took advantage of those opportunities, and this influenced the distribution of individual contributions. At the top end, 27 percent of all individual contributions to House candidates in typical races were made in amounts greater than $1,000 (see table 6-4). At the bottom end, only 23 percent of all individual contributions came in amounts of less than $200.

Incumbents, particularly those who had an easy road to victory, received most of the individual contributions regardless of size. However, there are some notable differences in the flow of individual contributions. More small contributions (less than $200) than modest and large contributions ($200 or more) went to candidates in competitive elections. The distribution of small contributions was also somewhat less favorable for incumbents. Although Republicans raised more individual funds of all sizes than did the Democrats, GOP House candidates did especially well with larger contributors, in part because of the differences in the two parties' constituencies. Individuals who believe they have the disposable income to contribute to a campaign are often well-educated and wealthy, two of the primary demographic groups of voters

Table 6-4. *Distribution of Individual Contributions in the 2004 House Elections*[a]

Percent unless noted otherwise

Election	Less than $200	$200–$749	$750–$1,000	More than $1,000
Competitive				
Incumbents				
Democrats	8	8	7	7
Republicans	12	11	13	12
Challengers				
Democrats	10	7	4	6
Republicans	5	6	5	6
Open seats				
Democrats	5	5	4	5
Republicans	4	3	3	4
Uncompetitive				
Incumbents				
Democrats	19	23	26	24
Republicans	21	26	30	26
Challengers				
Democrats	5	4	2	3
Republicans	7	3	2	4
Open seats				
Democrats	1	1	1	1
Republicans	2	3	3	3
Total (thousands of dollars)	72,725	74,916	80,236	83,793
(Percent of total individual contributions)	(23)	(24)	(26)	(27)

Source: Compiled from data provided by the Center for Responsive Politics.

a. See table 6-1 for cell N's and other information. Some columns may not add to 100 percent because of rounding. Calculated from preliminary data; some minor changes may result once final data are released.

who identify with the Republican Party. Because of the GOP's control of the chamber, its candidates were also positioned to raise more funds from individual donors, especially those who recognized that policy decisions in Washington could affect their financial well-being. In their contribution patterns, individuals are closer to access-oriented PACs than to parties or ideological PACs. Therefore most individuals making large contributions to members of the House appear to do so for policy or social reasons rather than for ideological ones.

Individual contributions to Senate candidates, however, were more likely to go to competitive races and to be in excess of $1,000. The proportionately more competitive races in the Senate and greater potential for chamber control to change hands probably help explain why Senate candidates raised substantially more from individuals than House candidates. Partisanship was also a factor. Democrats in Senate contests raised more in individual contributions across the board in House contests. Leading the pack was Barack Obama, who raised almost $5.7 million, much of which helped him win a hotly contested three-way primary.

There were also some similarities. Challengers for both the Senate and the House collected more funds through small contributions than larger ones. Democratic Senate candidates also raised more small rather than large contributions. Once again, the flow of money to incumbents, particularly those in safe seats, suggests that most individuals who make large contributions are more interested in forging bonds with incumbents than trying to influence the outcome of specific elections and the overall composition of the chamber.

The Money Chase

Even though contributions are most often discussed in terms of donors, congressional candidates are not passive spectators of election financing. They play active roles in the money chase, developing sophisticated fundraising strategies quite apart from those in the campaign for votes and involving distinct goals, tactics, and timetables. Furthermore, the campaign for resources addresses a nationally based financial constituency comprising political parties, PACs, and individual donors, whereas the campaign for votes focuses on the residents of a candidate's electoral district.

On average, House candidates spend 9.4 percent of their campaign budgets on fundraising, with incumbents spending ten times more and open-seat candidates five times more than challengers.[17] Some of these differences can be explained by the fact that virtually every House incumbent in a race contested by two major-party candidates relies on one or more paid professionals—a political consultant, campaign aide, or both—who specializes in fundraising. The same is true for roughly nine out of ten nonincumbents in competitive races. By contrast, fewer than 50 percent of the challengers in lopsided races hire a campaign professional for fundraising.[18] Not surprisingly, practically every Senate campaign, regardless of incumbency or competitiveness, places its fundraising in the hands of professionals.

Congressional candidates target fundraising appeals to individuals who are most likely to respond, including contributors who helped finance their previous campaigns. Incumbents and nonincumbents in competitive races use direct mail, telemarketing, receptions, and other fundraising events to collect money from individuals, parties, and PACs. Most candidates hold backyard barbecues, coffee klatches, and cocktail parties to raise small and moderate contributions in their districts or states. Incumbents and the small number of competitive nonincumbents who have national fundraising constituencies also hold "high-dollar" receptions in Washington, New York City, Hollywood, and other wealthy cities across the country.[19] These receptions often cost $250 or more per individual and $500 or more per PAC.

The intensity of the campaign for resources has pushed campaign costs up over the years. The fundraising efforts of House incumbents and candidates for open seats have borne the most fruit, and challenger fundraising has been largely stifled. In 1984 general election incumbents enjoyed a 2.4 to 1 fundraising advantage over challengers, which blossomed to 2.9 to 1 over the next decade and reached 4.8 to 1 by 2004. Differences in the campaign receipts collected by Senate incumbents and challengers vary according to the specific seats up for election in a given year, but they, too, have grown, albeit more modestly than in House elections.

Incumbents have this fundraising advantage over challengers largely because they are able to turn to more sources for campaign funds. Incumbents depend more on PAC money, whereas challengers turn to individuals, party committees, and the money that they donate to or lend their own campaigns (table 6-5). Some reformers have become concerned about self-financing in recent years, after seeing several congressional challengers (and others) invest millions of dollars in their own campaigns. This has alarmed incumbents as well, who would not like to find themselves running against a candidate willing to invest seemingly unlimited personal funds. The millionaires' provision of BCRA was designed to address this issue. When an opponent contributes or loans more than $350,000 to his or her own campaign in a race that meets the additional spending requirements discussed in chapter 2, the House candidate can raise individual contributions in excess of the normal limits and benefit from party coordinated expenditures in excess of the regular ceiling. Eight House general election challengers contributed or loaned their campaigns $350,000 or more in 2004, a substantially smaller number than had done so in 2002.[20] This preliminary evidence suggests that the provision had its desired effect. More elections will have to take place before the full effect of this aspect of the law can be determined.

Table 6-5. *Sources of House Candidates' Receipts, 2003–04*[a]
Percent unless noted otherwise

Source	Incumbents	Challengers	Open seats
Individuals	54	62	60
	($637,301)	($177,706)	($629,145)
PACs	40	14	25
	($420,217)	($39,731)	($269,948)
Party committees	1	3	2
	($10,593)	($7,878)	($24,370)
Candidates	1	18	7
	($5,885)	($51,798)	($71,975)
Miscellaneous	4	3	6
	($45,431)	($8,281)	($80,671)
Total resources	$1,169,428	$285,395	$1,076,100

Source: Compiled from Federal Election Commission data.
a. See Table 6-1 for cell N's and other information about the data.

The receipts of open-seat House candidates are yet another story. Like incumbent candidates, they usually raise substantial funds and often need to be more concerned with financing a high-spirited nomination race than an uncompetitive general election. Open-seat campaigns also resemble challenger campaigns in some ways, since their financing relies heavily on individual contributions and the candidates' own finances. During the 2004 elections, the typical open-seat candidate raised slightly less than the typical incumbent and substantially more than the typical challenger, reflecting the fact that open-seat races tend to be among the most competitive. Five candidates for House open seats contributed sufficient funds to exceed the threshold of the millionaires' provision.[21] Some met the provision's requirements in the general election, but others did so in the primaries.

Senators also enjoy important fundraising advantages over their challengers, but these are not nearly as substantial as those enjoyed by House members. During the 2004 elections, the typical Senate incumbent raised 160 percent more funds than his or her opponent (see table 6-6). Senators depended more on PAC contributions than their challengers but did not rely on PACs nearly as much as their House counterparts. Another major difference is that Senate incumbents contribute virtually nothing to their own campaigns, whereas some challengers dig fairly deeply into their own pockets. In 2004 four Senate challengers and two open-seat candidates contributed enough of their own money

Table 6-6. *Sources of Senate Candidates' Receipts, 2003–04*[a]
Percent unless noted otherwise

Source	Incumbents	Challengers	Open seats
Individuals	69	69	64
	($4,885,513)	($1,883,581)	($5,928,165)
PACs	22	8	12
	($1,518,113)	($210,810)	($1,120,979)
Parties	4	5	9
	($275,707)	($127,652)	($810,509)
Candidates	0	11	4
	($0)	($302,551)	($410,170)
Miscellaneous	5	7	10
	($375,273)	($191,451)	($953,922)
Total resources	$7,054,607	$2,716,045	$9,223,745

Source: Compiled from Federal Election Commission data.
a. See Table 6-1 for cell *N*'s and other information about the data. Some columns may not add to 100 percent because of rounding.

to trigger the millionaires' provision. For example, when Pete Coors, the Republican candidate for the open seat in Colorado, loaned his campaign more than $571,000, his opponent, Democrat Kenneth Salazar, was able to raise an additional $750,000 from individuals who had previously contributed to him. These funds were probably instrumental in leading Salazar to a 51 to 47 percent victory. Note, too, that open-seat Senate candidates collected substantially more money than challengers and incumbents in 2004, which means they were quite competitive financially.

Independent, Parallel, and Coordinated Campaigns

Congressional campaigns sometimes extend beyond party and PAC contributions and candidate fundraising and spending. Political parties and interest groups may run independent, parallel, and coordinated campaigns, any of which can change the tone and volume of communications in a congressional race.

Independent Campaigns

Independent campaigns, as defined by the Federal Election Commission, involve "independent expenditures," including radio, television, and direct mail communications that expressly call for the election or defeat of a federal candidate. These expenditures, instituted in 1996 under a ruling by the Supreme Court, must be made with hard money and flow directly from a party committee, PAC, or individual to voters without a candidate's prior knowledge or approval.[22] Planning these expenditures requires substantial organizational investment because teams of pollsters, media experts, and strategists must independently create and implement a communications plan designed to advance the cause of their preferred candidate. Independent expenditures are not without risk: the resulting advertisement may not coincide with the preferred candidate's message, might alienate that candidate's supporters, mobilize the opponent's supporters, or put the candidate at some other disadvantage.

Aside from the NRSC's $10 million outlay in 1996, party committees continued to rely more on soft money to finance issue advocacy advertisements right up to 2004. With BCRA's ban on such activity, party independent expenditures grew astronomically, rising to roughly $108 million in 2004's congressional elections from less than $4 million in the previous two cycles.[23] The parties had to jump through substantial legal hoops to make these expenditures. To avoid being charged with coordinating their efforts with their party's candidates, they had to create separate organizations that did not communicate with other party committees involved in federal elections.

Democratic Party committees spent roughly $28 million on independent expenditures in typical two-party contested House races in 2004.[24] The vast majority of these funds—more than 95 percent—were spent in a mere twenty-five competitive races. Because parties tend to make their independent expenditures late in the campaign season when there are fewer unpredictable elections, it is easier for them to concentrate these funds in close contests than in party contributions and coordinated expenditures.

Republican Party independent expenditures in the 2004 House races exceeded $40 million and also strongly favored nonincumbents. The GOP concentrated most of these funds—93 percent—in twenty-five elections, virtually all of them extremely close. Unlike the Democrats, Republicans channeled less of this money to their incumbents and considerably more to their open-seat candidates. The evidence suggests the parties may have perceived opportunities in the 2004 House elections differently. The Republicans, thinking they had a strong opportunity to defeat congressional incumbents, may have been encouraged to attack

Democrats in marginal districts. Democrats, however, may have responded by deploying their independent expenditures to shore up many of these same incumbents.

Both parties made substantial independent expenditures in contested Senate elections. The Democrats spent roughly $21.7 million in nine typical two-party contested elections, almost all of them competitive. The Republicans spent $11.5 million in these same contests (and about $22,000 in two others). Both parties made about 70 percent of their independent expenditures in open-seat races. Voters attuned to the Coors-Salazar race in Colorado witnessed a great deal of party independent spending. The DSCC aired television and radio advertisements early in the contest and continued to do so until it was over, spending $2.3 million on the effort. The NRSC spent $1.1 million—a considerable sum, but substantially less than the Democrats' expenditures. Thinking that their candidate could put more of his own vast fortune into the race if he felt it necessary, the Republicans did not match the DSCC outlay.[25]

In contrast to party committees, most PACs did not allocate large amounts to independent expenditures in 2004. They spent about $12.5 million for this purpose, slightly less than they had spent in the previous two election seasons. BCRA's ban on the use of corporate and labor funds to finance issue advocacy ads during the period before an election appears to have done nothing to stimulate more independent spending by most PACs. Various trade associations accounted for most of the independent expenditures in the 2004 congressional elections, including more than $11.3 million on 177 expenditures "for" specific candidates and almost $371,000 on 13 expenditures "against" them (see table 6-7). Most of this spending was intended to help Republican incumbents. Nonconnected PACs ranked next. Their spending was fairly evenly divided in races for the House but overwhelmingly intended to favor Republicans running for the Senate. Labor was positioned next, spending most of its funds to help Democratic candidates. Note that corporate PACs, which directly contributed the most to congressional candidates, invested very little in independent expenditures, and all of their expenditures were for rather than against candidates. Because corporate PACs participate in elections primarily to quietly gain access to members of Congress, most choose to avoid the negative publicity that often accompanies independent expenditures.

Table 6-7. *PAC Independent Expenditures in the*
2004 Congressional Elections[a]

Expenditure	For	Against
Corporate	$118,800	$0
	(63)	(0)
Trade association	$11,338,879	$371,195
	(177)	(13)
Labor	$170,482	$45,071
	(34)	(1)
Nonconnected	$2,500,563	$483,317
	(196)	(54)
Cooperative	$4,993	$0
	(1)	(0)
Corporation without stock	$62,478	$0
	(11)	(0)

Source: Compiled from Federal Election Commission data.
a. Number of expenditures is in parentheses.

Parallel Campaigns

Parallel campaigns, like independent campaigns, involve communications that flow directly from party committees or interest groups to voters. They differ in that they are financed with soft money and do not directly call for the election or defeat of a specific candidate. Party committees spent more than $100 million on the television advertising component of their parallel campaigns in 2002, but they could no longer conduct these activities in 2004 because of BCRA's ban on soft money fundraising and spending.[26] BCRA does not ban interest groups from spending soft money entirely; they may use such funds to finance a variety of election activities, including direct mail, telephone contact programs, and get-out-the-vote efforts. But mass media communications can only be financed with soft money before the federal advertising period, which begins thirty days before a primary and sixty days before a general election. Once this advertising period begins, interest groups may not use unlimited money from corporations or labor unions to finance broadcast advertisements. However, a small number of interest groups, labeled 527 and 501(c) committees (after the provisions of the revenue code that define them), worked to fill the void that resulted from BCRA's ban on party soft money and on issue advocacy ads financed by such money. Although they were not entirely successful in replacing party soft money activity, the 527s managed to raise $424 million in 2004, an increase of more than $274 million over the 2002 amount.[27] Most of this money was spent to influence the presidential contest, particularly through television advertising, but some funds were solely for specific congressional elections and for voter mobilization activities designed to affect elections at all levels.

Most of the 527 and 501(c) groups are closely aligned with the parties. They include groups such as America Coming Together and the Media Fund, which supported the Democrats, and Progress for America and Swift Boat Veterans and POWs for the Truth, which supported the Republicans. Some of the groups focus on advancing specific issues (for example, EMILY's List backs pro-choice Democratic women candidates), and others focus on broader ideological concerns (the Club for Growth, for instance, helps free-market Republicans). Several of these organizations are associated with PACs. The League of Conservation Voters (LCV), for one, has accomplished its objectives through a complex structure that includes a federal PAC to contribute to or make independent expenditures against congressional candidates, a 501(c)(3) organization to carry out its research and educational objectives, a 501(c)(4) organization to publicize politicians' environmental records, and a 527 organization to conduct issue advocacy. The LCV also has state-level affiliated organizations to influence state elections. Unlike the LCV, some 527 and 501(c) organizations adopt innocuous names to conceal the identities of their financial backers. Among these is the United Seniors Association, which is financed by the pharmaceutical industry. By forming complex legal entities, an interest group or a coalition of groups is able to take advantage of the tax incentives written into the revenue code and the various opportunities for political activity that exist within federal and state campaign finance laws and outside them.

Although most interest group parallel campaigning in 2004 focused on the presidential election, some also occurred in congressional races. Systematic data comparable to those for hard money contributions and expenditures are not available for parallel campaign activities, but there is sufficient evidence to demonstrate that a small number of well-financed groups were active in this regard, and that nearly all of their efforts took place in states hosting competitive races. According to one study of campaign activity, some fifty-four interest groups spent approximately $15.3 million on 60 television advertisements and $2.8 million

on 20 radio ads to influence the outcomes of fifteen close House and
Senate elections. These groups, and a few others, were also responsible
for 320 direct mail pieces and 46 newspaper and magazine articles.[28] In
some contests, interest group activity appears to have exceeded the level
of spending by the candidates' own campaign committees.

Interest group spending on parallel campaigns was divided along partisan lines, with few, if any, groups making significant expenditures to
help candidates of both parties. Groups allied with the Democrats spent
roughly 74 percent more on TV and radio ads than did groups allied
with the Republicans. Although the pro-Democratic groups spent more
on broadcast communications, the pro-Republican groups aired almost
twice as many unique TV and radio ads and distributed eighty-eight
more pieces of direct mail and purchased twenty-six more print media
ads than did the Democrats.[29] This suggests that spending by Republican-leaning interest groups was more finely targeted than spending by
Democratic-leaning groups.

The Coors-Salazar race provides an interesting example of interest
group parallel campaign activities. The contest drew the attention and
resources of several interest groups. Colorado Conservative Voters, a 527
organization, spent nearly $1 million during the Republican primary
attacking Coors for holding positions on drinking and other social issues
that the group deemed too liberal. Ironically, left-wing groups attacked
the candidate during the general election for being too conservative on
those same issues. One such group, Citizens for a Strong Senate, a 527
organization, spent almost $1 million on television ads criticizing Coors
for proposing to lower the drinking age and for pollution caused by his
beer company. The LCV also spent almost $800,000 on TV ads that
attacked Coors for his company's illegal dumping of waste into local
waterways and for helping to fashion a law shielding businesses that pol-
lute in Colorado from penalties. TV ads aired by conservative organizations were not as pervasive as those aired by liberal groups, but some
were quite visible. Americans for Job Security, a 501(c)(6) organization,
spent about $1 million on television ads and direct mail to criticize
Salazar's environmental record and link him to a cyanide spill that took
place while he headed the state's Department of Natural Resources. It
may be that more liberal than conservative groups mounted parallel campaigns in conjunction with the Colorado Senate race because like the
NRSC, conservative groups thought that since Coors could spend his
own money in the race, their funds would be better spent elsewhere.[30]

Coordinated Campaigns

Coordinated campaigns consist of traditional grassroots activities enhanced by innovations in voter targeting, communications, and mobilization. These efforts—which are generally coordinated with those of federal, state, and local candidates running in overlapping election districts—have been growing in importance in recent elections. Parties and interest groups have increasingly used voter files containing detailed information about individual citizens and sophisticated computer programs to locate and contact actual and potential supporters. Before the enactment of BCRA, party committees used a combination of hard and soft money to register voters, print and distribute leaflets, organize door-to-door visits, create and maintain Internet websites, and conduct other grassroots efforts. Most of these activities were financed with money that was raised by party organizations in Washington, D.C., and transferred to the state party organizations that spent it in accordance with the national party's wishes. In the wake of BCRA's ban on soft money, the parties must finance their coordinated campaign efforts with hard money in federal elections, while interest groups remain free to conduct coordinated campaign activities with either hard or soft money. Moreover, the law's prohibition against issue ads financed by interest group soft money during the final sixty days of a general election has encouraged groups to invest more in coordinated campaigns, particularly during the last two months of the election.

Responding to the changes in the regulatory environment, the national party organizations invested less money in coordinated campaigns in 2004 than they had in 2000. Most of this money was directed toward the presidential election, but some was applied to a few congressional contests. Lacking large infusions of national party soft money, state party committees had to find ways to increase the hard money receipts needed to finance their coordinated campaign efforts. Republican state party committees succeeded in raising sufficient funds to spend $58 million on voter mobilization and $9 million on organizing rallies, distributing bumper stickers and other paraphernalia, and engaging in other grassroots activities. Their Democratic counterparts spent $47 million and $8 million on such endeavors.[31] Although only a small portion of these efforts was intended to influence House and Senate elections, they did concentrate on competitive races. In fifteen of the most competitive contests, Democratic state party committees distributed two targeted e-mails, fourteen mass telephone calls, and four waves of personal contacts in connection with these races. The DCCC and the Abington-Rockledge Democratic Committee (a local party organization in Pennsylvania) also conducted one set of mass telephone calls each. Republican state committees carried out significantly more coordinated campaign activities in conjunction with the 2004 elections, including twenty-one targeted e-mails, seventeen mass telephone calls, and five sets of personal contacts. In addition, the NRCC and the Lower Providence Republican Committee (a local party organization in Pennsylvania) each transmitted a targeted e-mail. The NRCC and the NRSC also were responsible for thirteen and seven mass telephone calls, respectively.[32] For most of the twentieth century, the GOP lagged behind the Democrats and their labor allies in coordinated campaigning. During the 2002 and 2004 elections, the GOP used a number of new programs, including their much-vaunted 72 Hour Task Force and Strategic Taskforce to Organize and Mobilize People (STOMP) to match or exceed the Democrats' voter mobilization efforts in competitive House and Senate races.[33]

Both parties conducted impressive coordinated campaigns in Colorado to advance their candidates' prospects in races from the top of the ticket to the bottom. Fueled by roughly $891,000 from the DNC, $450,000 from the DSCC, and $57,500 from the DCCC, some money provided by the state party, funds provided by the Salazar campaign, and resources it raised on its own, the Democrats' Colorado Victory 2004 employed thousands of volunteers and hundreds of paid staff supervised out of eleven offices to conduct door-to-door voter identification and mobilization efforts. Similarly, the Republicans' coordinated campaign was fueled by transfers of approximately $819,000 from the RNC and $670,000 from the NRCC to the Colorado state party.[34] The GOP effort involved 8,000 volunteers who canvassed more than 1,000 precincts in order to contact in excess of 200,000 households. In addition to campaigning door-to-door, Republican volunteers made more than 300,000 telephone calls to mobilize the party's rank and file.[35]

Interest groups have a long tradition of working with candidates and political parties to reach out to voters. PACs, 527 committees, and 501(c) organizations, as well as the businesses, labor unions, religious organizations, and other interests that sponsor them, continued this tradition in 2004. These organizations conduct many of the same voter mobilization and grassroots efforts as the parties. Despite the fact that most campaign efforts coordinated by interest groups in 2004 focused on the presidential contest, several took an active role in congressional elections. Evidence drawn from fifteen competitive contests demonstrates that organizations such as the AFL-CIO, America Coming Together, and the LCV on the Democratic side, and the U.S. Chamber of Commerce, the National Right to Life, and Americans for Job Security on the Republican side, undertook considerable coordinated campaign efforts on behalf of House and Senate candidates in hotly contested races. The pro-Democratic groups conducted twenty-six e-mail campaigns, forty mass telephone call drives, and three waves of personal contacts; their Republican counterparts executed two e-mail campaigns, ten telephone drives, and thirteen sets of personal contacts.[36] In addition, a group of at least a dozen organizations, mainly unions, spent almost $10 million on internal communications in 2004 to educate their members about candidates for Congress and other offices.

Some of these groups were active in a number of elections, including the Senate race in Colorado. The LCV had volunteers going door-to-door for seven weeks to help Salazar and Democratic House challenger Dave Thomas. The AFL-CIO conducted a voter identification, education, and mobilization campaign that began about eight months before Election Day and culminated in a get-out-the vote blitz during the last four days of the election. Additional liberal groups that conducted coordinated campaigns include MoveOn.org, which traces its roots to the impeachment of President Bill Clinton, the New Voters Project, which focused on voters eighteen to twenty-four years of age, and America Forward, which targeted Hispanic voters. Conservative groups also were active in the race. Most of their efforts involved direct mail, e-mail, and mass telephone calls rather than door-to-door efforts.[37]

Winners and Losers

What impact did campaign spending have on the outcomes of the 2004 congressional elections? As is usually the case, the candidates who raised and spent the most money typically won, and most of these candidates were incumbents. Because most members of Congress have political clout and a high probability of electoral success, they are able to amass huge war chests, which they use to deter strong challenges and defeat their opponents. Nevertheless, not every incumbent was successful in 2004. Two House incumbents were defeated in their primaries. Another five lost their general elections to challengers, and two incumbents, Martin Frost and Charles Stenholm of Texas, lost to other incumbents in seats that were drastically altered as a result of the special redistricting session called for by Republican majority leader Tom DeLay. Despite the incumbent defeats in Texas and a few others across the country, incumbent House members enjoyed a 98 percent reelection rate in 2004. No senators lost their bids for renomination, and only one senator, Democratic leader Tom Daschle of South Dakota, was defeated in November.

Was money the major determinant of the outcomes of these contests? Probably not. Of the five incumbents who were defeated by a general election challenger, Representative Max Sandlin (Democrat of Texas) was the only one to be outspent by an opponent. Republican challenger Louis Gohmert Jr. outspent Sandlin by about 8 percent, $1,829,275 to $1,690,816. According to most political commentators, the major reason for the defeat was the partisan redistricting effort, which heavily favored a Republican candidate.[38] Moreover, when the election was over, Sandlin still had about $16,000 in campaign funds in the bank. In the one case of an incumbent senator losing to a challenger, Daschle outspent challenger Republican John Thune by a sizable amount, $19,975,170 to $14,660,167. In this case, too, at the end of the race both candidates had plenty of money left in their campaign accounts.

Inasmuch as most of the victorious congressional challengers had fewer resources at their disposal than did their opponents, it is not necessary for a challenger to outspend the incumbent in order to win. Once a challenger's spending reaches a threshold that enables the candidate to become visible among voters, that candidate has the possibility of mounting a viable campaign. Financially competitive challengers can discuss their qualifications for office, publicize issues, hold incumbents accountable, and increase voter interest in elections. These are often the keys to victory.

Conclusion

In many ways, the financing of the 2004 congressional elections resembled the financing of the elections that preceded it, despite the enactment of BCRA. Party committees and ideological PACs, which are strongly committed to electing candidates who share their partisan affiliations or policy views, continued to focus most of their resources on close elections. Access-oriented PACs continued to favor congressional incumbents, especially members of the majority party, because of the incumbents' influence over policymaking and excellent reelection prospects. Individual donors continued to favor incumbents as well, their contributions eluding the grasp of challengers who strongly needed them. The Republicans were the major beneficiaries of these donation patterns because they controlled the House and Senate. Even some labor unions stepped up their contributions to GOP members of Congress.

The elimination of national party soft money fundraising and expenditures forced party committees to depend less heavily on the abilities of party leaders, congressional committee chairs, and other members of Congress to raise huge sums of money from a few wealthy individuals and groups. The parties—and their leaders—thus had to step up their hard money efforts among individual donors. In response, the parties spent record amounts of hard money on independent expenditures. Among interest groups, the new constraints on the use of soft money to finance issue advocacy did not encourage PACs to increase independent expenditures but did persuade some groups, including many recently formed 527 committees, to spend large sums on television advertising before the federal spending period and then switch to other methods of political outreach, including grassroots voter mobilization, during the federal period. Individuals responded in different ways. A small number of extremely wealthy individuals continued to spend millions of dollars in congressional elections by contributing to the 527s. A significant number of well-off donors took advantage of the new contribution limits and gave the legal maximum to their preferred congressional candidates or contributed to other candidates, parties, and PACs. Many first-time donors also made small and not-so-small contributions.

As in previous elections, money influenced several congressional outcomes in 2004. Most incumbents enjoyed substantial financial advantages and were victorious. Nevertheless, not every incumbent outspent his or her challenger, and a few incumbents were defeated. Indeed, several challengers were able to spend sufficient funds, including some of their own money, to successfully deliver their message and win a congressional seat.

Notes

1. Scholars use a variety of measures to gauge the competitiveness of congressional elections. Measures based on the assessments of political journalists late in the campaign season are well suited to predicting the outcomes of these elections.

Because of their timing, however, these measures consider campaigns that were competitive early in the election cycle and later one-sided to be uncompetitive. The measure used here, which categorizes a larger number of campaigns as competitive than does the previous measure (and includes campaigns that were competitive early but not later), is particularly useful for assessing campaign financing because campaign money is raised and spent over the course of an entire election cycle, not just at the end.

2. For information on party goals, strategy, tactics, and contribution patterns, see Paul S. Herrnson, *Congressional Elections: Campaigning at Home and in Washington*, 4th ed. (Congressional Quarterly Press, 2004), chap. 4.

3. For information on PAC goals, strategy, tactics, and contribution patterns, see ibid., chap. 5. For information on individual donors' goals, motives, and strategies, see Peter L. Francia and others, *The Financiers of Congressional Elections: Investors, Ideologues, and Intimates* (Columbia University Press, 2003).

4. Leon Epstein, *Political Parties in the American Mold* (University of Wisconsin Press, 1986), chap. 1.

5. Herrnson, *Congressional Elections*, chap. 6.

6. The term "soft money" was coined by Elizabeth Drew in *Politics and Money: The New Road to Corruption* (New York: Macmillan, 1983), p. 15. See also Herbert E. Alexander and Anthony Corrado, *Financing the 1992 Election* (Armonk, N.Y.: M. E. Sharpe, 1995); and Robert Biersack, "The Nationalization of Party Finance," in *The State of the Parties,* 2nd ed., edited by John C. Green and Daniel M. Shea (Lanham, Md.: Rowman and Littlefield, 1996).

7. Party committees can also contribute $5,000 to candidates in primaries and runoff elections. However, they rarely make financial contributions until the general election.

8. Parties can only make coordinated expenditures for candidates in general elections. The limits for coordinated expenditures in states that have only one House district are twice the level in states with two or more House members. Party coordinated expenditures are indexed for inflation.

9. Federal Election Commission, "Party Financial Activity Summarized for the 2004 Election Cycle," March 14, 2005.

10. Diane Dwyre and Robin Kolodny, "The Parties' Congressional Campaign Committees in 2004," in *The Election after Reform: Money, Politics and the Bipartisan Campaign Reform Act,* edited by Michael J. Malbin (Lanham, Md.: Rowman and Littlefield, 2006).

11. The figures omit unusual elections, such as incumbent-versus-incumbent contests or elections in which candidates quit campaigns or died in the midst of the election season, allowing the reader to compare the distribution of funds in 2004 to previous elections. These can be found in Paul S. Herrnson, "Financing the 1996 Congressional Elections," in *Financing the 1996 Elections,* edited by John C. Green (Armonk, N.Y.: M. E. Sharpe, 1999), pp. 95–126; Paul S. Herrnson and

Kelly D. Patterson, "Financing the 2000 Congressional Elections," in *Financing the 2000 Elections*, edited by David B. Magleby (Brookings, 2002), pp. 106–32; and various editions of Herrnson, *Congressional Elections*.

12. Paul Farhi, "Bunning's Wild Pitches Tighten Kentucky Senate Race," *Washington Post*, October 15, 2004, p. A6.

13. Figure includes contributions to candidates not up for election in 2004.

14. For a discussion of PAC giving strategies, see Theodore J. Eismeier and Philip H. Pollock III, *Business, Money, and the Rise of Corporate PACs in American Elections* (New York: Quorum Books, 1988); Craig Humphries, "Corporations, PACs, and the Strategic Link between Contributions and Lobbying Activities," *Western Political Quarterly* 44 (June 1991): pp. 357–72; and Frank J. Sorauf, *Inside Campaign Finance: Myths and Realities* (Yale University Press, 1992).

15. Francia and others, *The Financiers of Congressional Elections*, p. 23.

16. Ibid., p. 107.

17. Herrnson, *Congressional Elections*, p. 83.

18. Ibid., pp. 72–73, 75.

19. See for example, ibid.,,, chap. 6.

20. Jennifer A. Steen, "Self-Financed Candidates and the 'Millionaires' Amendment,'" in *The Election after Reform*, edited by Malbin.

21. The thresholds for Senate elections vary in accordance with a state's voting-age population. See ibid.

22. *Colorado Republican Federal Campaign Committee* v. *FEC*, 116 S.Ct. 2309 (1996).

23. This figure includes spending in all congressional races, including those atypical races described in note 11.

24. See note 13.

25. Kyle Saunders and Robert Duffy, "The Colorado U.S. Senate Race," in *Dancing without Partners: How Candidates, Parties, and Interest Groups Interact in the New Campaign Finance Environment*, edited by David B. Magleby, J. Quin Monson, and Kelly D. Patterson (Brigham Young University, Center for the Study of Elections and Democracy, 2005), p. 187.

26. Ken Goldstein and Joel Rivlin, "Political Advertising in the 2002 Elections," unpublished manuscript.

27. Steve Weissman and Ruth Hassan, "BCRA and 527 Groups," in *The Election after Reform*, edited by Malbin.

28. David B. Magleby, J. Quin Monson, and Kelly D. Patterson, "Overview," in *Dancing without Partners*, edited by Magleby and others, pp. 57–62.

29. Ibid.

30. Saunders and Duffy, "The Colorado U.S. Senate Race."

31. Raymond J. La Raja, "State and Local Parties," in *The Election after Reform*, edited by Malbin.

32. Ibid. pp. 60–61.

33. See, for example, Herrnson, *Congressional Elections*; and David B. Magleby and Quin J. Monson, "Campaign 2002: The Perfect Storm," press release, National Press Club, November 13, 2005.

34. The NRSC chose not to participate in the Republicans' coordinated campaign in Colorado.

35. Saunders and Duffy, "The Colorado U.S. Senate Race."

36. Magleby and others, *Dancing without Partners,* pp. 60–61.

37. Saunders and Duffy, "The Colorado U.S. Senate Race."

38. "Texas 1," *Capital Eye* (www.capitaleye.org/hotraces.asp?txtState=TX [September 10, 2005]).

SEVEN   *A New Rule Book:*
          Party Money after BCRA

ROBIN KOLODNY AND DIANA DWYRE

For all the challenges of the 2004 elections, political
party organizations at the national, state, and local levels came through
the experience with an impressive adaptability. The long-promised campaign finance reform bill signed into law in March 2002 for the 2004
campaign cycle left party committees facing many uncertainties.
Although they had the law's provisions before them to help guide their
fundraising and expenditure planning, they would spend much of 2003
waiting for court decisions and specific rules from the Federal Election
Commission (FEC) to see if their plans would still be legal. Consequently, the cycle was filled with dire predictions of the effect on the
parties' ability to help their candidates. As this chapter shows, the parties did better than some observers expected, in some cases much better.
Despite the changes in fundraising and spending by the parties in 2004,
they continued to support only candidates in competitive races with an
eye to controlling governmental institutions, as they did in the past.

Fundraising

All party committees involved in federal elections adapted to the Bipartisan Campaign Reform Act (BCRA) by raising more hard money in the
hopes of making up for the loss of soft money, now prohibited. The two
national committees, the Democratic National Committee (DNC) and
the Republican National Committee (RNC), exceeded most expectations in 2004 by raising more in hard money alone than they had

acquired in both hard and soft money previously. This clearly con-
founded critics of BCRA who predicted that the loss of soft money
would weaken the national parties.[1] On the other hand, the congressional campaign committees—the Democratic Congressional Campaign
Committee (DCCC), the National Republican Congressional Committee
(NRCC), the Democratic Senatorial Campaign Committee (DSCC), and
the National Republican Senatorial Committee (NRSC)—did not reach
their previous combined hard and soft money fundraising levels.[2]
BCRA's impact at the state and local level was expected to be "a pro-
nounced reduction of party operations."[3] In fact, state and local party
committees adapted well. When transfers from the national party committees are set aside, Republican state parties raised 17 percent more
hard money in 2004 than they had in 2000, while Democrats raised
only 9 percent less in 2004 than they had in 2000.[4]

Since the 2002 election cycle was the last to be conducted before the
implementation of BCRA's ban on soft money, all of the national party
committees made a big push to collect those last soft money contributions. Thus they probably raised more money in 2002 than they would
have if soft money had not been on its way out.[5] Given this unusual situation, it is not surprising that the House and Senate party committees
fell short of their 2002 overall totals in 2004. The DNC and the RNC
did better in part because 2004 was a presidential election year, and, as
national party committees, they were primarily involved in the presidential contest. As discussed in chapters 1 and 3, the level of donor interest
in the 2004 presidential elections was high. The party committees
turned to individual contributors to help them adapt to the new rules.
The parties expanded and upgraded fundraising efforts, and they were
able to encourage donors to give more according to the higher party
contribution limits established by BCRA.

All of the national party committees did well under the new fundraising rules, particularly if only hard money receipts in other cycles are
considered. Quite notably, the 2004 election cycle marked the first time
since the FECA-mandated reporting requirements that the DNC raised
more than the RNC. Indeed, all of the Democratic Party committees did
exceptionally well against their Republican counterparts, primarily
because of Democratic success at raising both large and small individual
contributions. Many doubted the Democrats' ability to raise much in
small increments, for in the past the DNC had relied heavily on large
hard money contributions and even more on soft money contributions.

In 2004 the Democrats proved critics wrong by raising record amounts in small contributions.

The DNC and the RNC outperformed all other national party organizations. In fact, as shown in table 7-1, by the end of the 2004 election cycle, the DNC and RNC had raised more in hard money alone than they had *ever* raised in hard *and* soft money in the past. These 2004 totals, however, include millions of dollars in leftover presidential primary funds transferred from the Bush and Kerry campaigns to the RNC and DNC. John Kerry's campaign transferred $23.6 million to the DNC, $3 million to the DSCC, and $3 million to the DCCC; George Bush's campaign transferred $26.5 million to the RNC, $1 million to the NRSC, and $1 million to the NRCC.[6] Al Gore also transferred large sums from the money remaining from his 2000 presidential campaign, giving $1 million each to the DSCC and the DCCC and $4 million to the DNC.[7] Yet even if these transfers are subtracted, the national committees still raised almost $100 million more than they had in hard *and* soft money for the last presidential election in 2000. The DNC and the RNC more than made up for the loss of soft money with their successful hard money fundraising.

Even the senatorial campaign committees, which raised significantly less in 2004 than they had in combined hard and soft money in either the 2000 or 2002 election cycles, increased their hard money receipts considerably. The DSCC more than doubled its hard money receipts in 2004 compared with 2000, while the NRSC increased its receipts by more than 50 percent, and for the first time since 1988, the DSCC raised more money than the NRSC.[8] The House campaign committees fared better without soft money than their Senate counterparts. Indeed, the NRCC raised more in hard money in 2004 than it had in hard *and* soft money in 2000, but the committee did not exceed its 2002 hard and soft money receipts. The DCCC almost doubled its hard money receipts in 2004 over its 2000 and 2002 hard money totals, nearly compensating for the loss of soft money. In fact, their hard money receipts for 2004 were only 10 percent less than their hard and soft totals in the 2002 cycle.

State and local parties' hard money fundraising for federal elections was also quite impressive, with both Democratic and Republican state and local committees raising more hard money than they had in the past few election cycles. However, the state parties' total receipts reported to the FEC were down in 2004 because BCRA halted the flow of soft money transfers from the national party committees, which previously

Table 7-1. *National Party Committee Fundraising, 2000–04*[a]
Millions of dollars

Committee	2000			2002			2004	
	Hard	Soft	Total	Hard	Soft	Total	Hard	Total[b]
DNC	124.0	136.6	260.6	67.5	94.6	162.1	394.4	394.4
DSCC	40.5	63.7	104.2	48.4	95.1	143.5	88.7	88.7
DCCC	48.4	56.7	105.1	46.4	56.4	102.8	93.2	93.2
D S&L	149.3		149.3	114.2		114.2	171.2	171.2
Democrats	275.2	245.2	520.4	217.3	246.1	463.4	747.5	747.5
RNC	212.8	166.2	379.0	170.1	113.9	284.0	392.4	392.4
NRSC	51.5	44.7	96.1	59.2	66.4	125.6	79.0	79.0
NRCC	97.3	47.3	144.6	123.6	69.7	193.3	185.7	185.7
R S&L	176.6		176.6	132.5	· · ·	132.5	182.9	182.9
Republicans	465.8	249.9	715.7	441.6	250.0	691.6	840.0	840.0
Total	741.0	495.1	1236.1	761.9	496.1	1258.0	1587.6	1587.6

Source: Federal Election Commission data.

a. Column totals do not include transfers among the committees.

b. The 2004 Democratic totals include $29.6 million in excess primary funds transferred from the Kerry for President Committee ($23.6 million to the DNC, $3 million to the DSCC, and $3 million to the DCCC). The Republican totals include $28.5 million in excess primary funds transferred from the Bush-Cheney '04 Presidential Committee ($26.5 million to the RNC, $1 million to the NRSC, and $1 million to the NRCC).

accounted for as much as 40 percent of state party funds.[9] Note that state parties do not report all of their campaign finance activity to the FEC, only those funds that are for federal or joint federal/nonfederal activity.

Fundraising in a New Environment

Clearly, BCRA did not cripple the parties as some had predicted it might. Rather, it led all of the national party committees to change *how* they raised money to support their campaign activities since under BCRA they were only permitted to raise hard money.[10] The national parties were helped in part by changes in contribution limits. Recognizing that the ban on soft money fundraising could have a detrimental effect on parties and that contribution limits had not been increased since the 1970s, congressional reformers raised the limits on individual hard money contributions to party committees and candidates in the new law.

Before BCRA, an individual contributor could give a national party committee $20,000 a year in hard money, which counted against an individual's annual aggregate contribution limit of $25,000 a year ($50,000 every two years) for all hard money contributions, including those to PACs and candidates. The new law permitted an individual to contribute $25,000 a year to each party committee and established a separate sublimit within the new aggregate individual contribution limit of $95,000 per two-year election cycle of up to $57,500 for all contributions to party committees and PACs, with the remainder ($37,500) constituting the limit on an individual's total contributions to candidates (see chapter 2).

The new law actually established an incentive for individuals to contribute to parties by stipulating that $20,000 of the total aggregate limit for individuals could be given only to political parties.[11] Moreover, for the first time, the contribution limits were now indexed to inflation, so their value will not decrease from one election to the next because of inflation. For the 2006 election cycle, individual contribution limits were adjusted for inflation: individuals will be able to give $26,700 to each national party committee a year and a total of $61,400 to all parties and PACs in the 2006 election cycle.

These higher hard money limits could not completely compensate for the loss of soft money. Political scientist Anthony Corrado notes that even if the 429 soft money donors who gave more than $60,000 in 2000 all gave the maximum $57,500 in hard money in 2004, the parties would raise $100 million *less* from just this small group of donors.[12] Still, maximum amount contributions constituted a larger proportion of hard money than in past elections for all of the national party committees. For example, 12.4 percent of the DNC's individual contributions were at the maximum amount, up from 9.8 percent in 2000; and 17.4 percent of the RNC's were at the maximum, up from 6.5 percent in 2000.[13]

The parties also had raised millions in soft money from corporations, labor unions, and other groups, which they could no longer accept under the new rules. To make up for the millions lost, the parties had to do more than just ask past contributors to give more: they had to find more contributors, lots of them. Both parties' committees, but especially the RNC and the DNC, collected substantially more in contributions of $200 or less than they had in recent elections. The *amount* raised from these small contributors (reported as "unitemized" contributions in FEC filings) went way up, indicating a large increase in the number of small contributors. The DNC raised $166 million from these small contributors for the 2004 election, up from $38 million in 2002 and $60 million in 2000, while the RNC raised $157 million compared with $103 million in 2002 and $91 million in 2000.[14] As table 7-2 shows, all of the national party committees raised more from individuals in 2004 than in past election cycles, and the Democratic committees in particular saw a surge in small contributions. Congressional reformers designed BCRA to sever the link between big soft money givers and elected and party officials, as well as to stimulate growth in individual contributions by raising contribution limits and indexing them to inflation.[15] Fundraising patterns for the 2004 election confirm that their legislative goals were substantially met.

The strategic environment in 2004 was ripe for expanding the contributor base. Democrats were still angry about the 2000 election. A CBS/*New York Times* poll in August 2004 found that "70 percent of registered Democrats still thought that George W. Bush did not win the 2000 election legitimately."[16] Consequently, the Democrats had a natural issue for launching new donor appeals. In turn, the Republicans, particularly the Bush campaign, did not want to be outmobilized by the Democrats as they had been in 2000, and the party highlighted the need to expand its get-out-the-vote (GOTV) efforts, such as the 72 Hour Task Force, to mobilize voters in the last hours before Election Day.[17]

The Democrats needed to gain two seats to control the Senate and only one if they could win the White House (and therefore the vice president's tie-breaking vote). Although the Democrats fielded strong candidates

Table 7-2. *Sources of Receipts for National Party Committees, 2000–04*

Dollars

Year	Committee	Contributions from individuals	Contributions from office-holders and candidates	Contributions from PACs	Transfers from state or other national parties	Total receipts
2000	DNC	112,157,217	1,478,662	2,603,074	2,141,409	123,997,509
	DSCC	17,506,809	1,133,100	4,309,127	4,042,276	40,488,666
	DCCC	21,844,053	11,036,046	4,786,051	1,164,618	48,394,476
	RNC	193,181,420	56,050	1,630,105	11,237,797	212,798,761
	NRSC	33,999,707	2,960,305	4,027,375	2,623,620	51,475,156
	NRCC	67,010,001	14,816,796	4,593,138	4,575,539	97,314,513
2002	DNC	55,623,021	55,113	1,099,514	6,560,050	67,497,257
	DSCC	20,168,297	1,820,984	4,707,156	7,100,082	48,391,653
	DCCC	19,393,788	12,131,368	4,157,049	3,207,213	46,436,093
	RNC	157,825,892	160,250	703,084	3,522,399	170,099,094
	NRSC	41,533,725	1,621,321	4,206,101	6,580,615	59,161,387
	NRCC	79,175,374	14,077,114	4,661,590	4,454,900	123,615,586
2004	DNC	356,975,734	24,063,496	3,038,036	378,869	394,411,997
	DSCC	57,756,029	14,637,708	6,281,744	8,166	88,655,573
	DCCC	50,690,882	23,958,309	6,447,173	652,638	93,168,931
	RNC	350,368,907	26,678,514	2,970,840	4,655,873	392,413,393
	NRSC	60,811,444	3,846,670	7,714,233	501,961	78,980,487
	NRCC	145,858,047	24,247,276	8,595,727	1,204,620	185,719,489

Source: Federal Election Commission, "Party Financial Activity Summarized for the 2004 Election Cycle," press release, March 2, 2005 (www.fec.gov/press/press2005/20050302party/Party2004final.html).

and the Republicans had to recover from some hard-fought primary battles, it was clear to most observers as Election Day approached that the GOP would hang on to the Senate. Control of the House was not really up for grabs, particularly since the Republicans had gained six seats in 2003 with the Texas redistricting, but both parties fought to hold on to what they already had and battled hard over the few competitive and open-seat races (see chapter 6).[18]

The electoral stakes were high, and the new rules meant that the parties had to come up with new ways to wage their electoral battles. Post-BCRA fundraising strategies varied across party committees. Yet there were common approaches to raising more hard money for the 2004 elections: tapping new contributors; asking contributors for additional contributions; mobilizing grassroots supporters to contribute, particularly through the Internet; and relying more on elected officials and politicians for party fundraising.

Investing in Fundraising Paid Off

The parties began preparing for the new law even before it took effect. For instance, the DNC used some of its soft money in 2002 to construct a new party headquarters, saving the millions that had been spent annually to lease office space, and both parties invested heavily in solicitation efforts. The DNC invested approximately $15 million in new computer technology to create a centralized voter contact list and upgrade its Internet fundraising and direct mail capabilities. Informally dubbed "Demzilla" by the party, the database contained information on about 150 million potential voters.[19] The GOP established a similar data program in 2004 called "Voter Vault."[20] However, the RNC began building its database years earlier. During the 2002 congressional and 2003 gubernatorial races (in Kentucky and Mississippi), the GOP's 72 Hour Task Force used "block-by-block data" to register voters and get them to the polls on Election Day.[21]

The parties also improved their voter information files, mostly obtained from the state parties, by combining them with other information, including census data, information bought from private companies, and information acquired from allied groups. The parties thus constructed voter profiles that included data on marital status, educational level, ethnicity, home ownership, organizational affiliations, charitable donations, and recreational pastimes.[22] These robust profiles helped the parties target likely voters and contributors and enabled them to concentrate their efforts in the most efficient and profitable manner, just as corporations have marketed their products using similar computer-generated consumer profiles for some time.

Both parties tapped into the fundraising potential of the Internet. Their websites were set up to accept online contributions. In March of 2002, DNC chairman Terry McAuliffe set a goal of raising $12 million online for the 2004 election, up from the $2 million the party committee had raised online in 2000.[23] The DNC and RNC also developed large e-mail lists of party supporters, which were used to solicit contributions at a much lower cost than traditional direct mail or telemarketing methods. Given the public's increasing use of the Internet for various financial transactions, it is not surprising that the parties and their candidates were able to raise large sums of money in this way. Howard Dean surprised many pundits with his highly successful online fundraising efforts, and the Democratic Party benefited from his success. The quick implementation of online fundraising programs helps to explain the great increase in individual contributions the parties saw in the 2004 cycle. Yet the party committees spent millions on prospecting for online donors, reducing somewhat the efficiency of this fundraising approach.

The parties still raised money in more traditional ways as well—mail, phone, and events. In March of 2002, McAuliffe announced that the party would raise $100 million from direct mail (up from $31 million in 2000).[24] The GOP had long had the edge in direct mail fundraising, but the Democrats began to catch up. McAuliffe invested large amounts in lists to build the DNC's direct mail contacts.

Both national committees also enlisted large donors to raise funds for the presidential nominees. The DNC established the Presidential Trust, to which it directed $25,000-plus contributions and the funds collected by a new group of about 150 big-money fundraisers dubbed the Patriots, each of whom was expected to raise at least $100,000.[25] The RNC tapped into the Bush campaign's Rangers and Pioneers programs, which raised $100,000 and $200,000, respectively, for Bush's reelection effort.[26] The RNC invited them to become Super Rangers, expecting them to raise at least $300,000 for the RNC. Since the new law allows individuals to contribute up to $25,000 to a party committee, this high target was actually easier to reach with fewer contributors than the targets set for the Rangers and Pioneers, who had to raise funds for a candidate in $2,000 increments.[27]

The NRSC created the "Majority Makers" program, in which contributors would be required to give $25,000 (the maximum contribution) and in return would be invited to a private reception at Majority Leader Bill Frist's Washington area home for a meeting with President George W. Bush.[28] The DSCC's Majority Council sought $25,000 contributions from the personal funds of "allied lobbyists and consultants" rather than from the PACs they represent, promising monthly meetings with Senate Democratic leaders in Washington as a reward.[29]

The NRCC invested a reported $55.5 million in telemarketing to expand its small contributor base and thereby enhance its fundraising for House races in 2004 and beyond.[30] By early 2004, the NRCC boasted it had added 500,000 new donors.[31] Of course, these efforts involved some up-front costs that diminished the net returns. In the short run, the costs of new technology, list building, and solicitation reduced their benefits. However, the returns realized during the 2004 election (for example, 500,000 new donors to the NRCC) were apparently large enough to make these efforts worth the expense even in this first election cycle. There will be some recurring costs for each election, such as continuous list development and solicitation and mobilization costs. Yet the major investments in computer technology and advanced software made in 2003–04 will not have to be made again for a while. So in the longer run, these investments should produce even larger benefits. In addition, the parties held events aimed at attracting new low-dollar contributors. In one case, a wealthy Washington, D.C., real estate developer invited about seventy-five of his friends and business associates to his home and asked them for a small contribution for the Republican Party. Most of them were first-time political contributors.[32]

In previous election cycles, state and local party funds for federal elections came primarily from the national party committees, which transferred millions of dollars in hard and soft money to states with competitive federal elections. Much of the money transferred from the national committees was used to do the national committees' bidding, most often to run issue ads on radio and television to help federal candidates. Under BCRA, the state and local party committees were still permitted to raise and spend limited amounts of soft money strictly for voter registration and GOTV activities (see chapter 2). But these limited soft funds had to be raised by the state and local committees themselves; they could not be transferred from the national parties or raised by federal officeholders or party officials. Yet in the 2004 election cycle, state and local parties barely took advantage of these soft money funds, dubbed Levin funds after the sponsor of the provision, Senator Carl Levin (D-Mich.).[33]

However, the state and local parties did raise far more hard money than they had in recent election cycles (see table 7-3). State parties also received some hard money transfers from the national committees to help finance their federal election activities (see table 7-4). Not surprisingly, the three states considered most competitive in the presidential election—Florida, Pennsylvania, and Ohio—had the largest transfers from the national committees to the relevant state party committees.

Table 7-3. *State and Local Party Committee Receipts, 2000–04*[a]
Dollars

Committee	2000	2002	2004
Democratic S&L	71,549,811	75,166,730	105,157,670
Republican S&L	119,052,824	90,167,949	132,428,199

Source: Federal Election Commission, "Party Financial Activity Summarized for the 2004 Election Cycle," press release, March 2, 2005 (www.fec.gov/press/press2005/20050302party/Party2004final.html); Federal Election Commission, "Party Committees Raise More than $1 Billion in 2001–2002," press release, March 20, 2003 (www.fec.gov/press/press2003/20030320party/20030103party.html); Federal Election Commission, "FEC Reports Increase in Party Fundraising for 2000," press release, May 15, 2001 (www.fec.gov/press/press2001/051501partyfund/051501party fund.html).

a. This table includes only federal (hard) activity. These are amounts that the state and local parties raised on their own. The national party transfers were deducted from the Democratic and Republican state and local party receipts.

Sharing the Wealth: Officeholders and Candidates Support Their Parties

Because the law allows candidates and former candidates or officeholders to transfer unlimited amounts from their own campaign accounts to a party committee, party leaders were keen to tap this source of funds. As 2004 DCCC chairman Representative Robert Matsui (D-Calif.) noted, "Money from members is particularly important, because there [are] no costs of fundraising. . . . When a member gives a dollar, that entire dollar is spent on candidates, whereas with direct mail, there's the cost of stamps and printing."[34] The parties benefited greatly from the generosity of their own officeholders and candidates.[35] All of the national party committees raised a great deal more from federal candidates than they had in previous cycles (see table 7-2). As mentioned earlier, the presidential candidates of both parties transferred large amounts to various party committees, mostly from excess primary funds.

Members of Congress proved to be an important source of funding for the parties, especially for the congressional campaign committees and other congressional candidates.[36] While members of Congress have formed leadership PACs for many years and contributed to their parties from their own campaign committees, member giving has recently increased.[37] Officeholders were able to give more in part because BCRA doubled the amount individuals could contribute to candidates, from $1,000 per election (a limit that had remained constant since 1974) to $2,000 per election, and the new law indexed this amount for inflation. Furthermore, since individual contributors are motivated to give more

Table 7-4. *Top Twenty National Party Transfers Totals to State/Local Party Committees, 2003–04*[a]

Dollars

State	RNC	DNC	NRSC	DSCC	NRCC	DCCC	Total
Florida	11,276,106	6,438,728			105,000		17,819,834
Pennsylvania	4,205,909	5,302,210			620,000		10,128,119
Ohio	3,928,102	5,648,745					9,576,847
Michigan	2,050,962	4,909,955					6,960,917
Wisconsin	1,856,212	3,238,205		1,036,000			6,130,417
Colorado	944,281	2,198,434		1,000,000	670,000	75,000	4,887,715
California	1,256,000	333,226		3,000,000	72,500	155,259	4,816,985
Iowa	1,551,985	2,715,054					4,267,039
Alaska	60,000	14,663	192,494	3,402,000			3,669,157
Washington	879,181	1,031,543		1,290,579	352,000	25,000	3,578,303
North Carolina	535,300	661,205	25,000	2,342,600		10,000	3,574,105
Oklahoma	395,562	59,322	371,798	2,625,000			3,451,682
Nevada	1,412,239	1,721,286		55,000	150,000	25,000	3,363,525
New Mexico	447,979	1,786,098			300,000		2,534,077
Louisiana	960,000	576,673	138,940	671,500	175,000		2,522,113
Missouri	854,667	1,067,540		192,000	150,000		2,264,207
Oregon	1,025,539	1,162,542					2,188,081
New Hampshire	885,682	1,263,144					2,148,826
Minnesota	467,129	1,476,779			110,000		2,053,908
South Carolina	310,000	46,174	162,503	1,535,000			2,053,677
Total spent in top twenty races	35,302,835	41,651,526	890,735	17,149,679	2,704,500	290,259	97,989,534
Total spent in all races	43,583,917	47,576,443	1,198,769	17,865,349	5,734,500	632,359	116,591,337
Percent spent in top twenty races	81	88	74	96	47	46	84

Source: Federal Election Commission, "Party Financial Activity Summarized for the 2004 Election Cycle," press release, March 2, 2005 (www.fec.gov/press/press2005/20050302party/Party2004final.html).

a. All national party funds in 2003–04 were "hard money" raised under federal limits.

because of a personal connection to a candidate than they are to the broader concept of party loyalty or party majorities, members can often raise money for elections more easily than parties.[38]

In the early summer of 2004, the DCCC announced that it expected its 186 safe incumbents to transfer some of the $87 million in their campaign accounts to the party committee.[39] The DCCC also called on Democratic House members to pay their party dues, but this time the party was seeking more than the $70,000 to $400,000 it had asked for in the past, hoping to bring in a full one-third of the DCCC's funds this way. Requested contributions depended on one's seniority, committee posts, leadership roles, and fundraising history.[40] For the 2002 election cycle, the average member's contribution to the DCCC was $20,000, an amount significantly lower than the expected 2004 level. By November 2003, Democratic House leaders had already given substantial amounts to their party. Minority leader Nancy Pelosi (D-Calif.) led the way with $320,000 to the DCCC, and Robert Matsui had given $175,000.[41] While members' giving did not ultimately constitute one-third of the DCCC's receipts, in part because the committee raised so much from other sources, it did increase from $12.1 million in the 2002 cycle to $18.3 million in 2004. The NRCC also collected dues, and its members' transfers rose from $13.9 million to $19.4 million. GOP House committee chairpersons were expected to give $25,000 in dues. Representative Christopher Cox (R-Calif.), chair of the Republican Policy Committee, had given $100,000 by November 2003, and House Financial Services Committee chair Mike Oxley (R-Ohio) was up to $100,000 by then as well. The congressional campaign committees are likely to keep the pressure on their members to give to their parties. Whether member contributions to party committees will continue to grow is contingent on whether there is a real fight for the control of Congress. Future growth in such giving is made more likely by the new indexing of contribution limits, which means lawmakers can raise more from individuals each election cycle.

Although the senatorial campaign committees did not levy formal dues, the amount senators gave party committees from their personal campaign committees increased by an impressive 175 percent over 2002, growing from $5.9 million to $16.2 million.[42] DSCC chairman Senator Jon Corzine (D-N.J.), asked rank-and-file Senate Democrats to transfer $50,000 from their campaign accounts or leadership PACs and to raise an additional $100,000 for the party. Senate Democratic leaders were asked to give $100,000 and to raise an additional $250,000.[43]

Some even exceeded these lofty amounts: Charles Schumer of New York gave $2.25 million to the DSCC, Ron Wyden of Oregon gave $2.3 million, and Harry Reid of Nevada gave $1 million. In all, Democratic senators contributed $10.6 million to the DSCC. In contrast, Republican senators combined gave only $2.8 million to the NRSC. The top contribution from a Republican senator, $335,000, came from Mitch McConnell of Kentucky. NRSC chairman George Allen (R-Va.) implemented his "Team Ball" tracking system to keep track of what senators were doing for the party and its candidates and then shared the information with the entire Senate Republican Conference.[44]

Party leaders also tried to persuade retiring members to hand their excess campaign cash over to the party. Democrats had more retiring lawmakers and potentially more to gain from this tactic, but neither party got much from its retiring colleagues. Only three of the thirty-one retiring House members and three of the eight retiring senators gave significant amounts to their parties. From the House, Jennifer Dunn (R-Wash.) gave $386,550, Jim Greenwood (R-Pa.) gave $315,000, and Ed Schrock (R-Va.) gave $221,000. From the Senate, Don Nickles (R-Okla.) gave $465,706, John Breaux (D-La.) gave $254,978, and Ernest "Fritz" Hollings (D-S.C.) gave $273,500.[45]

Party Spending

One of the major reasons for passing BCRA was the lack of accountability in the use of soft money for issue advocacy advertising to help candidates. Because such activities were not considered to be "express advocacy" directly promoting the election or defeat of a federal candidate, parties did not have to specifically itemize the amounts spent on issue advocacy, even though the ads were usually aired in connection with federal elections. Parties were thus able to hide the amounts invested in particular candidates' campaigns, and in some cases what that money was used for. This was particularly true of money transferred to state parties, which were typically governed by inadequate disclosure laws. While records of television and radio spending are generally available to the public, finding out how money was spent on individual communication efforts (the ground war, including direct mail, phone calls, and door-to-door canvassing) is sometimes impossible.[46]

BCRA's elimination of soft money brought two major changes in party spending. First, federal and state expenditures could not be freely mixed. Second, federal expenditures would now be fully disclosed to the FEC. The parties could not rely on the various state laws to determine disclosure. Altogether, BCRA changed the parties' spending activities in the following ways:

—Hard money independent expenditures (IEs) substituted for issue advocacy, financed primarily with soft money.

—Independent expenditures meant limited contact between campaigns and the parties.

—With disclosure, party strategy became more transparent.

Before the 2004 election cycle, political party committees had four ways to spend money to help their candidates: direct contributions (limited, hard money), coordinated expenditures (limited, hard money), independent expenditures (unlimited, hard money), and issue advocacy (unlimited, a mix of soft and hard money). BCRA eliminated the last type of spending. Without soft money, IEs became the best option for helping candidates in competitive races because parties could spend unlimited amounts of hard money. The next few paragraphs explain how all categories of party spending changed.

Contributions

As noted in table 7-5, direct contributions to candidates were modest and resembled contribution patterns in previous cycles—with one exception. The senatorial campaign committees contributed more to candidates. BCRA raised the total amount that party committees could contribute to senatorial candidates from $17,500 to $35,000.[47] Thus contributions increased for most Senate races. Still, $35,000 contributions to multimillion dollar races are hardly significant, meaning that direct contributions accounted for the least important part of party spending.

Coordinated Expenditures

Coordinated expenditures, sometimes called 441a(d) funds after the section in the FECA regulating this activity, are disbursements made by the parties on behalf of candidates with the candidate's knowledge and consent. The expenditure amounts are limited in the law but indexed for inflation using the consumer price index. The limits for the 2004 cycle were $16.2 million for presidential candidates, $37,310 for House candidates, and a range from $74,620 to $1,944,896 for Senate races, depending on the number of persons of voting age in the state.[48] As is

Table 7-5. *How Party Hard Money Was Spent, 2000 and 2004*
Dollars

Party committee	2000				2004			
	Direct contributions	Coordinated expenditures	Independent expenditures	Transfers to states (hard and soft)	Direct contributions	Coordinated expenditures	Independent expenditures	Transfers to states (hard)
DNC	10,215	13,548,520	0	114,647,819	7,000	16,079,570	120,333,466	47,576,443
DSCC	290,530	127,157	133,000	62,975,797	694,500	4,394,396	18,725,520	17,865,349
DCCC	574,765	2,593,614	1,933,246	50,008,554	449,497	2,440,937	36,923,726	632,359
State and local	485,089	4,720,581	243,929	...	653,549	10,198,896	508,984	...
Total	1,360,599	20,989,872	2,310,175	227,632,170	1,804,546	33,113,799	176,491,696	66,074,151
RNC	400,000	23,670,006	0	129,060,394	251,992	16,143,042	18,268,870	43,583,917
NRSC	382,334	172	267,600	31,489,360	812,897	8,449,099	19,383,692	1,198,769
NRCC	698,769	3,696,877	548,800	26,810,663	545,693	3,184,358	47,254,064	5,734,500
State and local	812,647	2,231,910	740,402	...	965,534	1,324,897	3,125,756	...
Total	2,293,750	29,598,965	1,556,802	187,360,417	2,576,116	29,101,396	88,032,382	50,517,186

Source: Federal Election Commission, "Party Financial Activity Summarized for the 2004 Election Cycle," press release, March 2, 2005 (www.fec.gov/press2005/20050302party/Party2004final.html).

typical in a presidential year, both the RNC and the DNC spent nearly the maximum in coordinated expenditures in the presidential race. The senatorial committees spent more in coordinated funds than they had ever done before, while the House committees approached the levels of the 2000 cycle. Again, the change in senatorial committee spending is most noteworthy. In recent pre-BCRA elections, the senatorial committees had decided not to spend coordinated money; rather, they invested in a hard money match of soft money spending in issue advocacy advertising.[49] The DSCC spent about twenty-four times more on coordinated expenditures in 2004 than it had in 2002, and the NRSC spent about fifteen times more.[50]

Independent Expenditures

Party spending in 2004 experienced its greatest change in more independent expenditures, largely as a result of the BCRA ban on soft money. Unlike the pre-BCRA issue ads paid for with a mix of soft and hard money and run mainly through the state parties, independent expenditure communications may expressly advocate the election or defeat of a specific candidate. The party committees used IEs in 2004 directly for electioneering instead of using soft money matched with hard money for issue advertising.[51] The dramatic increases in independent spending reported by all national party committees (see table 7-5) showed that IEs were the parties' preferred mode of spending in this first post-BCRA election cycle.

The RNC and the DNC spent independently for the first time in this election, in accordance with a new regulation issued by the FEC as part of its BCRA rulemaking.[52] Earlier FEC regulations did not allow the DNC and RNC to run a campaign entirely independently of a publicly funded presidential candidate. The national committees took advantage of the new opportunity for independence, with the DNC spending $120 million in IEs for John Kerry and the RNC spending $18 million for George Bush. The RNC expenditure was more modest because of the use of generic or hybrid spending between the RNC and the Bush/Cheney campaign.[53] The RNC believed that it was allowable under federal law for ads to be coordinated with the Bush campaign yet contain language that referred to congressional candidates or Republicans generally. The money spent on these ads was not reported as independent expenditures.[54] The RNC spent $45.8 million on ads of this type in 2004, the DNC $24.0 million.[55]

On the congressional side, the senatorial committees spent similar amounts ($18.7 million for the DSCC and $19.4 million for the NRSC), while the NRCC outspent the DCCC by about $10 million ($47.2 million by the NRCC as opposed to $36.9 million by the DCCC). This extraordinary spending was tightly targeted on a handful of competitive House and Senate races, most of it on express electioneering via television and direct mail.

For Senate races, the $38 million spent independently was concentrated in twelve races, with a million dollars or more spent in eight of these races (see table 7-6). One benefit of IE disclosure is that it offers some sense of how extensive the undisclosed issue advertising efforts must have been before BCRA. For example, $8.3 million was spent by both sides of the U.S. Senate race in Florida through party IEs, or about one-third of what the candidates themselves spent in the entire two-year cycle. The great bulk of this money was spent on television advertising, followed by polling, direct mail, and phone banks. Furthermore, the parties became important players in media advertising in the late months of the election cycle.

On the House side, combined IEs of more than $80 million were concentrated in about thirty races, which meant that the party congressional campaign committees outspent the candidates in some of the most competitive races. The Democratic Party outspent its candidates in seven House races, while the Republicans did so in ten. Democrats won two of these seven races, Republicans five out of ten. In sixty-one races, the party spent $500,000 or more in IEs on its candidate's behalf.[56] Clearly, BCRA did not curtail party spending in competitive races.

Well before BCRA, in the first of two legal challenges involving the Colorado Republican Party, the Supreme Court recognized the right of parties to make IEs.[57] The Court found that existing law did not prohibit the parties from spending unlimited amounts of money to benefit their candidates as long as that money was not *coordinated* with the candidate's campaign but spent wholly independently by the party. One of the major drawbacks of such expenditures is that they must consist solely of hard money. Also, they must be made independently, which poses a significant constraint in that the candidate must not have any knowledge of, or consent to, the electioneering activities the party engages in on his or her behalf. Before BCRA, when party issue ads could be paid for with a mix of soft and hard money, both parties put more emphasis on soft money electioneering because they did not think

Table 7-6. *Party Independent and Coordinated Expenditures in Senate Races, 2003–04*[a]
Millions of dollars

State	Candidates	Party	Win/lose	Party independent expenditures	Party coordinated expenditures	Candidate spending
Alaska	Knowles, Tony	Dem	L	3.05	0.15	5.70
	Murkowski, Lisa	Rep	W	1.82	0.32	5.27
California	*Boxer, Barbara*	Dem	W	0.00	2.80	14.50
	Jones, Bill	Rep	L	0.14	0.39	6.93
Colorado	Coors, Peter	Rep	L	1.99	0.50	7.73
	Salazar, Ken	Dem	W	2.30	0.45	9.56
Florida	Castor, Betty	Dem	L	3.73	1.91	11.14
	Martinez, Mel	Rep	W	4.68	1.95	12.20
Georgia	Isakson, Jhon	Rep	W	0.00	0.16	7.87
	Majette, Denise	Dem	L	0.00	0.33	1.91
Kentucky	*Bunning, Jim*	Rep	W	0.05	0.47	6.04
	Mongiardo, Daniel	Dem	L	0.87	0.41	3.07
Louisiana	John, Chris	Dem	L	1.65	0.18	4.57
	Kennedy, John	Dem	L	0.00	0.00	1.89
	Vitter, David	Rep	W	1.35	0.50	6.99
North Carolina	Bowles, Erskine	Dem	L	2.53	1.47	13.28
	Burr, Richard	Rep	W	2.45	1.11	12.75
Oklahoma	Carson, Brad	Dem	L	2.32	0.58	6.05
	Coburn, Thomas	Rep	W	2.33	0.61	2.94
South Carolina	Demint, James	Rep	W	2.13	0.47	8.85
	Tenenbaum, Inez	Dem	L	3.86	0.24	5.99
South Dakota	*Daschle, Thomas*	Dem	L	0.94	0.15	19.74
	Thune, John	Rep	W	3.26	0.00	14.13
Washington	*Murray, Patty*	Dem	W	0.00	0.00	11.34
	Nethercutt, George	Rep	L	0.02	0.71	7.65

Source: Compiled from FEC Data; Diana Dwyre and Robin Kolodny, "The Parties' Congressional Campaign Committees in 2004," in *The Election after Reform: Money, Politics and the Bipartisan Campaign Reform Act*, edited by Michael J. Malbin (Lanham, Md.: Rowman and Littlefield, 2006), Table 3.2.
a. Incumbent names in italics.

they could cultivate enough donors to raise the same amounts in hard dollars exclusively. The fundraising results in 2004 suggest that this was not the case for either the DNC or the RNC.[58]

Under BCRA, the relationship between the party organizations and their candidates has become increasingly complex. Party committees try to help their candidates directly, working in coordination with them, but they also use electioneering techniques that cannot be coordinated with the candidates. How can parties do both at once? They do it by separating their internal operations to comply with the law. At the NRCC, for example, "the Republicans who handle independent expenditures are cordoned off from the rest of the campaign committee."[59] As a result, the parties make redundant outlays for polls and infrastructure before they make any meaningful IE investment in television ads or mail. As Don McGahn, general counsel of the NRCC, has confirmed:

> Going with independent expenditures causes a lot of . . . redundant spending; double polling, duplicative staff. In our case, . . . the actual dollars that went to the voter . . . at the end of the day, it was not nearly as much money as you would think. . . . We took the position that it made more sense to double poll, although it was much more costly because we really wanted to be able to talk to our campaigns about polling data. So the political division would do a poll, sometimes split the cost of [it with] the campaign, sometimes not, but at least get in a position where there [were] no secrets about what was in the data. . . . The other thing that was tricky was the candidates would occasionally not like the ads that were being run . . . —too negative, this or that—same general complaint . . . to me, the ads were not as punchy or as tight as they had been in prior cycles. Part of that is the coordination issue. It was very difficult to get good footage of candidates, both ones we were supporting and ones we were opposing. In prior cycles, it was easier—we had begun to buy b-roll from campaign staff—they weren't going to use it—in our issue ads. This time, the answer to the question was not nearly as clear.[60]

What proportion of IEs is spent on real campaign efforts rather than on the research required to set up electioneering efforts is not clear. In a few Senate campaigns where the NRSC used independent expenditures, the vast proportion of funds was spent on media advertising: 73 percent in Alaska, 86 percent in North Carolina, and 87 percent in South Dakota. While the percentage spent on polling was about 10 percent or less of outlays, those investments came almost entirely in September and were a necessary precondition of making media buys. Also, one polling firm did all the independent expenditure polls for the NRSC, for a total of $700,767. This is an explicit, added cost of independence.[61] Thus even if the figures devoted to the races might be comparable to pre-BCRA expenditures, less spending probably benefited candidates under independent expenditures. At the same time, issue advocacy spending was less effective, because parties needed to avoid the "magic words" of electioneering and thus could not make direct election appeals.

State Spending

State parties significantly altered their spending in the 2004 elections because of BCRA. They had to separate their money into three streams: federal (hard) money, Levin amendment funds (soft money), and non-federal funds. To participate in national elections, parties could raise hard money under federal guidelines or raise a limited amount of Levin soft money under strict controls, provided they used them only for generic party expenses (voter registration and GOTV efforts) that did not mention a federal candidate. The nonfederal money could only be used for local elections that did not share a ballot with a federal candidate.[62] BCRA "federalized" most campaign activity within 120 days of a federal election, making hard money even more important to the states.[63] Political scientist Raymond La Raja calculates that only $2.8 million of the more than $400 million spent by state parties in the 2004 cycle came from Levin amendment funds. Furthermore, only 17 percent of all state party money spent in 2004 was soft, compared with 62 percent in the 2000 cycle. Anecdotal evidence also indicates that state party staff found the Levin restrictions too daunting to pursue.[64] Future election cycles will tell whether this is true.

Conclusion

BCRA's ban on soft money and its other reforms did not cripple or even significantly weaken the political parties. Party committees at all levels raised more hard money than ever before, even if they did not all completely make up for the loss of soft money. Indeed, the national committees actually raised more hard money in 2004 than they had in hard and soft money combined in previous cycles. The parties adjusted to the new regulatory regime in some creative ways. For example, they effectively tapped into the Internet as a fundraising tool, invested in developing voter/contributor lists and in targeting many more small-dollar donors, capitalized on the increased amount individuals could give to parties, pressured their candidates and officeholders to give more than ever from their personal campaign committees to the party committees, and found new ways to use their money effectively, such as the joint hybrid or generic advertising pioneered by the RNC.

One development generally considered positive is the enhanced effort at party voter registration and mobilization during this election cycle. Reformers had hoped that with fewer avenues to spend their money (for example, no more issue ads funded with soft money), the parties would devote more resources to voter registration and GOTV efforts. As voter identification and contact methods become more high-tech and efficient, the parties may contact groups of voters that normally do not get mobilized and perhaps even increase voter turnout.

Of course, other developments, such as the RNC's hybrid advertising, which seems to get around coordination restrictions, suggest that the parties will still find more capital-intensive rather than labor-intensive ways to communicate with voters, Indeed, the Democrats left much of their voter identification and mobilization to a number of like-minded quasi-party 527 groups, such as America Coming Together. If the 527 groups continue to carry out "traditional" party activities, but without any of the accountability to which the parties might be subject, congressional reformers and their allied interest groups may well push and gain support for tougher regulation of these groups. As the 2004 election shows, campaign finance reform is inherently subject to unintended consequences—which is why continuous adjustment is necessary.

Notes

1. See for example, Raymond La Raja, "Why Soft Money Has Strengthened the Parties," in *Inside the Campaign Finance Battle: Court Testimony on the New Reforms,* edited by Anthony Corrado, Thomas E. Mann, and Trevor Potter (Brookings, 2003), pp. 69–96; Mitch McConnell, "Role of Federal Officials in State Party Fund-Raising," in *Inside the Campaign Finance Battle,* edited by Corrado and others, pp. 143–46; and Sidney Milkis, "Parties versus Interest Groups," in *Inside the Campaign Finance Battle,* edited by Corrado and others, pp. 40–48.

2. Diana Dwyre and Robin Kolodny, "The Parties' Congressional Campaign Committees in 2004," in *The Election after Reform: Money, Politics and the Bipartisan Campaign Reform Act,* edited by Michael J. Malbin (Lanham, Md.: Rowman and Littlefield, 2006).

3. Sidney M. Milkis, Rebuttal Declaration in *RNC v. FEC*, District Court Testimony (www.campaignlegalcenter.org/attachments/739.pdf).

4. Raymond La Raja, "State and Local Political Parties," in *Life after Reform: When the Bipartisan Campaign Reform Act Meets Politics*, edited by Michael J. Malbin (Lanham, Md.: Rowman and Littlefield, 2003).

5. Federal Election Commission, "Party Fundraising Reaches $1.1 Billion in 2002 Election Cycle," news release, December 18, 2002; and Diana Dwyre and Robin Kolodny, "National Parties after BCRA," in *Life after Reform,* edited by Malbin.

6. Federal Election Commission, "Party Financial Activity Summarized for the 2004 Election Cycle," news release, March 2, 2005 (www.fec.gov/press/press2005/20050302party/Party2004final.html [20 September 2005]); Paul Kane, "Kerry Transfers Surplus Money," *Roll Call*, September 22, 2004.

7. Chris Cillizza, "Gore Steers $6 M to '04 campaign," *Roll Call*, April 29, 2004.

8. David B. Magleby, J. Quin Monson, and Kelly D. Patterson, eds., *Dancing without Partners: How Candidates, Parties and Interest Groups Interact in the New Campaign Finance Environment* (Brigham Young University, Center for the Study of Elections and Democracy, 2005).

9. Suzanne Nelson, "BCRA Cuts into State Committee Coffers," *Roll Call*, May 26, 2005.

10. Note that under BCRA state and local parties are permitted to raise limited amounts of soft money on their own (not as transfers from national party committees or from fundraising by federal officials). These state and local soft money funds, called Levin funds, are discussed later.

11. David B. Magleby, J. Quin Monson, and Kelly D. Patterson, "Overview," in *Dancing without Partners,* edited by Magleby and others, p. 13.

12. Anthony Corrado, "Party Finance in the Wake of BCRA: An Overview," in *The Election after Reform*, edited by Malbin.

13. Federal Election Commission, "Party Financial Activity Summarized for the 2004 Election Cycle," news release, March 14, 2005.

14. Ibid.

15. Harvard University, John F. Kennedy School of Government's Institute of Politics, *Campaign for President: The Managers Look at 2004* (Lanham, Md.: Rowman and Littlefield, 2006), pp. 238–39.

16. Magleby and others, "Overview," p. 9.

17. David B. Magleby and J. Quin Monson, eds., *The Last Hurrah? Soft Money and Issue Advocacy in the 2002 Congressional Elections* (Brookings, 2004).

18. Magleby and others, "Overview," p. 11.

19. Chris Cillizza, "Critics Slam 'Demzilla'; DNC Defends Vast Voter, Donor ID Project," *Roll Call*, June 5, 2003.

20. Paul Farhi, "Parties Square Off in a Database Duel; Voter Information Shapes Strategies," *Washington Post*, July 20, 2004, p. A1.

21. Ibid.

22. Ibid.

23. Charles Lane and Thomas B. Edsall, "Campaign Finance Fight Not Over; Having Lost on Hill, Opponents Prepare Court Challenge," *Washington Post*, March 22, 2002, p. A04.

24. Ibid.

25. Sharon Theimer, "Democrats Start Presidential Fund," Associated Press Online, January 31, 2003.

26. Jonathan Kaplan, "RNC Offers 'Super Ranger' Status," *The Hill*, May 18, 2004.

27. Ibid.

28. Sharon Theimer, "Bush Raises Cash for Senate GOP Members," Associated Press Online, March 2, 2004.

29. Alexander Bolton, "The NRCC Closes in on $1M," *The Hill*, April 1, 2004.

30. Chris Cillizza and Ethan Wallison, "NRCC Touts Alliance with Infocision," *Roll Call*, November 29, 2004.

31. Alexander Bolton, "Meet the Leader, Only $25K: Senate Dems Sell Lobbyists Access for the Maximum," *The Hill*, April 29, 2004.

32. Eliza Newlin Carney, "In the Money," *National Journal*, July 10, 2004.

33. La Raja , "State and Local Political Parties."

34. Carney, "In the Money," p. 2170.

35. Marian Currinder, "Campaign Finance: Funding the Presidential and Congressional Elections," in *The Elections of 2004,* edited by Michael Nelson (Congressional Quarterly Press, 2005), pp. 127–28.

36. Dwyre and Kolodny, "The Parties' Congressional Campaign Committees."

37. Anne H. Bedlington and Michael J. Malbin, "The Party as an Extended Network: Members Giving to Each Other and to Their Parties," in *Life after Reform*, edited by Malbin.

38. Peter L. Francia and others, *The Financiers of Congressional Elections: Investors, Ideologues, and Intimates* (Columbia University Press, 2003).

39. Erin P. Billings, "Buoyed DCCC Raises Money Goal," *Roll Call*, June 22, 2004; see also Carney, "In the Money."

40. Carney, "In the Money," p. 2170.

41. Alexander Bolton, "Republicans Won't Escape Town before Paying 'Dues,'" *The Hill*, November 6, 2003.

42. Dwyre and Kolodny, "The Parties' Congressional Campaign Committees."

43. Carney, "In the Money," p. 2171.

44. Federal Election Commission, "Party Financial Activity Summarized for the 2004 Election Cycle," press release, March 2, 2005 (www.fec.gov/press/press2005/20050302party/Party2004final.html).

45. Dwyre and Kolodny, "The Parties' Congressional Campaign Committees."

46. See Magleby and others, *Dancing without Partners*.

47. U.S. Code, title 2, chap. 14, sec. 441a(h).

48. These figures effectively doubled because of agency agreements, written permissions from the RNC and the DNC, and the "federal" state party committees that allow the DSCC, the NRSC, the DCCC, and the NRCC to raise and spend coordinated funds on their behalf. The law only states that the RNC, DNC, and state party committees may make these expenditures; thus the CCCs may act as their agents. For more details, see Robin Kolodny, *Pursuing Majorities: Congressional Campaign Committees in American Politics* (University of Oklahoma Press, 1998). Also Federal Election Commission, "2004 Coordinated Party Expenditure Limits," *FEC Record* 30 (March 2004): 15.

49. See Diana Dwyre and Robin Kolodny "Throwing Out the Rule Book: Party Financing of the 2000 Elections," in *Financing the 2000 Election*, edited by David B. Magleby (Brookings, 2002), pp. 145–46.

50. Federal Election Commission, "Party Financial Activity Summarized for the 2004 Election Cycle," news release, March 14, 2005b.

51. Michael Malbin, "Assessing the Bipartisan Campaign Reform Act," in *The Election after Reform*, edited by Malbin.

52. See 69 *Fed. Reg.* 63919.

53. Michael M. Franz, Joel Rivlin, and Kenneth Goldstein, "Much More of the Same: Television Advertising Pre- and Post-BCRA," in *The Election after Reform*, edited by Malbin.

54. Corrado, "Party Finance in the Wake of BCRA."

55. Ibid., table 2.2.

56. Kolodny and Dwyre, "The Parties' Congressional Campaign Committees."

57. *Colorado Republican Federal Campaign Comm.* v. *Federal Election Commission*, 518 U.S. 604 (1996).

58. William Crotty, "Financing the 2004 Presidential Election," in *A Defining Moment: The Presidential Election of 2004*, edited by William Crotty (Armonk, N.Y.: M. E. Sharpe, 2005), pp. 87–107.

59. Peter Savodnik, "Democrats Cancel Ad Buy in Colo.," *The Hill*, September 28, 2004.

60. Donald McGahn, Comments to the Campaign Finance Institute, National Press Club, Washington, January 14, 2005.

61. Calculation by the authors from FEC data in March 2, 2005, press release.

62. La Raja, "State and Local Political Parties."

63. Sarah M. Morehouse, "State Parties Adjust to BCRA," paper prepared for the Annual Meeting of the Midwest Political Science Association, Chicago, April 7–10, 2005.

64. La Raja, "State and Local Political Parties."

EIGHT

Interest Groups and
Financing the 2004 Elections

ALLAN J. CIGLER

From the nation's beginning, political campaigns
have been a focal point for those interests that understood their fortunes
were dependent upon helping elect public officials sympathetic to their
values and policy preferences. But until relatively recently, that assistance was not typically delivered via widespread and organized group
participation in electoral activities. The groups that did participate were
ordinarily content to simply endorse candidates, encourage their members to vote and get involved in campaigns, and to contribute money to
parties and candidates. Organized interests historically have been sub-
servient to parties and candidate campaign organizations, supportive,
but normally not engaged in electioneering independently directed at the
broader electorate.

The pattern of group involvement in elections changed markedly
beginning in the late 1960s and early 1970s.[1] A number of factors contributed to the new trend. Most central was the expansion of government lawmaking and regulatory activity that raised the stakes of politics, creating incentives for groups of all kinds to participate in elections.
They were also encouraged by the electoral process itself, including
party nomination activity, which became more penetrable. By 2000,
there had been an impressive increase in the breadth and intensity of
group involvement in electoral politics. This escalation of activity was
accompanied by a huge rise in the amount of funds devoted to electoral
purposes, often independent of party and candidate campaign efforts.

The magnitude of spending by special interests to influence elections has been and remains especially controversial, contributing to widespread political cynicism among the electorate.[2] At base, the U.S. system of private funding of campaigns poses the dilemma of having to choose between two fundamental democratic values in conflict: the freedom to express political opinions and political equality. While the right to express political preferences and opinions is constitutionally protected, there is little doubt that the unequal distribution of wealth and resources enables financially advantaged interests to distort the "one person, one vote" principle that underlies political equality. Governments historically have tended not to intervene by limiting political expression during campaigns, but recent decades have elevated the status of political equality as a value to be protected and enhanced; campaign finance reform has periodically become part of the political agenda as a consequence.

The 2004 federal elections were the first held under the Bipartisan Campaign Reform Act (BCRA) of 2002. Like previous reform efforts, the new law was crafted with the explicit intention of curbing the excessive influence of moneyed interests in elections. The 2004 election can be viewed as the first test case of the new law's effectiveness. The analysis that follows suggests that for some groups it remained politics as usual. But the impact of the new law was clearly not neutral and altered the electoral landscape. The universe of group participants changed, as a few organized interests decreased their involvement or withdrew entirely from participation. On the other hand, a number of important new groups were formed in response to the new law and became major factors during the campaign. Almost all groups found that BCRA had an effect on their campaign strategies and tactics.

On the positive side, election activity by organized interests was better disclosed and grassroots participation was greater than it had been when issue advocacy by parties and groups was more prevalent. Party officers and elected officials were effectively banned from raising the unlimited contributions that came to be allowed under the old law (see chapter 7). Efforts to decrease the role of big money in elections were far less successful, however, as the upward spiral of large investments by special interests in federal elections continued, especially the investments of ideological interests. Organized interests with resources continued to have a powerful effect on election outcomes.

BCRA: A New Context for Group Involvement in Elections

BCRA was the first major campaign finance law enacted since the passage of the Federal Election Campaign Act (FECA) and its subsequent amendments in the 1970s. The original intent of the FECA, like BCRA, was to decrease the role of well-financed interests in elections and to inform the public of all campaign transactions. Unfortunately for reformers, the Supreme Court decision in *Buckley* v. *Valeo,* as well as later interpretative rulings by the Federal Election Commission (FEC), undermined much of the intent. Particularly troubling was the huge escalation of group fundraising and campaign spending not regulated by the FEC, much of it shielded from public scrutiny. One leading student of money and politics was led to remark after the 2000 election that the state of campaign finance "bore a greater resemblance to campaign finance prior to the passage of the FECA than to the patterns that were supposed to occur after it."[3]

Two so-called loopholes in existing law formed the crux of the problem. The first had to do with "soft money," or money contributed to national party committees for nonfederal election activity (see chapter 7). The major soft money donors to the party committees were organized groups, including unions and corporations that were allowed to contribute general treasury funds. Such funds had otherwise been banned from political contributions for decades. By the 2000 elections, soft money donations were the fastest growing form of organized interest money contributed in elections.[4] The largest contributions came from organizations such as individual corporations; single contributions frequently exceeded $1 million. In the 2000 election cycle, soft money contributions to national party committees had reached nearly half a billion dollars, even outstripping hard money contributions to candidates from political action committees (PACs). Such contributions, at a minimum, appeared unseemly, creating the impression that parties and their candidates were being bought by special interests.

The biggest soft money contributions were made typically by corporations or individuals connected to businesses, presumably for access reasons; not so subtle coercion by party and elected officials was apparently part of the process as well. From the perspective of many organized interests, if soft money was to be banned, resources could be freed up for other election activities where organizations had more direct control.

The second "loophole" dealt with issue advocacy electioneering.[5] The Supreme Court, in a footnote in the 1976 *Buckley* v. *Valeo* decision, outlined what came to be called its express advocacy guidelines. According to the Court's decision, the provisions of the FECA would apply only to communications expressly advocating the election or defeat of a candidate, using such terms and phrases as "vote for," "elect," "support," "cast your ballot for," "Smith for Congress," "vote against," "defeat," and "reject."[6]

It was more than two decades after *Buckley* before organized interests fully recognized the opportunities offered by the express advocacy standard, namely, that they could participate in more direct ways, campaigning for or against a candidate, if they simply avoided using the so-called magic words outlined in *Buckley*.[7] As long as these words were avoided, sponsoring organizations could claim the communication was merely an "issue ad," beyond the scope of government regulation, including required disclosure of donors or limitations on amounts spent.

These issue ads typically provided a picture of one or both of the candidates, sometimes in a positive but more often in a negative light. The identity of the group sponsoring the ad was often masked by an innocuous group name, and donor identities did not have to be disclosed, which provided groups engaged in issue advertising with a great advantage in raising money for hard-hitting negative ads. Rather than encourage voters to vote for or against a candidate, ads ordinarily asked viewers to write or call a candidate to register their support or opposition to his or her policy actions or pronouncements. There was no secret about the intent of the ads. The positive or negative tone toward the targeted candidate has been shown to be virtually indistinguishable from that of express advocacy ads issued by parties or candidates through television, radio, campaign flyers, or phone calls.[8]

Issue advocacy spending often consisted of big donations from organized interests. In 2000 one advocacy organization, Citizens for Better Medicare, a group representing the pharmaceutical industry, though this was not noted in the ads, had spent an estimated $65 million on issue ads alone.[9]

From the perspective of many interest groups, the attempt to eliminate or modify electioneering issue advocacy was not a good move. Some said any effort to set standards for campaign ads raised serious First Amendment objections. Others, such as the Cato Institute and American Civil Liberties Union, normally at different ends of the political spectrum, were philosophically opposed to any form of government intrusion on free expression. Still other equally diverse groups had been avid practitioners of electioneering issue advocacy, among them the

AFL-CIO, the National Rifle Association (NRA), the U.S. Chamber of Commerce, the Christian Coalition, and National Right to Life.[10] Like incumbent politicians, such groups do not like uncertainty, and many had come to view issue advocacy electioneering as an essential instrument in their arsenal of tactics to influence elections. Support for change came from a reform coalition, which included academics and public interest groups such as Common Cause and Public Citizen.[11]

Reform interests finally prevailed, however, and on March 27, 2003, President George W. Bush, calling the bill "flawed," signed BCRA into law, which was quickly challenged in the courts.[12] In December 2003, in *McConnell* v. *Federal Election Commission,* a divided Supreme Court upheld virtually all major provisions of the law, including the sections banning soft money contributions to the parties and those setting new standards for campaign advertising by organized interests.[13] Rejecting the "express advocacy" guidelines, the act set a new standard concerning the *content* of election-related political communications and the *period in which* organized interests could engage in advocacy electioneering. "Electioneering communication" was defined as any broadcast, cable, or satellite communication that referred to a clearly identified federal candidate within thirty days of a primary or within sixty days of a general election and was "accessible by" 50,000 or more persons in a district or state where a federal election is being held.

Under the new law, corporations and unions may form PACs and engage in hard money expenditures regulated by the FEC, but they are forbidden from using unregulated money from their corporate accounts or labor union treasuries to either directly or indirectly finance electioneering communications. Nonprofit corporations and incorporated political committees defined by section 527 of the Internal Revenue Code are covered as well.

Disclosure provisions of BCRA are more comprehensive than those of the FECA. Groups engaging in electioneering communications are required to file a disclosure report within one day of having spent an aggregate of $10,000 and to file a new report each time an additional $1,000 is spent. They also have to disclose the names of all donors contributing more than $1,000. The clear intent of BCRA was to lessen issue advocacy electioneering by organized interests near an election and outside of the hard money regulations of the FEC. But such restraints did not significantly reduce the role of organized interests in federal elections. Both regulated and unregulated funds were still raised and spent in a variety of ways, as groups either shifted their financial tactics or, in a number of cases, adopted organizational approaches that facilitated evasion of FEC regulation.

Interest Group PAC Contributions in 2004

The attempt to control the financial excesses of special interests in elections by encouraging them to channel hard money contributions to candidates through PACs, where contributions are limited and disclosure complete, was at the heart of the FECA and remained unchanged in BCRA. In a real sense, BCRA aimed to return campaign finance activities to where they had been before the early 1980s, when the soft money and electioneering issue advocacy loopholes were not yet being exploited, and when limited, disclosed hard money largely underwrote campaigns.

The guidelines under which PACs operate are pretty straightforward. PACs may raise unlimited funds for electoral purposes, but they face constraints on their direct contributions. They must disclose their donors and the recipients of their contributions and must file detailed reports periodically with the FEC. PACs are limited to contributing a maximum of $5,000 in a primary, $5,000 for each general election contest, and $5,000 in the case of a runoff election. Contributions may be made up to a total of $5,000 to a candidate in the presidential nomination contests and another $5,000 in the general election if the candidate elects not to accept public funding. Any registered multicandidate PAC may contribute up to $15,000 a year to each of the three Republican and Democrat national party committees; a non-multicandidate PAC may contribute even more ($25,000) to each. After 2004 this latter limit was adjusted for inflation. PACs may further increase their influence in elections by using hard money to engage in unlimited "independent spending," on behalf of or against a candidate as long as such efforts are not coordinated in any way with the preferred candidate or their representatives. This independent electioneering includes express advocacy advertising.

On its face, the passage of BCRA appears to enhance the PAC vehicle as a tool that organized interests can use to influence elections. With soft money contributions to the national parties outlawed, it is logical to expect some organizations to use the previously targeted funds to strengthen their PAC activity. It is also reasonable to think that the number of PACs might grow.

Yet in 2004 the PAC universe and strategies of group behavior experienced relatively modest changes, particularly in the patterns of campaign contributions. A number of interrelated factors were probably involved, most having to do with the competitive context of the presidential race during the 2004 elections. At base, PACs are largely vehicles that target congressional rather than presidential elections. Presidential candidates spend more of their time pursuing individual contributions since during the nomination season PAC contributions are not eligible for federal matching funds. And because BCRA raised individual contribution limits from $1,000 to $2,000, presidential candidates had an even greater incentive to seek individual contributions in 2004. Further, groups were probably less inclined to expand their efforts in congressional elections owing to the lack of competition in most individual congressional races in 2004 coupled with the fact that the Republicans were unlikely to relinquish their majority position in either the House or the Senate.

Still, PACs remained an important component of the campaign finance system.[14] Since the mid-1980s, the number of registered federal PACs has ranged from roughly 4,000 to 5,000. In the 2000 election cycle, 4,499 registered PACs were on the FEC books for at least part of the cycle. The number of PACs rose to 4,867 in 2004, and PAC contributions to candidates increased substantially, though not nearly as rapidly as overall spending on federal elections. In 2004 PACs made $310.5 million in direct contributions, a 19 percent increase over the previous presidential election and a 10 percent increase over the 2002 congressional year cycle. The growth in aggregate PAC contributions since the 1980 election cycle is presented in figure 8-1.

The overwhelming business bias in PAC contributions remained unchanged. Corporate PACs contributed over $115 million in the election, while trade associations contributed over $82 million; together this represented more than 63 percent of all PAC contributions. Labor PACs contributed $52.1 million, in the aggregate a mere half a million more than in 2000. For the first time, nonconnected PACs, usually issue- or ideologically oriented organizations set up to influence elections, outspent labor by contributing nearly $52.5 million to their preferred candidates. The "other" PAC category, which includes corporations without stock and cooperatives, contributed a little more than $7 million in the aggregate. Overall, PAC contributions by corporations grew by 26 percent in real dollars over the 2000 election, while independent PAC contributions increased by 37 percent. On the other hand, labor PAC contributions grew less than 1 percent.

PAC contributions to Republican and Democratic candidates in the 2004 election cycle continued the pattern that developed after the 1994

Figure 8-1. *PAC Candidate Contributions, 1979–80 to 2003–04*

Total in millions

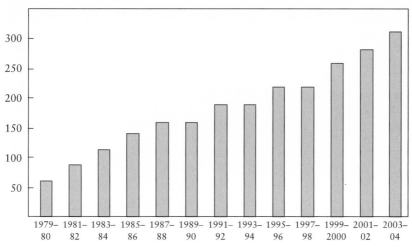

Source: Federal Election Commission, "PAC Activity Increases for 2004 Elections," press release, April 13, 2005 (www.fec.gov/press/press2005/20050412pac/PACFinal2004.html [April 2005]).

election, when Republicans first took control of both the House and the Senate. With more incumbents in Congress having majority status, Republicans have done increasingly well in raising PAC money over the past decade (see table 8-1).

The pattern for incumbents is also favorable. In the House, 83 percent of PAC contributions went to incumbents, and in the Senate 67 percent. Republican senatorial candidates garnered nearly $43 million in PAC contributions in 2004, while Democrats received a little over $33 million. In the aggregate, House Republican candidates in 2004 received over $30 million more in PAC contributions than their Democratic counterparts, the Republicans receiving $130.7 million and the Democrats $100.5 million. Overall, candidates for the House received $231.2 million from PACs in 2004, while Senate candidates received $76 million; each figure represents a 9 percent increase over the 2000 election. The $173.5 million received by Republican Senate and House candidates represented a nearly 24 percent increase over 2000. The House and Senate candidates for the Democrats received $134 million, which represented a mere 4 percent increase from 2000.

The overall incumbent bias of the PAC universe can obscure major differences in the giving behavior of the various types of PACs. Corporate

Table 8-1. *PAC Contributions to Candidates and Parties,*
2000 and 2004

Millions of dollars

Candidate/party	2000			2004		
	Democratic	Republican	Total	Democratic	Republican	Total
Senate	20.5	36.4	56.9	33.2	42.8	76.0
Incumbents	10.4	26.3	36.7	23.8	27.7	51.5
Challengers	5.7	2.1	7.8	2.1	3.5	5.6
Open seat	4.4	8.0	12.4	7.3	11.6	18.9
House	107.6	103.9	211.5	100.5	130.7	231.2
Incumbents	83.4	81.3	164.7	82.6	110.2	192.8
Challengers	14.2	7.7	21.8	8.7	7.3	16.0
Open seat	10.1	14.9	25.0	9.2	13.3	22.5
Presidential	0.0	2.2	2.2	1.0	2.0	3.0
Political parties	30.7	28.9	59.6	15.8	15.3	31.1

Source: Federal Election Commission, "PAC Activity Increases for 2004 Elections," press release, April 13, 2005 (www.fec.gov/press/press2005/20050412pac/PACFinal2004.html).

PACs, for example, tend to be both access-oriented and risk averse. In 2004 nearly 92 percent of their contributions went to incumbents, with only a little more than 2 percent going to challengers and 6 percent contributed in open-seat races. Trade associations followed a similar pattern, with nearly 88 percent of their funds going to incumbents. Labor PACs gave 77 percent of their funds to incumbents, with 12 percent going to challengers and nearly 11 percent invested in open-seat contests. The percentage of money going to incumbents from labor PACs was a record high, perhaps because so few contests were genuinely competitive. Only PACs in the "nonconnected" category, typically issue or ideological groups, are somewhat willing to invest in challengers. In 2004 over 17 percent of PAC money from such groups went to challengers, while nearly 22 percent was invested in open-seat races.

As table 8-1 indicates, PAC contributions to presidential contenders are a small proportion of the giving totals. But organized interests may be involved in funding presidential campaigns in more indirect ways. For example, many of the individual contributors to the presidential campaigns are closely connected to business interests, serving as CEOs, members of the board, or holding positions as major company officers.

The most significant difference between PAC contributions in 2004 and those in previous years was the steep decline in direct contributions to the national political party committees. PACs contributed only $31.1

million in 2004, down sharply from the $59.6 million that went into party coffers in the 2000 cycle. The decline may reflect in part the ban on soft money, which prohibited PAC gifts in excess of the federal limit. No doubt the decline was at least somewhat due to incentives for interest groups to contribute to the 527 committees, discussed later in the chapter.

Since the beginning of the PAC system in the 1970s, group giving has remained highly concentrated among a rather small proportion of PACs. The 2004 election was no exception. Forty-eight PACs, or less than 1 percent of the number registered, contributed over $1 million each in the election, which came to slightly over 25 percent of all money contributed. Of the forty-eight, twenty-one were labor PACs, ten were corporate PACs, and fifteen were affiliated with trade associations. Only two nonconnected PACs contributed more than $1 million; in fact, fifty-two of the groups in this category contributed nothing in the election cycle. Nonconnected PACs are at somewhat of a disadvantage. Unlike corporate, trade association, or labor PACs, which can fund their overhead from the parent organization, nonconnected PACs, by law, must fund their entire operation from donor contributions, leaving less money for direct contributions to candidates.

Forty-five percent of all PACs that contributed gave less than $100,000. Sixty-three percent of the total contributions came from the select group of 296 PACs that each contributed $250,000 or more: this group represents just 6 percent of the total number of registered PACS. Overall, one-third of all PACs, 1,648 registered organizations, made no direct contributions during the 2004 election cycle.

The top twenty PAC contributors in the 2004 elections are presented in table 8-2. The list looks roughly the same as it has for most recent elections. Heading the list is the National Association of Realtors Political Action Committee, which contributed nearly $3.8 million, almost exclusively to Republican incumbents. Both blue- and white-collar unions, which traditionally overwhelmingly favor Democrats, are found throughout the list. All of the top twenty contributing PACs gave disproportionately to one of the two major parties and all were largely incumbent-oriented. None of the more issue-oriented PACs were among the top twenty PACs in terms of contributions.

By themselves, however, the direct contributions of registered PACs greatly understate the influence of some organizations in today's federal elections, especially the more issue-oriented PACs. For example, PACs

Table 8-2. *Top Twenty PAC Contributors to Candidates, 2003–04*
Dollars

Rank	Name	Contributions
1	National Association of Realtors PAC	3,771,083
2	Dealers Election Action Committee of the National Automobile Dealers Association (NADA)	2,584,800
3	International Brotherhood of Electrical Workers Committee on Political Education	2,304,600
4	National Beer Wholesalers Association PAC	2,289,000
5	Laborers' Political League-Laborers' International Union of NA	2,249,000
6	Build PAC of the National Association of Home Builders	2,221,500
7	Association of Trial Lawyers of America PAC	2,170,499
8	United Parcel Service Inc. PAC	2,139,929
9	American Medical Association PAC	2,077,899
10	UAW-V-CAP (UAW Voluntary Community Action Program)	2,065,200
11	Credit Union Legislative Action Council of CUNA	2,005,385
12	Service Employees International Union Committee on Political Education (SEIU COPE)	1,929,000
13	Machinists Non-Partisan Political League	1,905,000
14	Drive (Democrat Republican Independent Voter Education) PAC for Int'l Brotherhood of Teamsters	1,890,441
15	Carpenters Legislative Improvement Committee United Brotherhood of Carpenters and Joiners	1,890,000
16	American Bankers Association PAC (BANKPAC)	1,809,845
17	SBC Communications Inc. Employee Federal PAC (SBC EMPAC)	1,787,116
18	American Hospital Association PAC	1,739,901
19	American Federation of Teachers AFL-CIO Committee on Political Education	1,700,322
20	NEA Fund for Children and Public Education	1,666,400

Source: Federal Election Commission, "PAC Activity Increases for 2004 Elections," press release, April 13, 2005 (www.fec.gov/press/press2005/20050412pac/PACFinal2004.html).

can make "in-kind" contributions to candidates and parties in a variety of forms, such as sharing poll results, training candidates in how to conduct their campaigns, or permitting candidates to use their phone bank facilities, at assigned costs far below the real market value.

In 2004 a number of registered PACs that made no direct contributions at all were still extensively involved in electoral politics. Under FEC regulations, PACs must not only list their contributors and direct contributions but also provide data on their receipts and disbursements for each election cycle. During the 2004 elections, MoveOn.org, an organization formed by progressive interests to help defeat President Bush, was the leading PAC in terms of FEC-reported money raised and spent (over $30 million dollars) yet made no direct contributions to any candidate. The PAC was an electoral arm of MoveOn.org, an Internet organization with reportedly two million or more members, which was originally formed (in 1995) to muster support for President Bill Clinton during the impeachment process. Their funds were largely used in concert with other progressive organizations to get likely anti-Bush voters to turn out by running independent expenditure ads and setting up a variety of vehicles outside of the FEC rubric to influence the election, most notably those in the 527 category.

The second leading PAC in terms of reported receipts and disbursements in 2004 was EMILY's List, which raised and spent a reported $26 million on the election. The group was founded in 1985 in order to give seed money to pro-choice Democratic women candidates, and it continues to make direct contributions to such candidates. The group is particularly adept at making in-kind contributions: sponsoring fundraising and meet-and-greet events for candidates, holding campaign training sessions for them, and providing support with polling and other research needs. The group is probably best known for its ability to get around the direct contribution limits that govern PACs. It engages heavily in "bundling," or collecting the individual contributions of its members made out to specific candidates and presenting them directly to those candidates.[15] For FEC compliance purposes, such contributions are considered individual contributions, not PAC contributions; no doubt the group receives the credit in the eyes of the recipient. In 2004 EMILY's List bundled $10.6 million in contributions.[16] Some conservative groups engage in the same kind of activity; Club for Growth bundled roughly $7.5 million in candidate contributions in 2004.[17]

Although PAC contributions got little attention in the presidency-focused 2004 elections, one should not minimize their importance, especially in House races. In the 2004 election cycle, 32 percent of the campaign contributions received by House candidates came from PACs, compared with only 13 percent of funds in senatorial campaigns. With most of the money going to incumbents, PACs remain a central part of incumbent advantage in elections.

Independent Expenditures and Internal Communications

The Supreme Court decided in *Buckley* v. *Valeo* and reaffirmed in *McConnell* v. *Federal Election Commission* that individuals and groups may spend unlimited sums of money in expressly advocating the defeat or election of a candidate for federal office, as long as such efforts are made without consultation or coordination with a candidate or a representing agent. Immediately after *Buckley*, ideologically oriented, nonconnected PACs were the first organizations to extensively engage in independent spending. One such PAC, the National Conservative Political Action Committee (NCPAC), was the leading fundraiser among all registered PACs in 1982: it spent more than $3 million in just six races, all against liberal senators running for reelection, including some who were defeated in close contests.[18]

The negative tone of much of the early independent spending caused a backlash against the activity, especially by the media but also by candidates themselves. Even candidates who were the beneficiaries of the advertising worried that the electorate might be confused about the sources of such ads and that they might be blamed for the negative campaigning. By the mid- to late 1980s, a number of the most aggressive ideologically oriented PACs, including NCPAC, had difficulty raising funds and went out of business. By the 1990s, when raising soft money for issue advocacy electioneering came into vogue, independent spending had lost much of its appeal. Unlike independent spending on campaign advertising, issue advocacy electioneering could accomplish virtually the same goal of supporting or opposing a candidate without disclosing contributors' identities, some of whom no doubt would have been uneasy about being associated with negative advertising. In the 2000 election, only 125 PACs reported engaging in independent spending, with a total of little more than $21 million in outlays.

If the FEC data on group expenditures in the 2004 elections are a good indication, BCRA's restrictions on broadcast advertising close to elections likely helped renew the attractiveness of independent spending, particularly in the presidential race, where it could be used within the BCRA window up to and including Election Day. Nearly $57.5 million of independent expenditures were made in the election cycle, including more than $10.8 million by MoveOn.org alone. Unions, in particular, utilized the independent spending route, but PACs of ideologically oriented groups like the NRA, National Right to Life, and Planned Parenthood were prominent as well.

The FEC asks those reporting to it to "self-classify" their independent expenditure activity as to its positive and negative intent; groups reported that $48.6 million was spent in support of candidates for public office, compared with only $8.8 million against. The competitive presidential race drew the most attention by far, with groups claiming that they spent over $35.5 million in support of their preferred choice compared with $7.8 million against a candidate. While total independent spending in 2004 more than doubled the aggregate in 2000, spending on House and Senate races was static in real dollars ($14.4 million in 2000; $14.5 million in 2004).

PACs also have to report to the FEC any money spent on "internal communications" expressly advocating the defeat or endorsement of any candidate, provided communication costs are greater than $2,000 per election. In 2004 more than $28.9 million was reportedly spent on this activity, mostly by groups like organized labor, teachers' organizations, business organizations, and some ideologically oriented entities like the Sierra Club and the NRA.[19] The figure represents a substantial increase over amounts reported in 2000.[20]

In reality, these reported data are highly unreliable and no doubt greatly understate the financial resources expended on communicating to members or employees about elections. If the primary reason for the communication is not a candidate endorsement, no reporting is necessary. And assigning a dollar value to such activities is a gray area: how are voter guides to be treated, for example, and how are expenditures assigned to e-mail communications? In practice, sophisticated internal communication within groups is probably on the rise. According to David Magleby and his colleagues, one group moving in this direction in response to BCRA restrictions is the Associated Builders and Contractors (ABC). The group utilized coordinators in its 23,000 or more member companies to contact their employees roughly twelve times between Labor Day and the election, using a combination of e-mail, phone, and direct mail. ABC also distributed nearly 900,000 voter guides in key presidential race swing states and in selected Senate contests, yet reported internal communications for the group did not come close to six figures.[21]

Independent expenditures and internal communications are targeted to select races and can be important. In the 2000 elections, close to 40 percent of independent expenditures reported by interest groups occurred in seventeen of the most competitive congressional races.[22] Similar strategic spending occurred in 2004, with groups like the American Medical Association (AMA) and other established organizations concentrating on a relatively small number of competitive states or districts. The AMA invested approximately $500,000 of its nearly $1 million in independent expenditures in a few competitive House and Senate races.[23] And in some cases, groups even targeted single candidates. In Colorado alone, the League of Conservation Voters (LCV), a longtime user of independent spending, invested over $1.1 million in targeting Republican Pete Coors.[24] Also, "You're Fired, Inc.," a one-time registered federal PAC operating only in South Dakota, invested $550,000 in independent expenditures in a successful effort to defeat Democratic Senate Majority Leader Tom Daschle.[25]

The Rise of 527 Committees as the Primary Conduit for Outside Money

While BCRA regulations regarding soft money and issue ads dramatically altered the electioneering activities of organized interests, it is important to understand what the new campaign finance reforms *did not* do. With the exception of "broadcast communications" aired within the BCRA window (thirty days before the primary and sixty days before the general election) and funded with soft money, all other forms of group electioneering remained intact. BCRA thus leaves a lot of campaign activity by groups unregulated. For example, get-out-the-vote (GOTV) activities and voter contact via phone, mail, and the Internet are not covered by BCRA's definition of broadcast communications. Disclosure of funds spent on such activities was not a part of BCRA either. In addition, the provision banning soft money contributions to the political parties in theory had the potential of adding to the coffers of some interest groups, particularly more ideologically oriented organizations that donors might envision as alternatives to parties for the purposes of political expression.

Analysis of electioneering activities by organized interests in 2004 strongly suggests that group involvement in the presidential election, especially in swing states, was greater than in any previous election in terms of the money raised and spent, as well as the intensity and breadth of both air war and ground war efforts. The primary means by which groups engaged in this widespread electioneering in battleground states was 527 committees. Contributions to 527 committees are unlimited. This fact together with the contested 2004 presidential election meant that outside money increased despite BCRA.

Even though provisions for setting up a 527 committee have been part of the U.S. Tax Code since 1974, it has only been recently that organized interests have learned to utilize the advantages these committees offer.[26] According to the code, a 527 committee is an independent political organization whose major purpose is to influence elections: as long as the committee does not engage in any hard money activity and refrains from express advocacy, it is totally exempt from federal taxation. The funds it receives from donors must be in non-interest-bearing accounts. Such political organizations must be certified by the Internal Revenue Service (IRS), but groups merely have to claim they meet the 527 provisions. And before August 2000, 527 committees did not even have to disclose their donors or expenditures; now both must be reported to the IRS and are made available for public scrutiny.

As noted, an advantage of 527s is that there are no limits on how much donors can contribute to such groups. In contrast, contributions to political parties, individual candidates, and PACs do have limits. Contributors to such groups also have a tax advantage compared with other nonprofit, advocacy organizations. For example, donors to social welfare groups, which typically register with the IRS as 501(c)(4) organizations, are not publicly disclosed but are confronted with an onerous federal gift tax if their contribution exceeds $10,000. The tax does not apply to 527 donors. Groups under various IRS classifications as nonprofits, including advocacy organizations, trade associations, and unions, are themselves taxed at a 35 percent rate on the lesser of their investment income or political expenditures. Clearly, 527 committees offer more bang for the buck both for donors and political organizations

The use of 527 committees did not begin with the 2004 elections. Groups on the political left such the Sierra Club and National Association for the Advancement of Colored People (NAACP) had active 527 committees by the late 1990s, as did the pharmaceutical industry and a number of other interests on the right. Organized labor noticeably stepped up its 527 activity soon after the 2000 elections. But the huge expansion of 527 fundraising and spending so prominent in the 2004 elections was the direct result of the new campaign finance law. It was BCRA's banning of soft money contributions to the national party committees that proved to be the catalyst for expanded soft money activity among interest groups, particularly for individuals and groups supportive of Democrats.

Democratic Allied Groups and Their Funding Sources

Democratic Party officials were well aware that BCRA provisions banning soft money contributions to party committees would put their party at a disadvantage more than Republicans, especially in the presidential race. Republicans were far less dependent on soft money for campaigns and had a larger, more reliable hard money pipeline from individual contributions (see chapter 7). Democratic National Party (DNC) chairman Terry McAuliffe, while publicly arguing for campaign finance reform during Senate and House deliberations in the early spring of 2002, was at the same time creating a special task force composed of some of the more prominent Democratic campaign operatives and consultants; the task force was charged with exploring ways to get soft money back into the system.[27]

Once BCRA was officially signed into law by President Bush in late March of 2002, the task force quickly decided to go ahead with plans to find funding for two new 527 groups, the Media Fund, which would concentrate on communicating the Democratic message using the mass media in federal elections, and another for grassroots Democrats, focusing on voter mobilization in nonfederal contests. Later in the spring a meeting was held in Washington of prominent leaders of Democratic interest group allies, which included such notables as Harold Ickes, an executive member of the Democratic National Committee and former official in the Clinton White House; Ellen Malcolm, president of EMILY's List; Carl Pope, executive director of the Sierra Club and head of Partnership for American Families; and Steven Rosenthal, former political director of the AFL-CIO. The primary purpose of the meeting was to develop a vehicle for coordinating interest group efforts to defeat President Bush.[28] The meeting's participants hoped to create a division of labor among the various organizations to avoid duplication. The results of this and subsequent meetings was the creation of America Coming Together (ACT), a 527 that would focus primarily on grassroots efforts to turn out Democrats and other anti-Bush voters in battleground states. Another new 527, Joint Victory Campaign 2004, was later created to raise money that was to be divided between the Media Fund and ACT.

While the new groups were officially independent from the Democratic Party, the overlap in personnel was apparent, but no one was ever charged with breaking any laws.[29] Ickes resigned his DNC position but remained a delegate to the Democratic Convention held in August 2004.

EMILY's List's Malcolm also resigned her DNC Executive Committee position after ACT was formed. Ickes and Malcolm each had key positions in both the Media Fund and ACT organizations and were instrumental in fundraising. Consultants and service providers to the new 527s were similar to those used by the Democratic Party, including Jim Jordan, who had been John Kerry's campaign manager, and Andy Grossman, who had worked for the Democratic Senatorial Campaign Committee. Throughout the campaign, Republicans and some in the press often referred to the new 527s as the "shadow Democratic Party."[30]

Despite the close party connections, these new 527s should be viewed not as vehicles of the Democratic Party, but as progressive organizations hostile to the reelection of George Bush; almost all of their money was spent on the presidential election, rather than for general Democratic Party purposes. Fundraising appeals were based on an anti-Bush message and were quite successful. The groups were careful not to use party appeals and took steps to avoid any appearance of coordination with the party.[31]

The list of the largest contributors to 527 committees in the 2004 election campaign (see table 8-3) is dominated by the anti-Bush groups. With the exception of Joint Victory Campaign 2004, a conduit organization that channeled most of its collected money to the Media Fund and ACT, the next six leading contributors to 527s were either Democratic-leaning unions or wealthy individuals committed to progressive causes. For some unions, money was simply transferred to 527 committee accounts from treasury funds. In the case of the Service Employees International Union (SEIU), all but about $4 million was transferred to its own 527. But more than the support of unions, it was the sheer magnitude of individual contributions to 527s that may have been the most startling aspect of group fundraising in 2004. The money appeared to represent an ideological "movement" rather than party money, with contributors more motivated by their principles and their dislike of Bush than by a desire for "access" to party or elected Democrats.[32]

Two individuals stood out for the size of their contribution to the anti-Bush 527s. Philanthropist and billionaire financial entrepreneur George Soros, who contributed nearly $24 million, and Peter Lewis, chairman of the Progressive Corporation insurance firm, who contributed over $22 million, targeted their money to a number of anti-Bush 527s. Both individuals were instrumental in providing early seed money; initially each pledged $10 million to get ACT off the ground.

Table 8-3. *Top Twenty Contributors to 527 Committees, 2003–04*
Dollars

Rank	Contributor	Total
1	Joint Victory Campaign 2004[a]	56,654,391
2	Service Employees International Union	53,187,817
3	AFSCME	30,327,630
4	Soros Fund Management/George Soros	23,881,000
5	Peter B. Lewis/Progressive Corporation	22,395,000
6	Shangri-La Entertainment/Steve Bing	13,802,381
7	Victory Campaign 2004	13,365,000
8	Golden West Financial	13,012,959
9	AFL-CIO	11,424,853
10	Perry Homes	8,085,199
11	Sustainable World Corporation/Linda Pritzker	7,205,000
12	Gateway Inc.	5,010,000
13	Ameriquest Capital	5,000,000
14	AG Spanos Companies	5,000,000
15	BP Capital	4,600,000
16	Sierra Club	4,383,099
17	August Capital/Andrew Rappaport	4,143,400
18	Amway Corporation	4,020,000
19	Chartwell Partners/Jerry Perenchio	4,000,000
20	Laborers Union	3,466,622

Source: Center for Responsive Politics, "Top-Twenty Contributors to 527 Committees" (www.opensecrets.org/527s/527contribs.asp?cycle=2004 [July 21, 2005]).

a. Joint Victory Campaign (JVC) 2004 is a joint fundraising committee run by America Coming Together and the Media Fund. Money raised by JVC is divided between these two beneficiaries. Combining receipts for these three groups would result in double counting.

Hollywood executive Steven Bing was fifth on the total giving list; he was particularly helpful in getting the Media Fund on firm financial ground. Overall, contributors to the anti-Bush 527s were overwhelmingly wealthy liberal donors. Over 90 percent of ACT's receipts for the election cycle came from contributions of $100,000 or more. While many of the contributors were previous donors to Democratic candidates and the party, their contributions to the new 527s far exceeded their previous party contributions.[33] As Democratic consultant Michael Lux noted, "The new big money to outside groups is more ideologically driven. Ideological donors are very highly motivated and very high profile. Some have really stepped up this year in a substantial way."[34]

A number of other important 527s operating in the campaign were clearly Democratic allies, but even more independent from party connections than the 527s discussed so far. The most notable was probably MoveOn.org Voter Fund, which supplemented that group's PAC activity and cooperated closely with both the Media Fund and ACT to avoid overlap in deciding where to focus its broadcast communications and grassroots mobilization activity. While Soros was also the largest contributor to its campaign coffers, the group was one of the few that relied extensively on small contributions gathered by Internet solicitation from its more than 2 million members. The group operated pretty much as an independent progressive entity, harsher than others in running its anti-Bush campaign, sometimes even embarrassing the anti-Bush coalition with its stridency. The group was also more active outside the presidential race than either the Media Fund or ACT.[35]

Some unions also capitalized on the use of 527 organizations, contributing to groups like the Media Fund and ACT as well as forming their own 527 organizations. Some traditional Democratic-leaning advocacy groups like EMILY's List (where Malcolm remained as president and chief fundraiser), the Sierra Club, and the LCV not only continued to have PACs contributing to candidates and spending independently, but also had their own 527s operating, which in many cases had already been part of their campaign arsenal for a number of election cycles. A number of the anti-Bush 527s were well funded by late 2003; a few started running ads attacking the president before the Democratic nomination had even been secured.

Republican Allied Groups and Their Funding Sources

Republicans relied far less on 527s than did the Democrats. Both Bush for President and Republican Party organizations had been remarkably successful in raising hard money going into the election year. While individuals close to House Republican leaders attempted setting up 527s after BCRA was passed, these groups failed to get off the ground.[36] Republicans eventually took the position that raising soft money through 527 committees violated both the intent and letter of BCRA itself. By early 2004, however, the activities of the anti-Bush 527s had clearly gotten the attention of Republicans by their aggressive broadcast ads attacking the president. But rather than copying the Democrats, in late March Republicans filed a complaint with the FEC accusing the Kerry campaign of violating BCRA by coordinating efforts with the anti-Bush 527s; the complaint cited the similarities between the Kerry campaign and that of the 527s in terms of strategies, fundraising solicitations, and timing of campaign ads as evidence of coordination. The lawyer representing the Republican National Committee (RNC) and the Bush campaign, Benjamin Ginsberg, charged that the activity of the 527s was an "unprecedented conspiracy" and "an illegal campaign finance scheme."[37] The appeal was rejected, and Republicans quickly turned to creating 527s of their own.

The anti-Kerry 527 with the closest connections to the party and the Bush campaign was Progress for America Voter Fund. The group had been formed in 2001 by Tony Feather, former head of the Bush-Cheney campaign in 2000 and a close confidant of Karl Rove. Originally registered as a 501(c)(4) social welfare organization, the group converted to a 527 committee in May 2004. Like the anti-Bush committees, it looked to individual big-money donors. The two largest contributors were Alex Spanos, owner of the San Diego Chargers (see table 8-3), and Dawn Arnall, chairperson of Ameriquest Capital Corporation, who each contributed $5 million. Both were also major fundraisers for the Bush campaign, listed as Rangers, an elite group of contributors who each raised a minimum of $200,000 in individual contributions for Bush. The cofounders of Amway Corporation, Richard DeVos and Jay Van Andel, each gave $2 million to the Progress for America Fund as well. Another anti-Kerry committee was Swift Boat Veterans and POWs for Truth, which ran anti-Kerry broadcast ads after the August Democratic convention. Oilman T. Boone Pickens was the largest contributor to the group, with donations of $500,000; the group also had close ties to the Bush campaign. Pickens, well known as a corporate raider, previously had contributed $2.5 million to the Progress for America Voter Fund. Other Republican-linked 527 committees, especially those representing more aggressive, ideologically oriented groups, also relied heavily on individual donor contributions

Overall, however, Republican efforts at creating well-funded anti-Kerry 527s were not nearly as successful as those of their Democratic counterparts. Besides starting late, fundraisers had to deal with the seeming inconsistency that they had earlier been opposed to 527s on the grounds of principle as well as law. Further, unlike labor money, corporate money was not as readily available in 2004.[38] A series of corporate scandals had made many businesses uneasy about contributing disclosed funds to 527s without FEC approval. Moreover, businesses are generally wary of funding new groups. Not surprisingly, 2004 saw many corporations withdraw from the direct big-money involvement in elections that had characterized the party soft money era.[39]

Like many of the Democratic donors, however, contributors to the anti-Kerry 527 committees were "true believers," in the words of

Table 8-4. *Top Twenty 527 Committees, by Receipts and Expenditures, 2003–04*

Dollars

Rank	Committee	Total Receipts	Total Expenditures
1	America Coming Together	79,795,487	78,040,480
2	Joint Victory Campaign 2004	71,811,666	72,588,053
3	Media Fund	59,404,183	54,494,698
4	Progress for America	44,929,178	35,631,378
5	Service Employees International Union	40,237,236	39,579,709
6	AFSCME	22,227,050	22,332,587
7	Swift Boat Veterans and POWs for Truth	17,008,090	22,565,360
8	College Republican National Committee	12,780,126	17,260,655
9	New Democrat Network	12,726,158	12,524,063
10	MoveOn.org	12,558,215	21,346,380
11	Citizens for a Strong Senate	10,853,730	10,228,515
12	Sierra Club	8,727,127	6,261,811
13	Service Employees International Union	8,148,131	8,115,937
14	EMILY's List	7,739,946	8,100,752
15	Voices for Working Families	7,466,056	7,202,695
16	AFL-CIO	6,583,572	6,473,110
17	Club for Growth	6,530,939	9,034,364
18	League of Conservation Voters	6,049,500	5,074,790
19	International Brotherhood of Electrical Workers	5,010,321	7,368,841
20	Club for Growth.net	4,115,037	4,039,892

Source: Center for Responsive Politics, "527 Committee Activity" (www.opensecrets.org/527s/527cmtes.asp [July 21, 2005]).

Grover Norquist, conservative Republican activist and founder of a 527 group named American Resolve: "It's not access money, it's movement money. They are not writing checks to sit down with congressmen."[40] Club for Growth, an aggressive conservative group, which had had a 527 committee in operation in previous elections, believed its fundraising efforts had been enhanced by BCRA's banning of party soft money.[41] Contributions to its PAC and 527 committee surged in 2004.

Expenditures, Activities, and Impact of 527s in the 2004 Elections

Of the top twenty 527 committees during the 2004 election, ranked by receipts and expenditures (see table 8-4), the first four are the ones with the strongest party connections, three of them linked to the Democratic Party. ACT was the leader, raising nearly $80 million and spending over $78 million, virtually all of which was directed toward voter registration and mobilization efforts. The organization claimed to have 2,500 full-time paid canvassers nationwide, plus paid part-timers, who were responsible for adding 500,000 citizens to the voter registration lists, all of whom were purportedly contacted periodically throughout the campaign season.[42] In Ohio alone, ACT opened fifteen offices, deployed 250 full-time field staff, hired 12,000 additional workers, and claimed to have knocked on 3.7 million doors and registered 85,000 potential voters.[43] Thousands of volunteers from out of state aided the group's efforts in Ohio as the election approached. During the last three weeks of the campaign, ACT's GOTV activity reportedly included making 16 million phone calls, dropping 11 million flyers during its canvassing, and sending out 23 million pieces of literature concentrated in a small number of swing states.[44]

ACT worked closely with a number of groups on GOTV efforts. Thirty-two progressive groups, including unions, women's groups, and environmentalists joined together under another coordinating 527, America Votes, to avoid overwhelming voters with too many mailings or phone calls at the same time.[45] The targets of the coalition's grass-roots efforts were divided up to avoid duplication. In Florida, for example, EMILY's List focused its efforts on Broward and Dade County (Miami), while LCV focused on Orlando, and the Sierra Club used its volunteers to canvass in the Tampa Area. Even though Kerry lost the election, Democratic turnout markedly increased in areas of ACT and America Votes involvement.

The anti-Bush GOTV activities overshadowed the broadcast advertising of the Democratic allies.[46] From the beginning, the Media Fund was the point group for advertising directed toward challenging the Bush record. It spent nearly all of its money for radio, TV, print, and Internet ads in twenty-one states: late in the campaign, swing states like Pennsylvania, Ohio, and Florida received almost all of the attention. The Media Fund was probably most important in the spring before the Kerry general election campaign was in gear, running hard-hitting ads against Bush at the very time the Kerry campaign lacked the funding to carry on an effective air war.[47] Media Fund messages concentrated on tapping into the public angst about the loss of American jobs, the president's spending priorities, and problems with Medicare and children's health care. All the group's early ads were negative, designed to make the Bush campaign respond to the charges rather than define Kerry.[48]

While many Democrat allies opted for a division of labor in 2004, some individual groups employed a comprehensive, mixed strategy in their anti-Bush efforts. MoveOn.org, which ranked tenth on the list of top 527s in receipts and eighth in terms of expenditures, relied on unpaid volunteers and on skillful use of the Internet to both raise funds and conduct a GOTV campaign. Web pages, videos, and audio downloads supplemented its ground war activity, which relied on bus signs, bumper stickers, and billboards. Broadcast advertising was part of the group's strategy as well, including five negative TV ads run in nine battleground states during and around the period of the Republican National Convention. These ads, which cost $3.2 million, focused on interviews with the group's members who had voted for Bush in 2000 but were now voting for Kerry.

Among the longtime Democratic allies, such as unions and environmental groups, the 2004 election continued the recent trend of devoting most of their resources to communicating with and mobilizing their members and other likely Democrat voters through GOTV activities rather than reaching the general public through broadcast media. Some of this was paid for out of 527 funds. Direct mail was extensive. Unions especially found that their efforts in past elections emphasizing broadcast advertising were not cost-effective since as many viewers were determined to oppose the union's choices as were willing to support them.[49] The bulk of union funds in 2004 was devoted to efforts like SEIU's "hero" program in Ohio, where union members worked full-time on grassroots mobilization, or the AFL-CIO's grassroots efforts in the same state called Take Back Ohio.[50]

The big national groups were not the only ones to have a 527. Like a number of PACs, some 527s were organized just to do business in one state. In Ohio, for example, local 527s such as Bring Back Ohio and Facts for Ohio participated in the air war in support of the anti-Bush campaign.[51]

Besides utilizing PACs and 527 committees, a number of the Democratic allies were involved in the presidential and congressional campaigns using their status as 501(c) organizations. Substantial electoral activity may be conducted under this rubric, including the same types of broadcast and GOTV activities that 527s engage in, but their activity falls largely outside of FEC regulation. Donors to 501(c) organizations are not disclosed, and the reports detailing a group's itemized contributions and expenditures are not routinely made public. Democrat allies such as labor unions, the Sierra Club, EMILY's List, NAACP, and

Human Rights Campaign all used the 501(c) vehicle in the 2004 campaign. Some groups engaged in electioneering solely through the 501(c) classification. At times it was difficult to discern whether an organization was operating through its 501(c) classification or through its 527 committee.

Overall, the actions of the anti-Bush groups were impressive, particularly in their scope and in the number of people involved in grassroots activities. Groups raised and spent more money than had been anticipated. For all intents and purposes, though technically separate from the party organization, interest group allies were the dominant force in the Democratic Party ground war effort in 2004, helping to counterbalance the massive grassroots effort by Republicans and their Christian Right supporters.

Republican interest group allies played a different role in 2004 than did their Democrat counterparts. The Bush for President campaign was awash in cash, quite able to run an extensive air war on its own. The RNC also was well funded and organizationally set up to run a wide-ranging GOTV campaign, fortuitously aided by one of the main issues during the election, gay marriage. Bush said he would support a constitutional amendment defining marriage as between a man and a woman; Kerry said such an amendment was unwise. The issue had the effect of energizing the Christian Right. Groups such as the Christian Coalition and Focus on the Family organized registration and GOTV activity, targeting Christian conservatives and thereby supplementing RNC efforts. In some states, conservative Christian groups were formed on an ad hoc basis to attempt to put statewide initiatives on the ballot to ban gay marriage. Even individual churches got involved in registering their parishioners in some areas.[52] The larger Christian Right groups typically organized as 501(c)(3) or 501(c)(4) tax-exempt organizations. All of this activity aided Bush and other Republican candidates by bringing to the polls many socially conservative voters who had not paid much attention to politics in the past.

Two Republican-allied 527s played especially important roles in the election by aiding the president's TV and radio campaign. The first, Progress for American Voter Fund, was the fourth wealthiest 527 during the 2004 campaign and fifth in terms of total expenditures (see table 8-4). The group aired nine ads during the election, all carefully designed to make the electorate focus on Bush's leadership in the War on Terror and to subtly ask questions about how Kerry would have responded to 9/11.

According to a number of postelection polls taken in battleground states, the group's "Ashley" ad was ranked by those interviewed as either the first or second most influential ad they had watched.[53] The ad, launched two weeks before Election Day, focused on a picture of a spontaneous moment on the Bush campaign trail when the president hugged a young girl whose mother had been lost on 9/11. The photo had been taken by her father. The carefully constructed ad tugged at the heart. After running the ad on TV, a banner campaign was conducted over the Internet that recorded 75 million impressions; 20 million e-mails of the ad were distributed as well.[54] The Progress for America TV ads were effective in conveying the image of Bush as a man of emotion, character, compassion, and leadership, in contrast to the more distant, hesitant Kerry.

But the 2004 presidential campaign may be most remembered for the ads sponsored by the Swift Boat Veterans for Truth (SBVT), later renamed the Swift Boat Veterans and POWs for Truth.[55] It ranks seventh on the list in table 8-4 in terms of money raised and spent. The numbers are deceiving, however, because most of the relatively large amount of money it amassed was collected and spent after the group had had its major impact using a minimal amount of funds.

The group was founded to plead the case of nearly 200 Vietnam Swift Boat veterans offended by the Kerry campaign's decision to make the Democrat contender's war record as a PT boat commander in Vietnam the central feature of his run for the presidency. Uniting the group was anger over Kerry's actions when he first returned from the war, which included participating in antiwar protests and testifying in Congress, where he charged that the U.S. troops engaged routinely in atrocities in the countryside. Some among the group even questioned whether the Democrat had lied about his service record by falsifying his injuries in order to get his Purple Hearts.

Between August 5 and 31, during the period after the Democratic Convention and before the Republican Convention, the group ran TV ads in only a few media markets, but the ads soon received national attention and put the Kerry campaign on the defensive. The first ad, aired in Wisconsin, West Virginia, and Ohio, was entitled "Any Questions." It first showed a videotape of Senator John Edwards praising Kerry's war record, followed up by comments from Swift Boat veterans accusing Kerry of lying, charging that in actuality he "betrayed his shipmates." Nearly three weeks later, a second ad appeared, this time in

West Virginia, Ohio, and Iowa, as well as on national cable, showing a videotape of Kerry's testimony before Congress, where he talked of U.S. soldier abuses of the civilian population in Vietnam. Kerry is then charged with "dishonoring his counry . . . and the people he served with." On August 31 a final ad, entitled "Medals," ran in Florida and in Nashville. This ad showed Kerry in a 1971 television interview saying he had given back several of his Purple Hearts in a symbolic gesture. Viewers were then asked whether a man who "renounces his country's symbols now can be trusted."

Polls indicated the ads were among the most influential during the campaign, while campaign professionals on both sides appeared to agree that the ads and the lack of a credible response by the Kerry campaign may have been the most defining moment of the election.[56] The ads got the Kerry campaign off message and received widespread coverage in the free press for days. The ads together cost the Swift Boat Veterans less than $2 million, but as soon as they gained national attention Kerry's standing in the polls started to sink.

No other Republican allies appeared to have the national effect of these two 527s. Hard money from Republican interest groups and wealthy donors enabled the Bush campaign and the RNC to pretty much control all aspects of the reelection effort; high-profile activity by Republican allied groups seemed less apparent in 2004 than in previous elections. Longtime Republican-leaning groups like the NRA and U.S. Chamber of Commerce were selectively active throughout the country, campaigning particularly in competitive congressional races such as Senate races in Alaska and South Dakota.[57] Both groups took advantage of 501(c) classifications.

One group that did appear more active than before was Club for Growth, which is an emerging powerhouse among Republican-allied interest groups. Not only did the group engage in hard money activity through its PAC, but it also had two 527 committees among the top twenty in terms of receipts. The group has antitax, free-market sympathies, and its decisions to become involved in a particular race are governed more by ideology than party concerns. Thus at times it has supported challengers against Republican incumbents in primaries. The group was active in 2004 in the presidential election, a number of competitive congressional and Senate races, and a few state legislative races. The group's two 527 committees together spent over $13 million, almost all of it on air war activities.

Conclusion

The involvement of organized interests in the 2004 elections represented both continuity and change. Hard money activity through PAC contributions to candidates, independent spending, and internal communications within membership groups remained important, and expenditures along such lines showed a marked increase over the previous presidential year. But hard money spending was not the focus of attention in 2004.

What reformers who had engineered BCRA through Congress failed to anticipate was that banning party soft money would spark the tremendous surge in 527 committee activity, which included soft money expenditures to underwrite extensive ground war and air war efforts by a variety of organized interests who evaded the intent of BCRA. With donor money to 527s unlimited, some of the larger 527s were able to attract six- and seven-figure contributions and engage in electioneering activity reminiscent of the pre-BCRA era, with its focus on issue advocacy electioneering, much of it of a negative variety. Even in the decade before BCRA, a time of soft money excess, no individual came close to investing the kind of money billionaires George Soros and Peter Lewis did in 2003 and 2004 in their failed effort to defeat President Bush. It has been estimated that 527s may have raised and spent over $424 million.[58] Of this amount, $146 million came from just twenty-five well-heeled individuals. The vast majority of the wealthy-donor money went to the anti-Bush groups.[59] Besides producing such a volume of money, 527 activity along the lines of TV ads by the Swift Boat Veterans for Truth played a role in reducing candidate and party control of the campaign issue agenda, which is crucial to electoral accountability.

Not surprisingly, talk of campaign finance reform was again on the table immediately after the election, as members of both parties expressed outrage over the role big money contributors played in underwriting 527 activities.[60] Still, changing the system would be difficult. On the positive side, President Bush, no friend of campaign finance reform during and after the 2000 election, argued in 2004 that 527s are "bad for the system" and indicated he would be willing to join with Senator John McCain to decrease the influence of such groups.[61] McCain, a potential presidential contender in 2008, may again attempt to make reform a centerpiece of his campaign as he did in the spring of 2000. But opposition can be expected from many in Congress, especially Democrats, who are well aware of how important the progressive 527s were to their side's grassroots mobilization efforts in 2004. Reformers would likely also face opposition from advocacy groups generally, including Republican-oriented groups worried that any attempt to restrict 527s might infringe on their efforts to promote specific issues or causes. At the time of this writing, campaign finance reform, while on the political agenda, is not a high priority.

More probably, the 527 universe will remain in a constant state of flux for the foreseeable future. Groups like the Swift Boat Veterans for Truth, which mobilized under unique circumstances to discredit John Kerry, had no other political goals. The group had focused on a single issue and disbanded shortly after the election. The Media Fund has disbanded as well, and ACT, faced with the withdrawal of support by its major patron, George Soros, and engaged in internal disputes over political direction, now retains only a token research staff, a far cry from being the lead group for a progressive movement, as envisioned by its founders.[62]

The donors underwriting some of the more prominent 527s, as well as the group activists themselves, were more concerned with ideology than with access to political officials; tangible material benefits were not the ultimate political goals, unlike those of political corporations or trade associations. Research suggests that groups that appeal to such expressive needs have a difficult time surviving, being especially prone to internal factionalism, and are likely to see their supporters drop out as passions wane.[63] Without an intense, polarizing environment comparable to that of the 2004 election, the propensity for big-money contributors to support ideological groups may be reduced. Interest in such organizations would be especially hard to sustain between elections.

Notes

1. Allan J. Cigler and Burdett A. Loomis, "The Changing Nature of Interest Group Politics," in *Interest Group Politics*, 6th ed., edited by Allan J. Cigler and Burdett A. Loomis (Congressional Quarterly Press, 2002), pp. 1–33; Mark Rozell and Clyde Wilcox, *Interest Groups in American Campaigns* (Congressional Quarterly Press, 1999).

2. *McConnell v. FEC*, 251 F. Supp. 2d 176 (D.D.C., 2003), note 80. For the full text of their report, see www.campaignlegalcenter.org.

3. Anthony Corrado, "Financing the 2000 Elections," in *The Election of 2000*, edited by Gerald M. Pomper (Chatham, N.J.: Chatham House, 2001), p. 95.

4. Diana Dwyre and Robin Kolodny, "Throwing Out the Rule Book: Party Financing of the 2000 Elections," in *Financing the 2000 Election*, edited by David B. Magleby (Brookings, 2002), pp. 133–62.

5. Allan J. Cigler, "Issue Advocacy Electioneering: The Role of Money and Organized Interests," in *Law and Election Politics*, edited by Matthew J. Streb (Boulder, Colo.: Lynne Rienner, 2005), pp. 50–76.

6. *Buckley* v. *Valeo* 424 U.S. 1[1976], note 52.

7. Tom E. Mann, "Linking Knowledge and Action: Political Science and Campaign Finance Reform," *Perspectives on Politics* 1 (January 2003): 74.

8. David B. Magleby, *Dictum without Data: The Myth of Issue Advocacy and Party Building* (Brigham Young University, Center for the Study of Democracy and Elections, 2000). For television ads specifically, see Craig B. Holman and Luke P. McLoughman, *Buying Time 2000: Television Advertising in the 2000 Federal Elections* (New York University School of Law, Brennan Center for Justice, 2000).

9. See Allan J. Cigler, "Interest Groups and Funding the 2000 Elections," in *Financing the 2000 Election*, edited by Magleby, pp. 180–81.

10. Derek Willis, "Broad Coalition of Groups Opposes Curb on Issue Ads in McCain-Feingold Bill," *Congressional Quarterly Weekly* 60 (February 6, 2002), p. 478.

11. Allan J. Cigler, "Enron, a Perceived Crisis in Public Confidence, and the Bipartisan Campaign Reform Act of 2002," *Review of Policy Research* 21 (March 2004), p. 249.

12. Karen Foerstel, "As Groups File Lawsuits, Bush Spurs Signing Ceremony for 'Flawed' Fundraising Law," *Congressional Quarterly Weekly* 60 (March 30, 2002), p. 868.

13. A good summary of the major provisions of BCRA and potential implications is found in Michael Malbin, ed., *Life after Reform: When the Bipartisan Campaign Reform Act Meets Politics* (Lanham, Md.: Rowman and Littlefield, 2003).

14. The 2004 data on PACs to be presented come from various official FEC reports and summaries made available during May through July of 2005. The data represent final information on the 2004 election cycle. The detailed information is available on the FEC website, www.fec.gov/press.

15. M. Margaret Conway, Joanne Connor Green, and Marian Currinder, "Interest Group Money in Elections," in *Interest Group Politics*, edited by Cigler and Loomis, p. 125.

16. David B. Magleby, J. Quin Monson, and Kelly D. Patterson, "Overview," in *Dancing without Partners: How Candidates, Parties and Interest Groups Interact in the New Campaign Finance Environment* (Brigham Young University, Center for the Study of Elections and Democracy, 2005), p. 23.

17. Ibid.

18. See Larry Sabato, *PAC Power* (New York: Norton, 1985). NCPAC directly contributed money to candidates of both parties who agreed with its issue positions, but it was the group's propensity to run aggressive, negative ads against those it opposed that drew the most attention.

19. See www.fec.gov/press.

20. Membership organizations spent a reported $17.9 million on internal communications in 2000. See Cigler, "Interest Groups and Financing the 2000 Elections," p. 175.

21. Magleby and others, "Overview," pp. 24–25.

22. David B. Magleby, "Election Advocacy: Soft Money and Issue Advocacy in the 2000 Elections," in *Election Advocacy: Soft Money and Issue Advocacy in the 2000 Elections,* edited by David B. Magleby (Brigham Young University, Center for the Study of Elections and Democracy, 2000), pp. 40–41.

23. Magleby and others, "Overview," p. 23.

24. Kyle Sanders and Robert Duffy, "The Colorado U.S. Senate Race," in *Dancing without Partners,* edited by Magleby and others, p. 184

25. Elizabeth Theiss Smith and Richard Braunstein, "The Nationalization of Local Politics in South Dakota," in *Dancing without Partners,* edited by Magleby and others, p. 241.

26. An excellent discussion of how 527 committees operate and their competitive advantages over other organizational influence vehicles is found in Center for Public Integrity, "Silent Partners, How Political Non-Profits Work the System" (www.publicintegrity.org/527/report.aspx?aid=7) [April 22, 2004]).

27. Harvard University, Institute of Politics, ed., *Campaign for President: The Managers Look at 2004* (Lanham, Md.: Rowman and Littlefield, 2004), p. 212.

28. Thomas Edsall, "Liberals Meeting to Set '04 Strategy," *Washington* Post, May 25, 2003, p. A1; Jeanne Cummings, "A Hard Sell on Soft Money," *Wall Street Journal,* December 2, 2003, p. A4;

29. Jim Rutenberg and Glen Justice, "A Delegate, a Fund Raiser, and a Very Fine Line," *New York Times,* July 30, 2004, p. A1

30. The term "shadow Democratic party" for the various progressive political groups was first used by Republican critics but soon was adopted by much of the press. See *"Washington Post* Again Labeled Progressive Groups with Political 'Foes' Term" (http://mediamatters.org/items/20040514004 [June 7, 2005]).

31. See, for example, Elisabeth Rosenthal, "In Pennsylvania Campaign Rolls on, Neither Neutral or Partisan," *New York Times,* July 24, 2004, p. A10.

32. See, for example, Matt Bai, "Wiring the Vast Left-Wing Conspiracy," *New York Times Magazine,* July 24, 2004, sec. 6, p. 30.

33. Ibid. Soros, for example, contributed $100,000 to the Democratic Party during the 2000 Campaign. Soros, whose motivation was to remake the Democratic Party in a progressive direction, was uneasy about the fact that direct donors to the party had no meaningful control over how funds were spent; they

were potentially being diluted by soft money contributions from large industrial concerns. See also Jane Meyer, "The Money Man," *New Yorker*, October 18, 2004, pp. 176–89.

34. Glen Justice, "New Pet Cause for the Very Rich: Swaying the Election," *New York Times*, September 24, 2004, p. A12.

35. Tim Dickinson, "The Online Insurgency," *Rolling Stone*, March 10, 2005, pp. 63–64.

36. Republicans apparently tried to set up a 527 called the Leadership Forum, started with $1 million contributed by the Republican Congressional Campaign Committee. Under criticism for its direct connection to a party committee, the Leadership Forum gave the money back, and Republicans quickly abandoned their early efforts to create 527s. See Harvard University, *Campaign for President*, p. 213.

37. Glen Justice, "Kerry and Democratic Groups Accused of Finance Violations," *New York Times*, April 1, 2004, p. A20.

38. Glen Justice, "Republicans Rush to Form New Campaign Finance Groups," *New York Times,* May 28, 2004, p. A1; Harvard University, *Campaign for President*, p. 213.

39. Steve Weissman and Ruth Hassan, "BCRA and the 527 Groups," in *The Election after Reform: Money, Politics, and the Bipartisan Campaign Act,* edited by Michael J. Malbin (Lanham, Md.: Rowman and Littlefield, 2006). None of the top ten party committee soft money contributors in 2000 gave any money to 527s in 2004.

40. Michael Janofsky, "Advocacy Groups Spent Record Amount on 2004 Election," *New York Times*, December 17, 2004, p. A31.

41. Magleby and others, "Overview," p. 24.

42. Glen Justice, "Advocacy Groups Reflect on Their Role in the Election," *New York Times*, November 5, 2004, p. A23.

43. Stephen T. Mockabee and others, "The Battle for Ohio: The 2004 Presidential Campaign," in *Dancing without Partners*, edited by Magleby and others, p. 146.

44. Justice, "Advocacy Groups Reflect on Their Role in the Election."

45. Ibid.

46. Unless specifically noted, all of the information dealing with 527 broadcast advertising by individual groups, including expenditures, content of the ads, and where run, comes from the Open Secrets website sponsored by the Center for Responsible Politics. The data come from IRS 527 disclosure records and from media reports. The site can be accessed through www.crp.org.

47. Harvard University, *Campaign for President*, pp. 221–24.

48. Ibid.

49. The change in strategy started after the 1998 election. See Frank Swoboda, "AFL-CIO Plots a Push for Democratic House," *Washington Post*, February 18, 1999, p. A1.

50. Mockabee, "The Battle for Ohio," p. 148.

51. Ibid.

52. See, for example, Allan J. Cigler, "The 2004 Kansas 3rd Congressional District Race: Déjà Vu All Over Again," in *Dancing without Partners*, edited by Magleby and others, pp. 285–98.

53. Harvard University, *Campaign for President*, pp. 214–15.

54. Ibid, p. 220.

55. As with the Democratic-allied groups, relations between the SBVT and Republicans were apparently close. For example, Benjamin Ginsberg, the Bush Campaign's top attorney, was originally a paid consultant to the group. When this was uncovered, he severed his connection to the president's campaign. See Jim Rutenberg and Kate Zernnike, "Veteran's Group had G.O.P. Lawyer," *New York Times*, August 26, 2004, p. A1. Also, Chris LaCivita, who had been the political director of the National Republican Senatorial Committee (NRSC) in 2002 and who headed Progress for America until the spring of 2005, later turned up as the senior media strategist for SBVT. See www.sourcewatch.org/index/php?title=Chris_LaCivita.

56. Harvard University, *Campaign for President*, p. 213.

57. Carl Shepro and Clive Thomas, "The 2004 Alaska U.S. Senate Race," in *Dancing without Partners*, edited by Magleby and others, pp. 166–77; Smith and Braunstein, "The Nationalization of Local Politics in South Dakota."

58. Weissman and Hassan, "BCRA and the 527 Groups."

59. David Broder, "Bipartisan Clout," *Kansas City Star*, March 15, 2005, p. B5.

60. Ibid.

61. Justice, "Advocacy Groups Reflect on their Role in the Elections."

62. Thomas Edsall, "Soros-Backed Activist Group Disbands as Interest Fades," *Washington Post*, August 3, 2005, p. A6.

63. See, for example, Mancur Olsen Jr., *The Logic of Collective Action* (Harvard University Press, 1965); Robert H. Salisbury, "An Exchange Theory of Interest Groups," *Midwest Journal of Political Science* 13 (February 1969): 1–32.

NINE   *Lessons for Reformers*

THOMAS E. MANN

The highly contentious debate associated with the passage and constitutional defense of the Bipartisan Campaign Reform Act (BCRA) not surprisingly carried over into analyses of the law's impact during the 2004 election cycle. Critics quickly unfurled their venerable banner—"The Law of Unintended Consequences"—to highlight developments that they saw undermining the objectives of BCRA's framers. They cited a surge in campaign fundraising and spending, the dominance of new 527 organizations financed largely by wealthy individuals, the collapse of the presidential public finance system, and the further decline of competition in congressional elections. Supporters generally took a more sanguine view of the new law's first test in the real world of campaigns and elections: the abuse of public power associated with party soft money fundraising has greatly diminished; parties have adapted well to the new rules by raising record amounts of hard money; the number of small donors has increased exponentially; and the long-standing statutory prohibition on corporate and union treasury contributions and spending in federal elections has been bolstered.

Disputes between BCRA supporters and opponents, in the scholarly as well as the policy community, have erupted over the objectives of the law, the relative importance of various campaign finance players in the 2004 cycle, and the connections between the new rules and practices. These disputes reflect a deep philosophical divide that produces *Rashomon*-like divergences in describing, explaining, and evaluating campaign finance practices and in drawing lessons for future reforms.

Advocates assert that BCRA aspirations were modest: to repair tears in the Federal Election Campaign Act (FECA) regulatory fabric by banning party soft money (a creation of the Federal Election Commission [FEC], not Congress), regulating (not prohibiting) a well-defined class of electioneering communications, and restoring bans on corporate and union financing of federal campaigns. Any system of regulation is bound to develop problems as new conditions arise, administrative agencies respond to their overseers and clients, and regulated actors wear down its constraints on their behavior. Effective regulation, they believe, requires ongoing maintenance and repair. The *McConnell* Court reflected this view when it concluded its majority opinion with these words: "We are under no illusion that BCRA will be the last congressional statement on the matter. Money, like water, will always find an outlet. What problems arise, and how Congress will respond, are concerns for another day."[1]

The law's objectives, advocates further argue, did not include reducing the overall amount of money in elections, limiting television advertising in federal campaigns, or preventing outside groups from participating in federal elections. And as much as they support steps to shore up the public financing system and increase competition in congressional elections, BCRA supporters have long acknowledged they chose not to include provisions in the legislation to achieve these objectives, leaving that battle for another day.

Critics view BCRA as more ambitious and more constraining on legitimate campaign activity than reformers typically claim. Many believe that reformers find campaigns distasteful and money inherently corrupting: BCRA, therefore, must be about reducing money, campaign activity, and political speech. They point to strident statements by some reform groups and to hyperbolic speeches by a number of BCRA supporters in Congress that support both propositions. In their view, the law's elaborate web of regulations threatens to discourage legitimate and constructive political activity and to entrap politicians in normal political behavior criminalized by the new law.

Critics of BCRA and campaign finance regulation more generally assert that efforts to restrict campaign contributions and expenditures are not only dangerous, but they are doomed to fail. First Amendment guarantees properly limit the reach of regulators. Political money is fungible, and legal constraints on its flow will merely divert it through less accountable passageways. Politicians and interest groups will exploit the weaknesses of the regulatory system to advance their interests. These overriding realities, they argue, ensure that new regulations will inevitably be overwhelmed by undesirable, unanticipated consequences. Better to reduce the rules on money in politics, move toward a deregulated system, and allow the political marketplace to discipline the campaign finance system.

The purpose of this volume and another sponsored by the Campaign Finance Institute is to try to get beyond these competing worldviews of campaign finance by marshaling evidence on the 2004 election cycle in as rigorous and objective a fashion as possible.[2] This is not an easy task since many of the contributors to both volumes, myself included, have weighed in on one side or the other of the reform debate. But that is the objective that motivates each of us.

Our task is further complicated by the reality that new campaign finance laws are neither self-executing nor hermetically sealed. Regulations are issued by the FEC, complaints are lodged and adjudicated, challenges are brought in the courts, and political actors calibrate how their interests are best served under the new legal regime. And the broader context within which candidates, parties, interest groups, and citizens make strategic decisions conditions the impact of laws on campaign finance practices. As documented in most of the chapters in this book, the intensely competitive and high-stakes presidential election led to an outpouring of political contributions, large and small, to candidates, parties, and groups, and to massive voter mobilization programs associated with both political parties. Both would almost certainly have happened had BCRA not been enacted, but changes in the law nonetheless affected the particular patterns of receipts and expenditures reported in this volume.

This concluding chapter reviews what we have learned about BCRA's impact in the 2004 elections, the controversies that arose about the new law's application during the course of the campaign, and the reform implications of these findings and ongoing debates. It begins with political parties since eliminating party soft money was the central pillar of BCRA and forecasts of its likely effect on the two major parties diverged so widely.

Political Parties

The passage of BCRA was preceded by an explosion of soft money fundraising (not subject to federal limits on the source and size of contributions because allegedly not used to elect federal candidates) by party and public officials from corporations, unions, and individuals.[3] The new law was designed to eliminate this regulatory loophole allowing unlimited contributions. By all accounts it succeeded.[4] The national party committees kept only one set of accounts, which recorded the receipt and expenditure of federal funds. Federal officeholders ceased raising soft money for these party committees or for their own leadership political action committees (PACs). And, as recounted by Anthony Corrado in chapter 2, despite a dispute between BCRA authors and the FEC over the wording of the regulation governing the appearance of federal officeholders at state party nonfederal fundraising events, the intent of the new law appears not to have been undermined in 2004 through the state parties.

To one degree or another, critics worried that parties would be weakened, Democrats in particular would suffer (one author referred to BCRA as a "Democratic Party Suicide Bill"), voter identification and mobilization activities would be diminished, and party soft money donors would redirect their contributions to outside groups.[5] The worst fears of these critics did not materialize. In the 2004 election cycle, both the national parties raised more hard money than they had collected in hard and soft dollars in previous election cycles.[6] The Democratic National Committee (DNC) and Republican National Committee (RNC) had the most impressive fundraising records; the surge in receipts by the DNC allowed it to achieve parity with its Republican counterpart after many years of trailing far behind. As David Magleby notes in chapter 1, the DNC initially cultivated large donors (those who could contribute up to $25,000 per year), expanded their small donor lists, and then reaped the surge in direct mail and Internet contributions. Each of the four congressional party campaign committees enjoyed substantially higher hard money receipts, although not sufficient to compensate fully for the abolition of soft money. State parties raised roughly the same amount in the 2004 cycle for federal and shared party activities as they had in the previous presidential election, once the funds transferred by the national committees to the states are removed.[7] Those transferred funds were used primarily to finance television advertising in federal campaigns, predominantly with soft money.

Forecasts of the political suicide of the Democratic Party proved to be wrong. While Republicans retained an overall advantage in party fundraising, it was the smallest in decades. Democrats matched the Republicans at the national committee level, where most resources are directed at the presidential election, and they maintained their lead over the Republicans in the senatorial party committee sweepstakes. However, they failed to put a dent in the traditional GOP advantage with the two House campaign committees, and they trailed their Republican counterparts at the state party level in direct hard money fundraising. Both parties greatly increased the number of donors; but Democrats, who had traditionally trailed the Republicans in small donors, made up substantial ground (see chapters 3 and 7).

Some have suggested that the relative fundraising success of the Democratic Party in 2004 was entirely a function of the competitive, high-stakes presidential election. From this perspective, the 2006 midterm election cycle is likely to see a decline in Democratic fortunes. Figures released by the FEC for the first six months of the 2006 election cycle suggest otherwise.[8] Democratic Party committees increased their receipts by 53 percent over a comparable period in the 2004 election; Republicans, by comparison, had a 2 percent increase in contributions. To be sure, Republicans retain a substantial advantage in both receipts and cash on hand, one that could persist over the entire two-year cycle. Nonetheless, the success of the two parties in the first half of 2005 compared with their performance in 2003 should be encouraging to Democrats.

The elimination of party soft money did not diminish grassroots campaign activity, as some had feared (see chapter 1). The extraordinary focus on and investment in voter identification and get-out-the-vote (GOTV) efforts in 2004 was not solely a consequence of BCRA, but the new law reinforced rather than deterred these activities. Thanks in part to path-breaking experimental research on field activities and turnout by political scientists Donald Green and Alan Gerber, both parties had concluded well before the passage of BCRA that additional investments in grassroots voter contact were likely to pay substantial dividends.[9] Both parties had ample hard money to invest in voter mobilization programs. The size of their investments and the strategies they pursued were not obviously constrained by BCRA. The Republicans, having developed and tested voter mobilization programs in the 2002 election, launched an ambitious effort in 2004 that was financed and implemented within their party organizations.[10] Republicans spent $125 million on this program, triple the amount they invested in 2000.[11] The Democrats spent $80 million on their field operation in 2004, much more than they had in 2000. Democrats relied more on the independent efforts of labor unions, the new 527 America Coming Together, and aligned liberal interest groups to carry out the same functions, a decision that may have put them at a relative disadvantage.

A final prediction of critics of the new law was that the ban on soft money would simply divert large contributions from parties to less transparent and accountable entities. In one respect, this forecast was realized. Initially the Democratic and eventually the Republican Party encouraged the formation of new 527 organizations to compensate for the loss of party soft money. As Allan Cigler documents in chapter 8, these organizations succeeded in raising and spending substantial sums of unlimited contributions for television advertising and grassroots activities designed to influence the 2004 presidential and to a lesser extent congressional elections. These organizations are discussed in more detail in the next section

At the same time, the new 527 organizations in 2004 neither matched the party soft money receipts and expenditures of recent elections nor relied on diverted party soft money donations.[12] These groups made up less than half of the party soft money that was eliminated by BCRA. Moreover, their donors had a very different profile. Virtually all of the corporate party soft money donors retained these freed-up funds, choosing not to contribute them to other groups. Unions shifted some of their soft money contributions to Democratic-leaning 527s emphasizing voter mobilization but chose to spend much of these funds directly. Most individuals who donated soft money to parties did not give to 527s. And while many of the mega-donors to the new 527s, those contributing six-, seven-, and eight-digit amounts, had previously contributed to party soft money accounts, their 527 donations in 2004 dwarfed their earlier gifts to the parties.

Given the broadly salutary consequences of BCRA's soft money ban during the 2004 election cycle, advocates saw little reason to push for additional changes in the law as it related to political parties. One exception was a proposal that built on the surge in the number of individual donors in 2004 by providing tax credits for small contributions made to parties and candidates.[13] Another was to rein in soft money contributions to the national party conventions raised under the guise of local organizing committees.[14] BCRA critics, on the other hand, in response to the notoriety of several 527 groups financed largely by huge contributions from a small number of wealthy liberal donors, proposed major changes in the law to level the playing field between parties and

527s. Two of the provisions of "The 527 Fairness Act," sponsored by Representatives Mike Pence (R-Ind.) and Albert Wynn (D-Md.), directly affect the political parties.[15] The first would repeal the aggregate limit on contributions by individuals. BCRA increased the aggregate limit from $25,000 a year to $95,000 over the two-year election cycle (indexed for inflation), with sublimits for candidates, parties, and PACs that allow national party committees to raise up to $57,500 from one person over the cycle. By repealing the cap on total contributions by an individual, the Pence-Wynn bill would allow an individual in the 2006 election cycle to contribute $53,400 to each of his or her party's three national committees and $20,000 to each of the fifty state party committees, for a total of $1,160,000. Since there is no restriction on the transfer of funds among party committees, all of the funds received by a party's committees from that individual could be gathered in a single party committee and spent on behalf of one candidate favored by the donor. Nothing would prevent that candidate from establishing a joint fundraising committee and soliciting in this fashion a $1 million plus check from a single donor.

The second major provision of Pence-Wynn would repeal the limit on the amount of coordinated party expenditures on behalf of candidates in general elections. The 1974 FECA set limits indexed for inflation or population on what parties could spend in coordination with their candidates. The Supreme Court later ruled in *Colorado I* that parties have the constitutional right to spend unlimited sums on behalf of their candidates if it is done independently, a ruling codified in BCRA.[16] *McConnell* established that parties could make both limited coordinated and unlimited independent expenditures, and the FEC's new regulations dropped an earlier provision that prohibited party independent expenditures in presidential general election campaigns (see chapter 2). In 2004 parties were free to spend unlimited amounts on behalf of any presidential or congressional candidate, provided they used only hard money and spent those funds independently of that candidate. Pence-Wynn would eliminate the need for parties to spend independently.

The House Republican leadership embraced the Pence-Wynn bill, moved it quickly through committee, and reported it to the House. But strong opposition among Republican and Democratic BCRA supporters, who argued the bill would effectively repeal the ban on party soft money as applied to individual donors, made its passage in the House more perilous.

One little-noticed provision of the Pence-Wynn bill, permitting unlimited transfers from leadership PACs to party committees, was added in committee as a rider to a Senate appropriations bill (though ultimately removed under pressure from opponents). Under current law, federal candidates may make unlimited transfers from their campaign committees to their party committees. In fact, as Robin Kolodny and Diana Dwyre document in chapter 7, member financing of the congressional party campaign committees has become increasingly important in recent elections. Since most incumbents face no serious opposition, it makes sense for their war chest surpluses to be redistributed through the parties to the most competitive races. This new provision would apply the same rule and opportunity to members' leadership PACs. The advantage of the latter is that it can receive contributions of up to $5,000 per person a year, compared with $2,000 per election for candidate committees. Opponents, led by BCRA authors John McCain and Russ Feingold, see this provision as a giant loophole, one that allows officeholders to steer larger contributions through party committees to their own benefit.[17] And since leadership PACs are a mechanism available only to sitting members, it constitutes yet another advantage of incumbents over challengers. Supporters respond that these funds are most likely to be spent only on the most competitive races, including those of a substantial number of challengers.

Corporations and Unions

Another major objective of BCRA was to repair the long-standing prohibition on the use of corporate and union treasury funds in federal elections. Both entities could participate in federal elections by forming political action committees financed by voluntary contributions and by communicating with their members or restricted classes. Treasury funds could be used to cover the administrative costs of PACs and to finance internal political communications, but not for contributions and expenditures defined by federal election law. The rise of party soft money and the use of those funds for issue advocacy electioneering created gaping holes in the legal wall severely limiting treasury funds in presidential and congressional campaigns.

As just mentioned, the ban on party soft money was particularly effective in stemming the flow of corporate treasury funds into federal elections. The Committee for Economic Development reports: "Corporate executives and other members of the business community are no longer being 'shaken down' by elected officials and party leaders for soft money contributions in ever-increasing amounts."[18] Soft money contributions from corporations to parties have ended. And little of this money found its way into the coffers of the new 527 groups.[19] In the case of labor organizations, the flow of treasury funds to political parties was also halted, but most of these dollars appear to have been spent elsewhere, either directly or in the form of contributions to Democratic-leaning 527s.

The second way of repairing the breach in regulation of corporations and unions under federal election law was to prohibit these entities from financing a class of broadcast ads defined as electioneering communications. Broadcast ads that named or clearly identified a federal candidate, targeted that candidate's constituency, and ran thirty days before a primary or sixty days before a general election were subject to disclosure and limits on contributions. The latter included an explicit ban on financing by corporations and unions, directly or indirectly through contributions to other organizations. Both profit and nonprofit corporations were included in this provision, except for that limited set of MCFL corporations the Supreme Court has long exempted from campaign finance regulations.[20]

Since the 1996 election, unions and corporations had funded issue advocacy electioneering widely acknowledged to influence federal campaigns. BCRA ended that practice for the set of campaign communications explicitly defined in the law. The evidence available on campaign advertising in 2004 shows there was no diminution in the air wars in federal election campaigns but there were changes in the way they were financed.[21] Television and radio ads run in close proximity to the election, the period judged most crucial by political consultants, were financed without corporate and union treasury funds. Some of these groups, however, used hard money in their PACs to run independent ads near the election. The parties also ran extensive independent ad campaigns in the two months before the election, relying exclusively on limited individual contributions. Several unincorporated 527 organizations not registered with the FEC used large individual contributions but no corporate or union funds to finance ambitious television advertising campaigns during the thirty- and sixty-day windows. A somewhat higher percentage of television ads were run outside the electioneering communications window, when the BCRA disclosure requirements and contribution limits did not apply, but the hotly contested presidential election ensured there would be no falloff in the absolute number of ads broadcast near the election

In a strict sense, therefore, the BCRA electioneering communications provision worked as intended. Corporate and union treasury funds were no longer used to finance a specific set of broadcast communications that had assumed increasing importance in recent elections. But numerous options remained for the electoral use of these funds: broadcast ads outside the window, nonbroadcast electoral communications (such as newspaper ads, direct mail, telephone banks, and personal voter contact via paid staff) that did not expressly advocate the election or defeat of a candidate, and inside communications with executives, stockholders, and union members. It should have been no surprise to discover that the ground war in presidential battleground states and in a small number of competitive House and Senate races in 2004 was intense and well financed, as demonstrated in chapter 1. The trend toward more sophisticated and vigorous field operations has been under way for some time.[22] The high-stakes presidential election reinforced and accelerated that trend; nothing in BCRA prevented or seriously constrained candidates, parties, and interest groups from taking an active role in the 2004 election.

Apart from issues surrounding 527 groups, which are considered in the next section, a number of questions emerge from the role of corporations and unions in 2004. One deals with the status of 501(c) nonprofit corporations. An amendment to BCRA by Senator Paul Wellstone (D-Minn.) included them in the universe of corporations covered by the electioneering communications section of the new law. Some consider this an inappropriate restriction on political speech and favor its repeal. Others have just the opposite concern: they see 501(c) organizations, with fewer transparent reporting requirements, as an increasingly utilized means for groups to avoid disclosure. Another question arises with respect to the ability of unions to use treasury funds on voter identification and mobilization programs aimed at nonmembers. Current law appears to forbid the practice, but a number of unions contributed such funds to support programs run by America Coming Together. Can labor organizations do indirectly what they are prohibited from doing directly? On the other side of this argument, how can the constitutional rationale for regulating corporate-funded election activity apply to election activity funded by labor unions?

A final question is already working its way through the courts. In upholding the electioneering communications section of BCRA, did the *McConnell* Court rule permissible a per se ban on speech that appears to refer solely to lobbying members of Congress on legislation? Or does such speech have to be judged on a case-by-case basis?

527 Groups

The emergence of several new 527 organizations proved to be the most controversial campaign finance development in the 2004 election cycle. BCRA's ban on party soft money was a primary consideration in the formation of entities that could both receive funds not subject to limits on the source and size of contributions and expend them in federal elections. After false starts by both parties in launching 527s focusing on congressional elections, Democrats were the first to exploit this possibility.[23] They feared their eventual presidential candidate would be at a distinct financial disadvantage in comparison with President Bush, who was certain to opt out of the presidential public finance system and be in a position to spend tens of millions of dollars on campaign ads from March to the national party conventions.[24] Their candidate, likely to take public funds and live with the spending limit that comes with them, could no longer count on issue ads financed by party soft money to keep his campaign on the airways during this critical period. Harold Ickes, a longtime Democratic political operative and a DNC member, started the Media Fund to fill this gap.[25]

Ickes chose to enroll his new group as a political organization under Section 527 of the Internal Revenue Code. This designation allowed the Media Fund to pay no taxes on its revenues and for its donors to be exempted from the gift tax. But he declined to register his organization as a political committee with the FEC, arguing that an organization making no contributions to federal candidates, operating independently of those candidates, and engaging in no express advocacy was not required to do so. Another Democratic-leaning 527 group, America Coming Together (ACT), was started by former AFL-CIO political director Steve Rosenthal to strengthen the ground operations of labor-favored (that is, Democratic) presidential candidates. Part of the motivation for ACT was fear that the loss of soft money would lead to a substantial underinvestment in voter mobilization by the Democratic Party. Another motivation had nothing to do with BCRA: a desire to extend labor's successful GOTV program for its members to other Democratic constituencies. Almost all of ACT's operations were financed with soft money, but it also formed a federal political action committee registered with the FEC.

As recounted by Anthony Corrado in chapter 2, the FEC was soon embroiled in a highly contentious dispute over whether 527s such as the Media Fund and ACT were required to register as political committees and abide by the restrictions of federal election law, including limits on contributions. BCRA's primary authors and the Republican Party argued that they should. The question is a complex one since the purposes of the IRS Section 527 and the FECA are different: the former affords favorable tax treatment to political organizations, the latter regulates groups engaged in election activity without imposing undue burdens on political speech.[26] It turns on the legal meaning of "contributions" and "expenditures" under federal election law and whether a group's "major purpose" is the nomination or election of a candidate, or both. In the end, the FEC declined to intervene in this dispute in a way that would alter the practices of 527s during the 2004 elections. The FEC did approve a new allocation rule effective in the 2006 cycle that requires groups with federal and nonfederal accounts to use at least 50 percent federal (that is, hard) funds to pay for voter mobilization activities. Had this been in effect in 2004, ACT would have been forced to rely much more heavily on hard money or to cut back its operations severely. Republicans responded to the FEC decision by moving quickly to energize their own 527 organizations, most importantly Progress for America. As was the case with the Democrats, they lent support to these ostensibly independent groups with "a wink and a nod," sharing political consultants, party activists, and prominent former officials. Representatives Christopher Shays and Martin Meehan, BCRA coauthors, filed suit in the U.S. District Court to require the FEC to issue regulations defining a political committee and specifying when a 527 organization becomes a political committee. This litigation is still pending.

Shays and Meehan also pursued legislative remedies. They introduced a bill in the House, a companion to "The 527 Reform Act of 2005" submitted in the Senate by McCain and Feingold, to achieve that same purpose legislatively. In the House, the Pence-Wynn bill was offered by BCRA opponents as an alternative to Shays-Meehan. In the Senate, Rules Committee chairman Trent Lott offered an alternative grab bag of campaign finance provisions, some of which were sure to reduce support among Democrats. Senator Charles Schumer (Democrat of New York), once a supporter of the McCain-Feingold 527 bill, announced he no longer favors requiring voter mobilization groups such as ACT to register with the FEC. Neither chamber seemed poised at the end of 2005 to act on the 527 bills or on related legislation (introduced by BCRA's four authors) meant to radically restructure the FEC.

While the Congress seemed unlikely to rein in the new 527 groups in time for the 2006 elections, the FEC surprised many observers by filing suit in September 2005 against the Club for Growth, which the FEC alleges was clearly out to influence primarily federal elections and so should have registered with the FEC as a political committee.[27] The case could ultimately define the limits of 527 activity. In the meantime, signs of a bear market in 527s abound. George Soros, who contributed $24 million to Democratic-leaning 527s in the 2004 election, reportedly has decided to invest his money elsewhere in the future, emphasizing nonelectoral ventures such as liberal think tanks and media outlets.[28] Of course, Soros, like every other American citizen, retains the right to act alone to influence federal elections by making unlimited independent expenditures. The Media Fund, at least for now, has closed its shop, and ACT has laid off most of its employees.

A clear-eyed view of the actual influence of 527s in the 2004 elections suggests why the incentives to harness these organizations for electoral purposes may have diminished. While the Media Fund ran ads in early 2004 during a financially difficult period in John Kerry's campaign, the rationale for its role was largely eliminated by Kerry's flush campaign coffers and the DNC's ability to raise ample hard money to finance independent expenditures on behalf of its presidential candidate. By most accounts, the most influential advertising in the presidential campaign was done by the Swift Boat Veterans and POWs for Truth, which scored spectacularly in August with a minimal ad buy and much free media coverage.[29] Big money spent on independent ad campaigns is not as valuable (and may sometimes be counterproductive) as resources controlled by the presidential campaigns. Much the same may be true for voter mobilization activities. Republicans appear to have profited by building their GOTV program into the party and presidential campaign, not outsourcing it to independent organizations with paid staff.[30] Democrats may well draw a lesson from this experience.

Presidential Campaign Finance

John Green and Anthony Corrado document in chapters 4 and 5 the extraordinary developments in presidential campaign finance in 2004: the decision of both major party nominees (as well as another Democratic candidate, Howard Dean) to opt out of the public funding system for the nomination process; the unprecedented fundraising success of George Bush and John Kerry, who both raised about five times the spending limit in place for candidates accepting public funds for the nomination contest; the ability of the candidates and their parties to sharply expand the number of small donors through direct mail and the Internet; the surge in party assistance to the presidential candidates via independent expenditures; the increased activity of outside groups in the presidential campaign through independent expenditures, electioneering communications, and other unregulated forms of political communications; and the initiation of a new form of hybrid expenditures, which allowed presidential campaigns to control the use of party funds well beyond the limits on coordinated spending.

BCRA was a factor in most of these developments, but by no means the dominant one. The increase in the individual contribution limit from $1,000 to $2,000 boosted the fundraising ability of the candidates and made the public match less attractive and less essential. Yet George Bush would have opted out of the public funding system in 2004 in any case, as he had in 2000. Howard Dean declined public funds because of his phenomenal success attracting small donations through the Internet, not $2,000 contributions through a network of fundraisers. John Kerry's hand was forced more by Bush and Dean, not BCRA, and his ability to use some of his personal wealth to jump-start his campaign made his decision a logical one. Similarly, the elimination of party soft money stimulated the parties, especially the Democrats, to beef up their small-donor capacity. The 2004 election was a highly charged and competitive presidential contest that allowed the parties and groups, as well as the presidential candidates, to reap the benefits. BCRA and the Supreme Court together allowed the parties in 2004 to substitute hard money independent expenditures for soft money issue advertising, thereby ensuring them a significant role in the presidential campaign, but the magnitude of that role was made possible by the intense interest of contributors, large and small. And as discussed earlier, the new 527s were stimulated in part by BCRA's ban on party soft money, but organizational form and activities had little to do with the new law.

The big question coming out of this experience is whether the presidential public financing system can be salvaged. It is near death in the nominating process and increasingly vulnerable in the general election. If action is not taken by Congress to adapt the system to the realities of contemporary presidential campaigns, it will soon pass from the scene. Proposals to repair the public financing system have been offered by the Campaign Finance Institute, various public interest groups, FEC commissioners Scott Thomas and Michael Toner, and several members of Congress.[31] Most include provisions to replenish the tax checkoff fund, eliminate state spending limits, raise the overall limit, increase the value of the public match, and raise the spending limit for participating candidates who face an opponent opting out of the public funding system. Some would link the availability of the public grant in the general election to participation in the public matching program in the primaries.

Support for public financing among majority Republicans on Capitol Hill is limited, and no action to consider various legislative remedies has been taken in the 109th Congress. Ominously, a report on possible budget savings by the conservative House Republican Study Committee includes a recommendation to eliminate the entire system of public financing in presidential elections. One Republican member of the House has circulated a "Dear Colleague" letter proposing this idea as a down payment for the costs of recovering from Katrina.[32]

Another reform idea emerging from both the presidential and congressional election experience in 2004 concerns spending by parties on behalf of their candidates. The last election confirmed a new reality: there is no limit on what parties can spend in hard dollars for their candidates in federal elections, only restrictions on the legal form of those expenditures. Parties can make limited contributions to candidates, limited coordinated expenditures spent with candidates, unlimited independent expenditures, and presumably unlimited hybrid expenditures. The idea of a party spending independently of its own candidates, affirmed in *Colorado I*, strikes many as preposterous, especially once the party's nominee is selected.[33] What public good is served by forcing parties to set up entirely independent operations, which avoid any coordination with that candidate? It is a perversion of the whole purpose of political parties. One reform idea meant to remedy this forced separation between parties and their candidates is to eliminate the caps on party coordinated spending, thereby eliminating the incentive to engage in independent spending.

Congressional Campaign Finance

As Paul Herrnson discusses in chapter 6, the role of money in the 2004 congressional elections reflected more continuity than change. BCRA was not explicitly directed at altering the structure of House and Senate elections; it included no provisions that promised to reverse the trend of declining competitiveness. The ban on soft money meant the congressional party campaign committees would have to redouble their hard money fundraising efforts and set up independent expenditure operations for those contests in which it wanted to invest beyond the coordinated spending limits. The increase in the individual contribution limit was expected to modestly ease the fundraising burden on congressional candidates but not to alter the gap between incumbents and challengers. Outside groups retained multiple options after BCRA for participating in congressional campaigns, meaning their presence was unlikely to change much as a result of the new law.

All of these modest expectations were largely realized. Parties found ample ways and means to engage actively in the small number of contests they judged competitive.[34] While the $2,000 individual contribution limit made fundraising by incumbents, serious challengers, and open seat candidates a bit easier, incumbents continued to enjoy their huge money advantage over challengers. PAC contributions and ground war operations kept interest groups involved in competitive contests.

Increasing competition in congressional elections will require steps that go well beyond BCRA. Eliminating the caps on party coordinated spending could help, partly by increasing the efficiency of party investments on behalf of candidates. It might even encourage the parties to target their resources in a less concentrated fashion. Expanding the number of seriously contested races must be a priority for any political party hoping to build a comfortable majority. Other measures proposed to increase resources available to challengers include tax credits for small donors, public subsidies, and free air time.

The Internet

The Internet grew in importance during the 2004 election, primarily as a means of fundraising but also as an important communications device for candidates, parties, and groups to inform and mobilize activists.[35] It has remained largely free from considerations of campaign finance regulation, but that may be about to change. While BCRA made no explicit mention of the Internet, the FEC initially included in its regulations implementing the new law a provision excluding paid Internet advertising from the definition of "public communication," thereby permitting such ads to be paid for with soft money (see chapter 2). A U.S. district court (subsequently upheld by an appellate court) struck down that provision and others in *Shays* v. *FEC,* holding that it impermissibly excludes all Internet communications from BCRA's restrictions on funding of federal political activity and directed the FEC to rewrite the provision.[36]

In the spring and summer of 2005, the FEC held hearings on a proposed rule that would subject paid Internet advertising to the same regulatory and disclosure requirements imposed on television and other media advertising. This stimulated an impassioned debate between proponents, who argued the proposed regulation closes a vast soft money loophole and simply brings the law up to date with new technology, and opponents, who contended that any regulation of Internet communications is a precursor to wholesale free speech violations.[37] Bloggers weighed in heavily against any form of regulation. The FEC subsequently approved an advisory opinion that appeared to grant a broad press exception for Internet bloggers. Hearings before the House Committee on Administration revealed some bipartisan support for exempting the Internet from campaign finance regulation. A bill to do just that attracted majority support in the House but fell short of the supermajority required for bills on the consent calendar. It is very likely to reemerge in the next session of Congress.

The Future of Campaign Finance Reform

As the dispute over Internet regulation underscores, the two communities discussed at the outset of this chapter continue to diverge in their views about money and politics: whether in regard to regulation versus deregulation, corruption versus free speech, or political equality versus economic inequality. The philosophical divide is deep. And the political obstacles to resolving the debate decisively in one direction or the other are enormous.

The coalition that came together to pass BCRA in 2002 has since frayed. None of the high priorities of the reform community—reviving the presidential public finance system, defining 527 organizations involved in federal elections as political committees, restructuring the FEC, aiding challengers in congressional elections—have bright prospects of being adopted by the present Congress. Instead, narrowly tailored initiatives to weaken the FECA and BCRA are likely to appear with more frequency. Much of the energy of the reform community will perforce be devoted to rearguard actions. On the other hand, there is no realistic prospect of Congress's repealing the entire edifice of campaign finance law and thereby moving to the deregulated world that would follow.

The Supreme Court is another matter. The replacement of the Rehnquist Court by the Roberts Court introduces great uncertainty in campaign finance jurisprudence. Justice Sandra Day O'Connor's resignation and the confirmation of her replacement, Samuel Alito, could lead to a reversal of the 5-4 decision in *McConnell* upholding BCRA. The Court's acceptance for its new term of the Vermont case on contribution and spending limits provides an opportunity to reconsider the constitutional logic of *Buckley* and its progeny.[38] And the lower courts and the states will also shape the pace and direction of campaign finance regulation.

At this point it is virtually impossible to forecast the broader political environment in which these campaign finance issues will be debated and resolved. Corruption charges against House Majority Leader Tom DeLay and super-lobbyist Jack Abramoff could spark a Teddy Roosevelt–like movement for broad political reform. Or we could fall back into an ongoing struggle—in Congress, the FEC, and the courts—to define the meaning of the existing law. In either case, tracking the effects of campaign finance regulation in the real world of campaigns and elections, to which this volume and the series of which it is a part are devoted, remains a useful exercise.

Notes

1. *McConnell v. FEC*, 124 S. Ct. 619 (2003).

2. Michael J. Malbin, "Assessing the Bipartisan Campaign Reform Act," in *The Election after Reform: Money, Politics and the Bipartisan Campaign Reform Act*, edited by Michael J. Malbin (Lanham, Md.: Rowman and Littlefield, 2005).

3. Thomas E. Mann, "The Rise of Soft Money," in *Inside the Campaign Finance Battle: Court Testimony on the New Reforms*, edited by Anthony Corrado, Thomas E. Mann, and Trevor Potter (Brookings, 2003).

4. Anthony Corrado, "Party Finance in the Wake of BCRA: An Overview," in *The Election after Reform*, edited by Malbin.

5. Seth Gitell, "The Democratic Party Suicide Bill," *Atlantic Monthly*, vol. 292, July/August 2003, p. 106.

6. Corrado, "Party Finance in the Wake of BCRA."

7. Raymond J. La Raja, "State and Local Political Parties," in *The Election after Reform*, edited by Malbin.

8. Federal Election Commission, "FEC Releases 6-Month Fundraising Figures for Parties," July 21, 2005 (www.fec.gov/press/press2005/20050721party/20050721party.html [January 5, 2006]).

9. Donald Green and Alan Gerber, *Get Out the Vote* (Brookings, 2004).

10. David B. Magleby and J. Quin Monson, eds., *The Last Hurrah? Soft Money and Issue Advocacy in the 2002 Congressional Elections* (Brookings, 2004).

11. Corrado, "Party Finance in the Wake of BCRA."

12. Steve Weissman and Ruth Hassan, "BCRA and the 527 Groups," and Robert G. Boatright and others, "Interest Groups and Advocacy Organizations after BCRA," in *The Election after Reform*, edited by Malbin.

13. H. Rept. 157, 108 Cong. 1 sess. (January 7, 2003). Also David Rosenberg, *Broadening the Base: The Case for a New Federal Tax Credit for Political Contributions* (Washington: American Enterprise Institute, 2002).

14. Campaign Finance Institute, "The $100 Million Dollar Exemption: Soft Money and the National Party Conventions" (www.cfinst.org/eguide/party conventions/financing/cfistudy.html [October 3, 2005]).

15. H. Rept. 1316, 109 Cong. 1 sess. (March 15, 2005).

16. *Colorado Republican Federal Campaign Committee v. Federal Election Commission et al.*, 518 U.S. 604 (1996).

17. "The 'Show-Me-the-Money' Bill," *Public Citizen*, June 30, 2005 (www.citizen.org/congress/campaign/legislation/pence_wynn/articles.cfm?ID=13 426 [October 3, 2005]).

18. Committee on Economic Development, "Building on Reform: A Business Proposal to Strengthen Election Finance" (www.ced.org/projects/cfr.shtml [January 5, 2006]), p. 1.

19. Weissman and Hassan, "BCRA and the 527 Groups."

20. MCFL corporations, named after a Court decision in Massachusetts Citizens for Life, are formed for purely ideological reasons and have no business activity or business income.

21. Michael M. Franz, Joel Rivlin, and Kenneth Goldstein, "Much More of the Same: Television Advertising Pre- and Post-BCRA," in *The Election after Reform*, edited by Malbin.

22. Magleby and Monson, *The Last Hurrah?*

23. Examples of failed Democratic-leaning congressional 527s include the New House PAC and the Democratic Senate Majority Fund. Congressional-oriented failed Republican 527s include the Leadership Forum and the national

Committee for a Responsible Senate. See Chris Cillizza, "Congressional 527s Are a Flop," *Roll Call*, April 26, 2004.

24. Harold Ickes, president, Media Fund, National Press Club event transcript, "Dancing without Partners," Brigham Young University, Center for the Study of Elections and Democracy, February 7, 2005, p. 37.

25. Ibid.

26. Miriam Galston, "527 Groups and Campaign Finance: The Language, Logic, and Landscape of Campaign Finance Regulation" (http://ssrn.com/abstract=798984 [January 5, 2006]).

27. Federal Election Commission, "FEC Files Suit against Club for Growth Inc.," September 19, 2005 (www.fec.gov/press/press2005/20050919suit.html [October 3, 2005]).

28. Alexander Bolton, "Soros Dives into Midterms: Smarting over 527s' $25M, Billionaire Now Turns to Party," *The Hill*, September 22, 2005, p. A1; and Thomas B. Edsall, "Rich Liberal Vows to Fund Think Tanks," *The Hill*, August 7, 2005, p. A1.

29. Harvard University, Institute of Politics, ed., *Campaign for President: The Managers Look at 2004* (Lanham, Md.: Rowman and Littlefield, 2006), pp. 214–18.

30. David B. Magleby, J. Quin Monson, and Kelly D. Patterson, eds., *Dancing without Partners: How Candidates, Parties, and Interest Groups Interact in the New Campaign Finance Environment* (Brigham Young University, Center for the Study of Elections and Democracy, 2005).

31. Campaign Finance Institute, "So the Voters May Choose: Reviving the Presidential Matching Fund System," 2005 (www.cfinst.org/presidential/report2/index.html [October 3, 2005]), pp. 15–17.

32. H. Rept. 3960, 109 Cong. 1 sess. (September 29, 2005). Also Randy Neugebauer, "Check off Taxpayer Financing of Presidential Election Campaigns and Conventions," Dear Colleague letter received through e-mail but not otherwise published. Citable source: Randy Neugebauer, "Neugebauer Proposes Reform to Help Pay Costs of Katrina Recovery," September 21, 2005 (http://johnshadegg.house.gov/rsc/word/Neugebauer—OpOff.doc [October 3, 2005]).

33. *Colorado Republican Federal Campaign Committee et al.* v. *Federal Election Commission*, 518 U.S. 604 (1996).

34. Magleby and others, *Dancing without Partners*.

35. Karen White, political director, EMILY's List, National Press Club event transcript, "Dancing without Partners," Brigham Young University, Center for the Study of Elections and Democracy, February 7, 2005, p. 64.

36. *Shays and Meehan* v. *FEC* (1:02CV01984).

37. Kenneth P. Doyle, "House Administration Hears Debate over FEC Regulation of Online Politics," *BNA Money and Politics*, September 23, 2005.

38. Linda Greenhouse, "Justices Take on Spending Limits for Candidates," *New York Times*, September 28, 2005, p. A6.

Contributors

Allan J. Cigler is the Chancellor's Club Teaching Professor of Political Science at the University of Kansas.

Anthony Corrado is professor of government at Colby College and a nonresident senior fellow at the Brookings Institution.

Diana Dwyre is associate professor of political science and director of graduate studies at California State University, Chico, and coauthor of *Legislative Labyrinth: Congress and Campaign Finance Reform.*

John C. Green is professor of political science and director of the Ray C. Bliss Institute of Applied Politics at the University of Akron.

Paul S. Herrnson is director of the Center for American Politics and Citizenship and professor in the Department of Government and Politics, University of Maryland.

Robin Kolodny is associate professor of political science at Temple University and the author of *Pursuing Majorities: Congressional Campaign Committees in American Politics.*

David B. Magleby is dean of the College of Family, Home and Social Sciences, distinguished professor of political science, and senior fellow of the Center for the Study of Elections and Democracy at Brigham Young University.

Thomas E. Mann is the W. Averell Harriman Chair and senior fellow in the Governmental Studies program at the Brookings Institution.

Kelly D. Patterson is associate professor of political science and director of the Center for the Study of Elections and Democracy at Brigham Young University.

Index

Smith, Bradley, 47

Soft money: amounts raised in *2000*, 32, 210; amounts raised in *2002*, 184; expenditures in *2000* and *2002*, 5, 32; interest group contributions of, 210; interest group use of, 172–74, 223; issue ads funded, 6, 136, 170, 172, 196; motives for donations, 210; problems with, 5, 196–97; raised by state parties, 202; raised just before ban, 190, 243–44; uses, 190

Soft money ban, 4–5, 32–37; constitutionality, 44, 45; exemptions, 35–37; FEC rules, 47–48; goals, 5, 195–96; legal cases, 44, 45; Levin funds exemption, 19, 36–37, 192, 202; success, 244; supporters, 5–6

Soft money ban, effects of: on advertising by parties, 136, 170; on congressional campaign financing, 154, 156, 170, 256; on coordinated campaigns, 175; on corporations, 5–6, 10; on Democratic Party, 11; on *527* groups, 254–55; on fundraising, 9–14, 185–87, 243–44, 254; on interest groups, 78, 223, 235; on national parties, 11, 224; on party spending, 197, 199; on unions, 6

Soros, George: criticism of Bush administration, 2; donations to *527* groups, 3, 85, 225, 227, 235; future donations, 253; independent expenditures, 77, 141

South Dakota Senate races, 21, 88, 178, 222

Spanos, Alex, 3, 86, 228

Special interests. *See* Interest groups

State parties: BCRA provisions affecting, 33–35, 39; coordinated expenditures, 175–76; effects of BCRA, 184, 185–86; federal and nonfed-

eral election activity, 33–35; federal and nonfederal funds, 202; fundraising for *2004* campaigns, 155, 184, 185–86, 192, 203, 244, 245; funds transferred from candidates, 132; funds transferred from national parties, 34, 156, 192, 196–97; hard money expenditures, 33–34, 39; Levin funds, 19, 36–37, 192, 203; limits on contributions to, 8, 39; spending in *2004* elections, 69, 203; voter mobilization efforts, 33, 34, 175–76, 192

Stenholm, Charles, 157–58, 178

Stern, Andrew, 6

Stevens, John Paul, 44–45

Strategic Taskforce to Organize and Mobilize People (STOMP), 176

Super Rangers, 191

Supreme Court: *Colorado Republican Federal Campaign Committee* v. *FEC*, 9, 43, 74–75, 136–37, 200, 247, 255; express advocacy guidelines, 37, 45, 210–11, 212; future decisions on campaign finance, 258. *See also Buckley* v. *Valeo*; *McConnell* v. *FEC*

Survey research expenditures: by campaigns, 134; independent expenditures, 202, 203

Swift Boat Veterans and POWs for Truth, 173, 228, 233

Swift Boat Veterans for Truth (SBVT): activities in *2004* campaigns, 88; ads attacking Kerry, 118, 133, 134, 233–34, 253; disbanding, 236; donors, 85, 228; expenditures, 110, 118, 140, 233; fundraising, 23

Tax-exempt groups. *See* Section *501*(c)(3) groups

Tax returns, Presidential Election Campaign Fund checkoff, 70–72